The Ogre's Progress

The Ogre's Progress

Images of the Ogre in Modern and Contemporary French Fiction

Jonathan F. Krell

Newark: University of Delaware Press

© 2009 by Rosemont Publishing & Printing Corp.

All rights reserved. Authorization to photocopy items for internal or personal use, or the internal or personal use of specific clients, is granted by the copyright owner, provided that a base fee of $10.00, plus eight cents per page, per copy is paid directly to the Copyright Clearance Center, 222 Rosewood Drive, Danvers, Massachusetts 01923. [978-0-87413-065-2/09 $10.00 + 8¢ pp, pc.]

Other than as indicated in the foregoing, this book may not be reproduced, in whole or in part, in any form (except as permitted by Sections 107 and 108 of the U.S. Copyright Law, and except for brief quotes appearing in reviews in the public press).

Associated University Presses
2010 Eastpark Boulevard
Cranbury, NJ 08512

The paper used in this publication meets the requirements of the American National Standard for Permanence of Paper for Printed Library Materials Z39.48-1984

Library of Congress Cataloging-in-Publication Data

Krell, Jonathan F., 1952–
  The ogre's progress : images of the ogre in modern and contemporary French fiction / Jonathan F. Krell.
      p.   cm.
  Includes bibliographical references and index.
  ISBN 978-0-87413-065-2 (alk. paper)
  1. French fiction—20th century—History and criticism.   2. Ghouls and ogres in literature.   3. Violence in literature.   I. Title.
PQ673.K74   2009
843'.9140937—dc22
                                                                                        2009000563

PRINTED IN THE UNITED STATES OF AMERICA

For KAN and DFK

Contents

List of Illustrations	9
Acknowledgments	11
Introduction	15
1. Appetites: "ingestion-digestion-defecation"	25
2. The Ogre as Sexual Predator	49
3. Avatars of Cronus: Time, Totalitarianism, and the Scapegoat	77
4. The Dark Side of Aphrodite: The Ogress	107
5. Conclusion: *JE est un ogre*	123
Appendix: The Resurgence of the Ogre: Interviews with Michel Tournier and Pascal Bruckner	133
Notes	143
Bibliography	156
Index	163

Illustrations

1. Gustave Doré, engraving, p. 8, "Le Petit Poucet" 14
2. Francisco Goya, *Saturn Devouring His Child* 24
3. Gustave Doré, engraving, p. xiii, "Le Petit Chaperon rouge" 48
4. Kindlifresserbrunnen (Ogre Fountain), Bern, Switzerland 76
5. Paul Lacombe, wood sculpture, *Isis*. 106
6. Gustave Doré, engraving, p. 9, "Le Petit Poucet" 122

Acknowledgments

I WOULD LIKE TO THANK THE UNIVERSITY OF GEORGIA RESEARCH FOUNdation for research and travel grants that facilitated my work at the Bibliothèque Nationale in Paris, and interviews with Pascal Bruckner and Michel Tournier in Paris. I am also indebted to the Jane and Harry Willson Center for Humanities and Arts at the University of Georgia for a faculty research grant that helped me pursue my ogres.

Other friends and colleagues were enormously helpful. Jeff Clippard and Jerry Daniel provided invaluable technical assistance. Many thanks to Catherine Jones, Doris Kadish, and Kristin Nielsen for reading, questioning, and critiquing various parts of the manuscript. Also, the readers of the University of Delaware Press gave me invaluable suggestions for improving the manuscript. Finally, I am especially grateful to my brother David Krell for his close reading of the entire book, which greatly benefited from his expertise in French, German, Greek, and many areas of philosophy and psychology.

The Ogre's Progress

Gustave Doré, p. 8, "Le Petit Poucet," by Charles Perrault. Bibliothèque Nationale de France, Paris, France.

Introduction

> The primordial crime is the action that makes something in existence disappear: the act of eating. Guilt is thus obligatory and inextinguishable.
>
> —Calasso 1993

> We are all meat, trembling and fresh, dying and spasming, and we enter into our humanity, as we leave it, by way of our animalness. We are beasts eating beasts, and the real bestiality . . . lies in avoiding the truth of it.
>
> —Gopnik 2005

> Every pregnant woman carries *two* children in her womb. But the stronger will not tolerate the presence of a brother with whom he will have to share everything. He strangles him in his mother's belly and . . . eats him. . . . Mankind is made up of ogres, strong men, yes, with stranglers' hands and cannibal teeth. And these ogres roam the world, in desperate loneliness and remorse, having by their original fratricide unleashed the torrent of crime and violence we call history.
>
> —Michel Tournier, *Gemini*[1]

ON THE MORNING OF JANUARY 3, 2007, A PRISON GUARD IN ROUEN, France, made a gruesome discovery. A schizophrenic prisoner, Nicolas Cocaigne, had strangled a cellmate, and then eaten parts of his lungs and chest, sautéed in onions. (Details of the cooking privileges in the French prison system are unfortunately missing.) *Agence France Presse* wrote that the incident "brings back memories of [the] Japanese Issey Sagawa, who twenty-five years ago killed his Dutch girlfriend in Paris, ate much of her body over three days and went on to become a celebrity at home" (Hecker 2007).

Occurrences such as these, along with those portrayed in *Silence of the Lambs* and its sequels, remind us that the taste for human flesh is not solely a phenomenon of ancient primitive societies. Nor is it merely the stuff of the myths, legends, and tales that stoke every child's imagination with the universal fear of being devoured. For the psychoanalyst Christiane Olivier, the "inner ogre" is no more than a metaphor to describe one aspect of Freud's death instinct: the desire to do violence to ourselves and to others. Yet the crimes of Sagawa and Cocaigne shock us as makers of metaphors because they show how the vehicle (the ogre) and the tenor (violence) can become one and the same, and with chilling realism prove the latent savage potential—what one might call the ogre instinct—of human beings.

What is an ogre? The *Oxford English Dictionary* tells us that ogre is an Old French word from the twelfth or thirteenth century meaning "fierce pagan" or "man-eating giant." Although the etymology is uncertain, it could derive from the classical Latin *Orcus*, "god of the infernal regions," or perhaps from the postclassical Latin *Ugri*, referring to "Hungarians or Magyars." Gustav Körting, in his 1891 etymological dictionary of romance languages, maintains that ogre originates from the Latin *augur*, evolving from "seer" to "magician" to "sorcerer," and finally to "evil supernatural being" (Bouloumié 1985–86, 27). In France, the most recognizable ogres are those in the seventeenth-century tales of Charles Perrault: French children all know the fearsome giants in "Little Tom Thumb" ("Le Petit Poucet") and "Puss in Boots" ("Le Chat botté"), the murderous nobleman called "Bluebeard" ("La Barbe bleue"), and the cunning wolf in "Little Red Riding Hood" ("Le Petit Chaperon rouge").

Readers of modern French fiction have recently witnessed a curious renaissance of the ogre as a metaphor. In the early 1970s, two stories of ogres were granted France's most prestigious prize for the novel. The French author Michel Tournier won the coveted Prix Goncourt in 1970 for *The Ogre* (*Le Roi des Aulnes*), and Jacques Chessex of Switzerland won the same award in 1973 for *A Father's Love* (*L'Ogre*). Thus the new age of the literary ogre was inaugurated. Since then many authors have employed this powerful metaphor to illustrate the act of devouring in its myriad forms.

All of the writers in the present study have been strongly influenced by the devouring monsters of fairy tales, such as the mighty ogre of "Little Tom Thumb," the cannibalistic witch of "Hansel and Gretel," and the strangely seductive wolf of "Little Red Riding Hood." The child psychologist Bruno Bettelheim, in *The Uses of Enchantment*, has shown that such figures, wicked as they are, are not without their attractions (1989, 9); children—who tend to admire those in a position of power—may even temporarily take their side. Bettelheim remarks that "in fairy tales evil is as omnipresent as virtue" (1989, 8); tales thus teach children at an early age about life's ambiguities. The ogres of modern French fiction are similarly complex: some have appetites we might call consummately evil, but others resemble humans in possessing a few redeeming qualities.

Of our authors, only Pierrette Fleutiaux and Pascal Bruckner have invented literal ogres who, like those in fairy tales, actually eat children. What we are calling ogres are, for the most part, characters, or even ideas—like war or National Socialism—whose viciousness is in its essence an act of devouring.[2] My purpose, then, is to examine how writers have appropriated the ogre figure in order to evoke the voracious aspect of violence—be it political, sexual, or familial—as well as the destructive nature of time itself. Time is personified by the prototypical ogre of Western literature, Cronus, devourer of his own children.

The inspiration for this essay came while researching the writings of Michel Tournier. After studying *The Ogre,* I began to notice how often French authors employ the ogre as a metaphor for countless types of violence and abuse. In the many conversations I have had with Tournier at his home, the immense importance and pervasiveness of the ogre character—unfortunately trivialized in some modern films and fiction[3]—has become apparent to me. As Tournier states in the interview reproduced in the appendix to this study, the ogre is a ubiquitous figure who appears not only as the monster of myths and folk tales, but also in real life. For Tournier and other authors similarly haunted by the horrors of the Second World War, he symbolizes the abominations of the Nazis and those who collaborated with them; for other writers, the ogre is the sexual deviate who preys upon the innocent. To my knowledge, however, no scholarly book has studied this metaphor that speaks to so many authors who wish to describe indescribable evil.

The ogre personifies the "demonic imagery" that Northrop Frye detects in the realist or "ironic"[4] literature of Europe and America, typical of late nineteenth-century authors like Gustave Flaubert or Emile Zola but alive and well in French prose of the late twentieth and early twenty-first centuries. In Frye's theory of myths, demonic imagery stands in stark contrast to what he calls the "apocalyptic imagery" (Frye 1957, 141–46) of those literary works of the Occident that present the world as a place where the desires of Christian humanity are fulfilled. The latter is a world of tranquil gardens and farms, of ideal cities like the Celestial City of Bunyan's *The Pilgrim's Progress,* and ideal love reminiscent of the biblical "'one flesh' metaphor of two bodies made into the same body by love" (1957, 143).

Demonic imagery, by contrast, presents a world that the Christian fears and rejects: "the world of the nightmare and the scapegoat, of bondage and pain and confusion; the world as it is before the human imagination begins to work on it and before any image of human desire, such as the city or the garden, has been solidly established" (1957, 147). Whereas in apocalyptic imagery the world approximates heaven, demonic imagery reveals life's hellish aspects. Apocalyptic symbolism is centered on wholeness and unity, reflecting the dogma of the Holy Trinity, in which three separate persons form one God. Demonic symbolism, on the other hand, represents fragmentation and chaos: the bucolic garden is now the sinister forest; the ordered city is destroyed by unruly mobs and damned like the City of Destruction in *The Pilgrim's Progress;* love degenerates into "a fierce destructive passion" (1957, 149). The apocalyptic world's "Eucharistic symbolism" (1957, 148), by which plants, animals, and humans are all metaphors of the divine, is inverted into images of cannibalism, of gods dying and devoured. This is the world of the ogre, writes Frye: "The imagery of cannibalism usually includes, not only images of torture and mutilation, but of what is technically known as *sparagmos* or the tearing apart of the sacrificial body, an image found in the myths of Osiris, Orpheus, and Pentheus. The cannibal giant or ogre of folk tales, who enters literature as Polyphemus, belongs here, as does a long series of sinister dealings with flesh and blood from the story of Thyestes to Shylock's bond" (1957, 148).

Frye identifies the naturalistic, "ironic" novel of the waning nineteenth century as the most likely genre to be dominated by the tyrants, monsters, and ogres of demonic imagery. Yet modern and contemporary French literature also abound in such fiction, and it is not difficult to see why. Metaphorical ogres are everywhere: interminable violence against others and the self—from war, ethnic cleansing, hate crimes, and child abuse, to eating disorders and obesity—is fodder for hungry authors of fiction.

In order to understand the place of the ogre in the literary imagination, it is useful to return to the roots of Western literature: early Greek philosophy and tragedy. Long before the gods took their place on Olympus, and the Greek and Christian cultures became intertwined, the Titans and Giants ruled, and Prometheus, Cronus, Atlas, and their kin were celebrated by such writers as Aeschylus and Empedocles. The eventual demise of the Titans—fathers of half-human monsters and, as sons of the Earth, reminiscent of the ancient mother goddesses—corresponds to basic terrors that underlie the Western imagination: fear of the earth and of the mortality of all earthly beings; fear of the body, of the feminine, of the genetically "impure."

The authors we will examine bring these old fears to the surface; in their fiction the solar hero gives way to the earthly, shadowy antihero, the heavenly gods to the terrestrial Titans. Marginals take center stage, celebrating the body and the bawdy. The ogre's appetite may be for the flesh of children or for excessive and violent sex. Yet in spite of his crimes, we will see how the ogre's nature remains ambivalent. For this monster also embodies the rebel's liberating joy, a love of the present that refuses to think of the future, of the inevitability of death. His transgressions do not wholly efface his glorious beginnings as a revolutionary dedicated to the regeneration of his society. Cronus, wielding Gaea's sickle, appallingly mutilated his father Uranus, but in so doing inaugurated a new divine order: the reign of the Titans.

My study will not be encyclopedic; I have made selections that will leave out some of the classic ogres of French literature. With the exception of Emile Zola, I concentrate on post-1970 prose fiction in the French language, when Tournier and Chessex brought their ogres to the summit of literary success in France. Thus I will not study early prose like Rabelais's *Gargantua* (1534), Charles Perrault's tales (1697), or modern plays like Alfred Jarry's *Ubu* series (1896–1901) or Sartre's *The Flies* (1943).[5]

Chapter 1 ("Appetites: 'ingestion-digestion-defecation'"), opens with a study of Zola's *The Belly of Paris,* followed by analyses of *The Ogre* and Daniel Zimmermann's *Le Dixième Cercle* [The tenth circle]. The chapter is organized around those novels that demonstrate the ogre's enormous appetite for living prey. I broach scatological and cannibalistic themes, as well as the anti-Semitic tendencies that they sometimes reveal.

I begin with Zola's *The Belly of Paris* for two reasons. First, Zola is the primary representative of what Gilbert Durand calls the Dionysian period of modern literature (1992, 264–65), during which decadent and naturalist authors infuse their works with an erotic and intoxicated frenzy that underscores the tragedy of the human condition. For Frye, tragic stories, especially those related to divinities, are Dionysian "stories of dying gods" (1957, 35); the ironic literature of Zola displaces these myths and transports them to the human level. As we will see in chapter 1, the savage Dionysus, "eater of raw flesh" (Detienne 1998, 62), is, along with Cronus, one of the principal mythical incarnations of the ogre. And although other novels by Zola express a more intense Dionysian eroticism,[6] none articulates the ogre's prodigious appetite quite like *The Belly of Paris.*

A second reason to begin with Zola is that most of the post-1970 authors who comprise the bulk of my study—even though one would never classify them as naturalists—are indebted in some way to the father of naturalism. Some shock the reader with their frank descriptions of the body and sexuality, as did Zola, condemned as obscene by many of his contemporaries.[7] Others create characters whose nature, like that of Zola's heroes of naturalism, is rooted in the profoundly dark, bestial, demonic shadow of humanity. So it is not surprising that these stories, even those that are ostensibly realistic, should conjure up images of the mythical ogre. As Frye notes, "Irony . . . begins in realism and dispassionate observation. But as it does so, it moves steadily towards myth, and dim outlines of sacrificial rituals and dying gods begin to reappear in it" (1957, 42). In a letter to his friend Henry Céard in 1885, Zola belies his claim to a rigorously scientific writing method: "I have hypertrophy of the true detail, a leap to the stars on the springboard of exact observation. With the stroke of a wing, truth ascends to meet the symbol" (Zola 1985, 249). In naturalism, stark reality swells to an unrecognizable state, so that trivial objects—like the foods of the great market place in *The Belly of Paris*—metamorphose into the great archetype of the devouring ogre.[8]

Zola's protagonists in the twenty *Rougon-Macquart* novels are most often marginal beings, relatively poor workers or peasants, often drifting into the madness they have inherited from their ancestor Aunt Dide. Madness haunts the characters of our recent novels as well, from Tournier's well-meaning but delusional protagonist in *The Ogre*, who assures us, unconvincingly, "My name is Abel Tiffauges, . . . and *I'm not crazy*" (1997b, 4), to the bitter old man in Sylvie Germain's *Days of Anger*, a novel we will study in chapter 2: "Madness had burst upon Ambroise Mauperthuis, progressed by leaps and bounds, and then tautened like a bow, with contained violence. A frenzied madness, like a flash of lightning frozen in the sky. . . . He had confused beauty with crime, love with anger—and desire with death" (Germain 1993, 13).

Chapter 2 ("The Ogre as Sexual Predator") examines the relationship between sexual and alimentary appetites. The ogre is represented by his double the wolf—like the one in "Little Red Riding Hood"—hungry for young bodies. Once again, I study Tournier's *The Ogre*, in which the protagonist, Abel Tiffauges, equates eating and loving. Then I turn to works by a trio of contemporary women: Pierrette Fleutiaux, Sylvie Germain, and Muriel Cerf. Fleutiaux's "La femme de l'Ogre" [The ogre's wife] is a whimsical, but still disturbing, tale of an ogre's vegetarian wife who becomes the lover of the diminutive and ingenious Little Tom Thumb, whose small size belies his sexual prowess. Incest haunts Germain's *Days of Anger* and *The Medusa Child*. The former depicts the mad, murderous love of a man for his granddaughter; in the latter a little girl falls into what Julia Kristeva calls the "black sun" of depression, her life ruined by her sadistic half-brother, an ogre lurking within the walls of her own house. Cerf's *Ogres et autres contes* [Ogres and other tales] and *Le Verrou* [The bolt] portray the ogre in love: an obsessive, devouring love that destroys the object of its desire—often, but not always, an adolescent or pre-adolescent girl.

Time and mortality are the subjects of chapter 3 ("Avatars of Cronus: Time, Totalitarianism, and the Scapegoat"). For time, famously incarnated as Saturn or Cronus in Goya's painting *Saturn Devouring His Child* (1821–23), is the greatest ogre, eating up the seconds of our lives as we march toward death. Tournier's Tiffauges feels he has a special relationship with time, having lived on this planet, he claims, for millions of years. He believes he can suspend time through the act of "phoria" (carrying a child), and capture time in his photographs of children. In Jacques Chessex's *A Father's Love*, a castrating father holds sway over his weak son even in death; as many ogre tales do, this novel recounts the Oedipal rivalry between generations. In Daniel Pennac's *The Scapegoat*, a sinister group of Nazis holds a perverse power over time. Sex and violence combine in their rituals to free them from historical time; they aspire to live in an orgiastic eternal present. Pascal Bruckner's "Les Ogres anonymes" tells the story of a dashing Parisian modern-day ogre. Joining "Ogres Anonymous" does not help him break the habit; indeed, as we will see, he even organizes an extravagant suicide to ensure the perpetuation of his bloodthirsty race. Time and memory hold the key to Pierre Péju's *Le Rire de l'ogre* [The ogre's laugh]. His protagonists share inherited memories of a war experienced by their fathers. War is an ogre, and its devastation persists long after the cessation of hostilities.

Chapter 3 also examines the paradox of the ogre-scapegoat. The murderous tyrant and the innocent scapegoat, the two poles of character in the ironic mode of literature, are at times merged in the same individual (Frye 1957, 148). When this occurs, persecutor and persecuted are simultaneously polarizing and polarized: similar and dissimilar doubles, united but separated, they strangely combine identity and alterity in one being. If the "normal" relationship between ogre and victim is metonymical (based on their physical contiguity at the moment of the crime), the two have a metaphorical relationship when they are fused in one character. At any moment, the persecuted can be transformed into the persecutor: an insidious and paradoxical relationship ensues, which in effect makes evil the substitute for, and thus the equivalent of, good. The ogre is rehabilitated and, as René Girard explains in his essay *The Scapegoat*, given the honorable role of victim or scapegoat.

Chapter 4 ("The Dark Side of Aphrodite: The Ogress") examines the feminine side of the ogre in Chessex's *A Father's Love,* Tournier's "Veronica's Shrouds," and Cerf's *Ogres* and *Le Verrou*. Chessex's Thérèse, Tournier's Veronica, and Cerf's Nora contrast sharply—at least physically—with the beastly mythical ogre. Beauties rather than beasts, they bear no resemblance to the ghastly Saturn of Goya. They are femmes fatales more in the tradition of Aphrodite and the great goddesses who give death as readily as they give life and love. Thérèse shares certain aquatic attributes with Aphrodite; like the goddess, she consumes her lover by her infidelity, driving him to suicide. Veronica is a photographer, and her abuse of her model and lover illustrates the aggressiveness inherent in photography, which can capture a person's image, and use it to destructive ends. Finally, young Nora Neumann is both victim and ogress; she is prostituted by her mother and abused by older men, but in the end this girl of insatiable appetites gains revenge on her oppressors. These ogresses star in stories of pathological love, illustrating the inseparability of Freud's Eros and Thanatos instincts—what Freud himself called, cryptically enough, *Triebmischung*, a fusion of the drives. In the end, the male protagonists succumb to the ogress's superior energy, beauty, and inner strength.

In chapter 5, I conclude that the ogre metaphor is so compelling because ogres are a part of us as much as they are the monstrous Other. Like the Titan Cronus, they incarnate the ambiguity of humanity, capable of both immense good and immeasurable evil. I also address a crucial historical question: why did the ogre metaphor began to blossom in French fiction precisely during the last third of the twentieth century, continuing to this day? As we will see, this time period is characterized by a "cult of memory" (Todorov 1995, 51), that is summoning up shrouded realities from a somber past. France is finally acknowledging its willful participation in the Holocaust, as well as its disconcerting history of violence against women and children. These two crimes—personified by what I call the "political ogre" and the "sexual ogre"—have motivated much of the literature we are about to examine.

I give the last word to two authors who inspired this study. In separate interviews, Michel Tournier and Pascal Bruckner comment on what the ogre myth represents for them. For Tournier the ogre of folklore is an anal character, dominated by "digestion and defecation." The ogre's sense of smell is extraordinary, his eyesight weak. As a child, Tournier frequently visited Germany, and witnessed the rise of the Nazi ogre. The "biological obsession" that is Nazism starts with children; with militaristic fanfare, it seduces the young who correspond to its very narrow "Nordic ideal."

According to Pascal Bruckner, the ogre in literature reacquaints us with the dark side of human nature, explicitly present in old myths and tales, but lacking in our modern "Rousseauan" society, which views humans as good, while evil is a product of social institutions that can infect people "like a sickness." Finally, Bruckner sees the ogre as an illustration of the very fine line between Eros and Thanatos. As we will see in the chapters that follow, ogres kill not only with hate; they can also smother their victims with love, suffocating them with possessiveness, or consuming them with a passion gone awry.

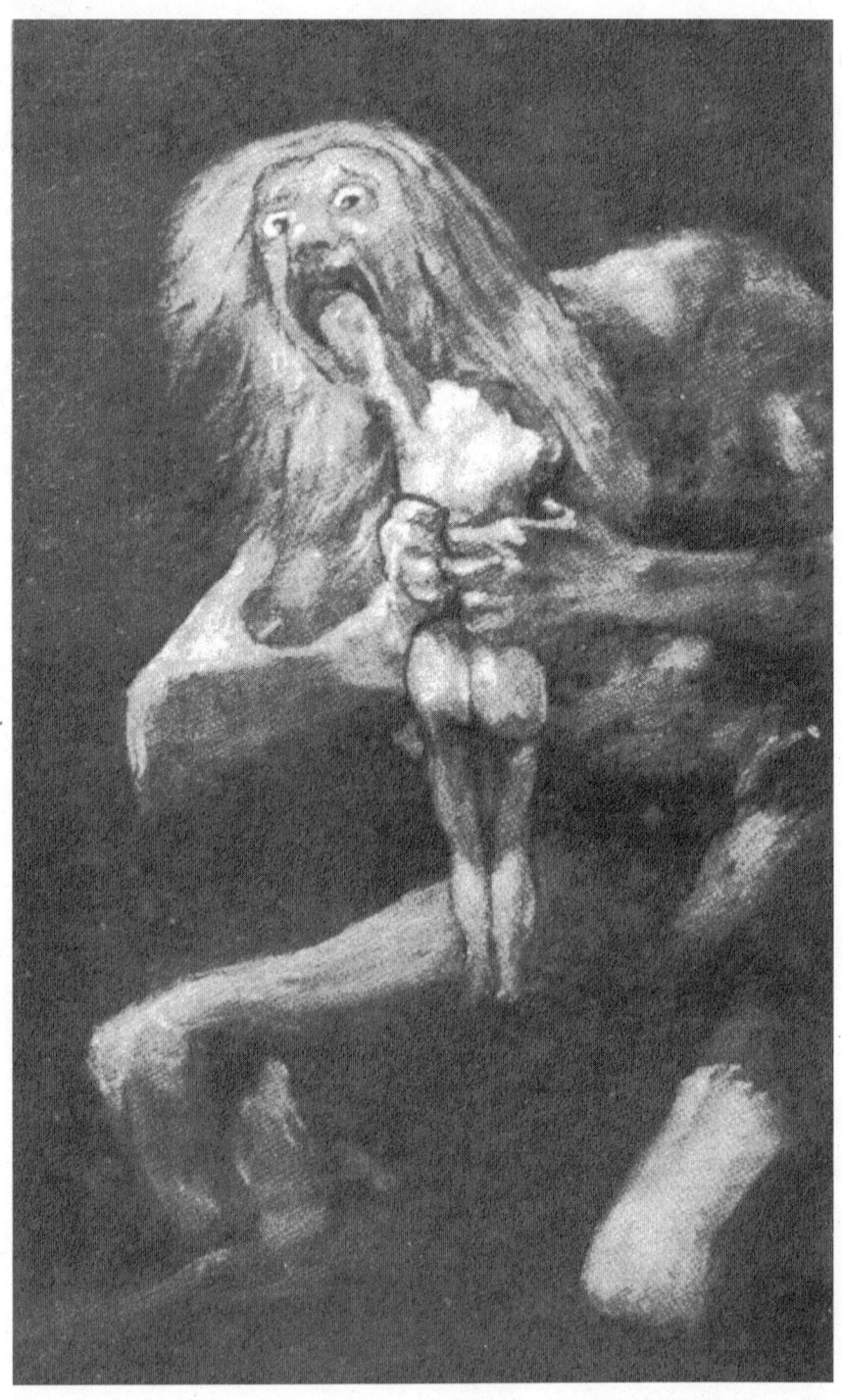

Francisco Goya, *Saturn Devouring His Child*, Museo del Prado, Madrid, Spain. Scala / Art Resource, NY.

1
Appetites: "ingestion-digestion-defecation"

> We have landed in the moment when the metaphors begin to devour themselves, the moment of rhetorical self-annihilation.
> —Eugenio Donato in Gopnik 2000, 154

> I marveled at the empirical, tranquil wonders of nature: how we chew food without thinking; how it unfailingly makes its way down to our stomach; how it stays there long enough to undergo subtle, almost alchemical transformations; how we extract life-giving elements from the food; how the residue of these mysterious operations is driven outside our body: to me everything—even the excrement—seemed deserving of interest and admiration.
> —Audeguy

THE OGRE'S APPETITE IS MONSTROUS. YOUNG, RAW FLESH IS HIS FOOD OF choice, taken in the most violent of ways. Yet the act of consuming is only a part of his nature; the victim descending the digestive track metonymically produces a myriad of themes. The ogre not only bites, he swallows, he digests, he defecates, and revels in his excrement. As Tournier writes of the schoolboy Nestor in *The Ogre,* "the trilogy ingestion-digestion-defecation" (Tournier 1997b, 20) governs the ogre's life.

EMILE ZOLA: *THE BELLY OF PARIS*

In *Figures mythiques et visages de l'oeuvre* (Mythic figures and faces of the work), the sociologist and literary critic Gilbert Durand analyzes the dominant literary myths of the last two hundred years. Early nineteenth-century France is the era of Prometheus, who symbolizes an optimistic belief in human progress and "the victory of historic man," who is a "rebel against the reign of the bad gods" (Durand 1992, 274). The high point of this Promethean art is Victor Hugo, in whose poetry Durand detects a plethora of antitheses, poetic expressions in which opposites are always contradictory and rarely combinatory. In Baudelaire and

Zola, however, Durand senses the end of the Promethean and the beginning of the Dionysian age. Hugo's antitheses yield to the oxymorons—figures in which contrasting elements are blended, rather than opposed—of Baudelaire, the poet who claims to be the "perfect chemist" (Durand 1992, 272). In his *Fleurs du mal* (*The Flowers of Evil*) he upholds his promise to intermingle gold and filth, beauty and evil.

Baudelaire's oxymorons typify the blurred boundaries that critics have noted in recent works of the postmodern age, and which also characterize the Dionysian era of late nineteenth-century France, exemplified by Emile Zola. Zola publishes the first volume of his enormous *Rougon-Macquart* project just a few months after the debacle of the Franco-Prussian War. France has been humiliated by Germany: Napoleon III is captured at Sedan, Lorraine and Alsace are lost; it is a time of national disillusion and despair. Zola represents with Baudelaire the end of Platonic dualism and the optimistic Promethean myth. The world is no longer black and white, but gray, and the Zolian antihero lives in a Dionysian blur, marked by sexual ambiguity and the excesses of violent crime, alcoholism, incest, adultery, and insanity.[1] As Zola condemns France's Second Empire (1852–70), writes Durand, he destroys the illusions of "the great titanic myths of Romanticism: Prometheus or Jesus," myths that were "bastardized in a 'decadence' confirmed by the monopoly of a myth: that of Dionysus" (1992, 264–65). Durand associates the Dionysian with ugliness and decadence, echoing the speculations of Nietzsche—Zola's contemporary—that the source of early Greek tragedy lay in the "demand for ugliness, . . . severe will to pessimism, to the tragic myth, to affirm the image of all that is fearsome, wicked, mysterious, annihilating and fateful at the very foundations of existence." Tragedy was born from "Dionysiac madness," which was perhaps "a symptom of degeneration, of decline, of a culture that has gone on too long." Or conversely—and this appears to be Nietzsche's conclusion—the Dionysian spirit, as a source of great art, might lie in "desire and delight, in strength, in overbrimming health, in an excess of plenitude" (Nietzsche 1999, 7). Indeed, Nietzsche finds a deep pessimism in both contemporary culture and in archaic Greece, but in the case of the Greeks, it was a paradoxically healthy pessimism: "Is pessimism *necessarily* a sign of decline, decay, malformation, of tired and debilitated instincts . . . ? Is there a pessimism of *strength*? An intellectual preference for the hard, gruesome, malevolent and problematic aspects of existence which comes from a feeling of well-being, from overflowing health, from an *abundance* of existence?" (1999, 4).

One can argue that, like ancient Greek tragedy, the "Dionysian" literature of nineteenth-century France was a fruitful by-product of the pessimism that resulted from political, social, and military upheavals and failures. And nowhere is the god of excess more powerful, more terrible than in Zola's *Rougon-Macquart* novels, which narrate the unbridled appetites and ambition of five generations of one family living under the oppression of Napoleon III.

The ogre is one incarnation of the fearsome madness of Dionysus, and Zola uses it to represent the degeneracy of Napoleon III's Second Empire. It is frequently places, rather than persons, that assume the mantle of the ogre. Zola's proletariat is devoured by its surroundings. For example, at the beginning of *Germinal,* Zola describes the ogreish mine that will eventually consume so many workers: "And Le Voreux[2] lay lower and squatter, deep in its den, crouching like a vicious beast of prey, snorting louder and longer, as if choking on its painful digestion of human flesh" (Zola 1993, 15). At the end, the protagonist Etienne has barely survived a mining accident, and he and his co-workers have suffered a bitter defeat at the hands of the mine owners. Nevertheless, he is still optimistic that the proletariat, dangerous and voracious, will prevail under his leadership: "He already saw himself on the rostrum leading the people to triumph, if the people didn't eat him alive before he got there" (1993, 521). After serving as fodder for the rich, the miners will at last consume their enemy: "If one class had to go under [*fût mangée*], wouldn't the people, who were still fresh and vital, trample [*mangerait*] all over the bourgeoisie, who were debilitated by their endless pleasure-seeking?" (1993, 521).[3]

Like *Germinal*'s mine, Père Colombe's distillery in *L'Assommoir* reeks of death. When Gervaise first visits the dram shop, she is overcome by anxiety in this hellish place. She cowers beneath the copper still that seems to conjure up devouring demons: "the shadow of the machinery against the back wall outlined abominable shapes, creatures with tails, monsters opening their jaws as though to swallow everyone up" (Zola 2000, 338).

But it is *The Belly of Paris* (*Le Ventre de Paris*), Zola's "gastric poem" (Guillemin 2002, 10), that best demonstrates the novelist's use of the ogre metaphor to describe a place. Paris's belly is *les Halles,* the huge market that occupied the center of Paris from the twelfth century until it was transferred to Rungis, near Orly Airport, in the 1960s. Zola's Paris is a beast, and les Halles are its digestive system. Florent, a political prisoner arrested in December 1851 during Napoleon III's brutal repression of a demonstration on the boulevard Montmartre, has recently escaped from Devil's Island. Weak with hunger as he approaches Paris on foot, he hitches a ride on a vegetable cart. When he finally arrives in the center of the city, he is overwhelmed by the sight of the enormous market at night:

No, Florent had never again been free from hunger. . . . And now that he was back in Paris once more, he found it fat and sleek and flourishing, teeming with food in the midst of the darkness. He had returned to it on a couch of vegetables; he lingered in its midst encompassed by unknown masses of food which continually increased and disquieted him. . . . Once again he saw the glittering windows on the boulevards, the laughing women, the luxurious, greedy city which he had quitted on that far-away January night; and it seemed to him that everything had expanded and increased in harmony with those huge markets, whose gigantic breathing, still heavy from the indigestion of the previous day, he now began to hear. (Zola 1996, 18)

Although vaguely disturbing, the market is not yet a truly threatening place; to the famished protagonist, back in the city after nearly eight years in the ghastly penal colony off French Guiana, it represents the possibility of a new life, from which hunger will be banished. Its "colossal jaws" are more nurturing than devouring. They nourish Paris, giving life to the city like "some huge central organ beating with giant force and sending the blood of life through every vein of the city" (1996, 43). Indeed, at times it seems a joyous place, as in this passage where two children born and raised in les Halles lead a carefree life in the belly of the beast: "They felt no fear of the huge monster; but slapped it with their childish hands, treated it like a good friend, a chum whose presence brought no constraint. And the markets seemed to smile at these two light-hearted children whose love was the song, the idyll of their immensity" (1996, 232–33). Similarly, Logre, a hunchback whose name, appearance, and fearsome demeanor would seem to incarnate the negative connotations of the market where he works as a fish auctioneer, is nonetheless a sympathetic character, one of Florent's comrades.[4]

Yet the escapee will always remain an outcast, even as he settles into the neighborhood, living with his brother and his family upstairs of their butcher shop. They, along with most people he meets in and around les Halles, are bourgeois "respectable people" [*honnêtes gens*] (1996, 397), wellfed and content to live in the Second Empire of Napoleon III. Florent, with his dreams of revolution, is their opposite not only politically but also physically. For he is a thin person [*un maigre*] out of place in this milieu of food and fat people [*les gras*]. This he realizes at once when, reunited with his brother, he meets his sister-in-law and niece for the first time: "He had now seated himself, and his glance turned from his brother to handsome Lisa and little Pauline. They were all brimful of health, squarely built, sleek, in prime condition; and in their turn they looked at Florent with the uneasy astonishment which corpulent people feel at the sight of a scraggy person [*un maigre*]. The very cat, whose skin was distended by fat, dilated its yellow eyes and scrutinized him with an air of distrust" (1996, 53–54).

1: APPETITES: "INGESTION-DIGESTION-DEFECATION"

Zola had hinted at the significance of the thin/fat opposition for his literary project a few years earlier, in his preface to *La Fortune des Rougon*, the first of the twenty novels that comprise the *Rougon-Macquart:* "The characteristic of the Rougon-Macquarts, the group, the family that I propose to study, is an insatiable appetite, the great upheaval of our age which rushes after pleasure. . . . Historically, the Rougon-Macquarts emerge from the masses, they radiate throughout contemporary society, . . . and thus through their individual dramas they tell the story of the Second Empire, from the ambush of the coup d'Etat to the treachery of Sedan" (Zola 1969, 35–36). The individual tragedies of the Rougon-Macquart family thus "tell" the tragedy of late nineteenth-century France, which for Zola suffers from its ravenous appetite for the pursuit of pleasure. But for every ogre chasing after his pleasure there is a victim, a fact of life that the artist Claude Lantier explains to his friend Florent:

> "Do you know the 'Battle of the Fat and the Thin'?"
> Florent, surprised by the question, replied in the negative; and thereupon Claude waxed enthusiastic, talking of that series of prints in very eulogical fashion. He mentioned certain incidents: the Fat, so swollen that they almost burst, preparing their evening debauch, while the Thin, bent double by fasting, looked in from the street with the appearance of envious stick figures. . . .
> In these designs Claude detected the entire drama of human life, and he ended by classifying men into Fat and Thin, two hostile groups, one of which devours the other and grows fat and sleek and enjoys itself.
> "Cain," said he, "was certainly one of the Fat, and Abel one of the Thin.[5] Ever since that first murder, there have been rampant appetites which have drained the lifeblood of the small eaters. It's a continual preying of the stronger upon the weaker; each swallowing his neighbor, and then getting swallowed in his turn. Beware of the Fat, my friend." (Zola 1996, 275–76)

Little by little, Florent realizes the danger that faces him in this world of fat. The voluptuous fishmongers he works with are giant ogresses; he is intimidated by the "savagery of these fishwives, the cruel tenacity of these huge females, whose massive figures heaved and shook with a giant-like joy whenever he fell into any trap. . . . Florent, who had always been afraid of women, gradually felt overwhelmed as by a sort of nightmare in which giant women, buxom beyond all imagination, danced threateningly around him, shouting at him in hoarse voices and brandishing bare arms, as massive as any prizefighter's" (1996, 161–62). This thin, unhappy man is right to fear the women of the market, including his beautiful sister-in-law Lisa, presiding like a priestess over the marvelous "sanctuary of gluttony" (1996, 51) that is her butcher shop. For the women will eventually denounce him to the police for fomenting a workers' rebellion. Les Halles gradually lose their protective quality as a potential shelter; they become an aggressive beast that Florent grows to fear and hate. Abhorring the injustices of Napoleon III and the Second Empire, he nevertheless finds himself working among its friends, and living in the belly of a politically conservative ogress:[6]

> To Florent [the markets] appeared symbolical of some glutted, digesting beast, of Paris, wallowing in its fat and silently upholding the Empire. He seemed to be encircled by swelling forms and sleek, fat faces, which over and over protested against his own martyr-like scragginess and sallow, discontented visage. To him the markets were like the stomach of the shopkeeping classes, the stomach of all the folks of average rectitude puffing itself out, rejoicing, glistening in the sunshine, and declaring that everything was for the best, since peaceable people had never before grown so beautifully fat. (1996, 182)

In *The Belly of Paris* then, the ogre metaphor is twofold. First, the great market is the digestive organ of Paris, with all the positive and negative connotations that this designation implies. It nourishes Paris, but as nourishment entails the death of the food source, so the market possesses a dark, threatening side, its "colossal jaws" (1996, 43) ever devouring victims. And who—or what—are these victims? Some are the fruits and vegetables that Claude Lantier imagines waiting for their death: "He stoutly maintained that they were not yet dead, but, gathered on the previous evening, waited for the morning sun to bid him good-bye from the flagstones of the market. He could observe their vitality, he declared, see their leaves stir and open as though their roots were yet firmly and warmly embedded in well-manured soil. And here, in the markets, he added, he heard the death-rattle of all the kitchen-gardens of the environs of Paris" (1996, 39).

More disquieting are the fish and meat, victims of les Halles whose deathly stench sickens Florent: "The masses of food amongst which Florent lived now began to cause him the greatest discomfort. The disgust with which the pork shop had filled him came back in a still more intolerable fashion. He almost sickened as he passed these masses of fish, which, despite all the water lavished upon them, turned bad under a sudden whiff of hot air" (1996, 178). The "victims" of the belly of Paris—living creatures sacrificed to feed Paris—are in turn the persecutors of Florent; they "revolt" and "suffocate" this "ascetic outlaw, in his way a modern Christ" (Mitterand 2002, 445).

But these persecutors will always remain victims in Florent's mind. In order to escape the "abominable odor" (Zola 1996, 178) of the fish,

Florent takes a walk, and finds relief as he observes the play of the setting sun on the intricate architecture of les Halles. But his relief is short-lived, and the stench of rotting flesh inspires in him images of a suffering people: "[B]ut on the flaming evenings, when the foul smells arose and forced their way across the broad yellow beams like hot puffs of steam, Florent again experienced discomfort, and his dream changed, and he imagined himself in some gigantic knacker's boiling-house where the fat of a whole people was being melted down" (1996, 179).

The second aspect of the ogre metaphor is political. The decomposing meat and fish sicken Florent, as does the repressive political system that most of the market workers espouse. "Evil smell" (1996, 179) describes not only the overwhelming attribute of the market, but also the discourse of the women who despise Florent, and plan to denounce him to the police as an escaped convict: their "words and gestures seemed to be infected with the evil smell of the place" (1996, 179). In a remarkably odoriferous and synesthetic metonymy that has been called a "symphony of cheeses" (Guillemin 2002, 10), the market women sing the stench of the cheeses around them:

> It was a cacophony of smells. . . . From the Cantal, the Cheshire, and the goats' milk cheeses there seemed to come a deep breath like the sound of a bassoon. . . . And then the different odors appeared to mingle one with another, the reek of the Limbourgs, the Port Saluts, the Géromés, the Marolles, the Livarots, and the Pont l'Evêques uniting in one general, overpowering stench sufficient to provoke asphyxia. And yet it almost seemed as though it were not the cheeses but the vile words of Madame Lecocur and Mademoiselle Saget that diffused this awful odor. (Zola 1996, 313)

The stinking discourse of the two women is that of all the "Fats" of the market: plump, healthy and content, defenders of the status quo, ever suspicious of change. These are the "respectable" or "honest" people whom Zola despises. They are relieved when Florent, who had threatened their way of life, is finally arrested and sent back to Devil's Island. The last words of the novel belong to Claude Lantier, who cannot resist one last meager insult, even as he admits defeat: "What scoundrels these honest people are!" (1996, 424). They are the defenders of the real ogre of *The Belly of Paris,* the Bonapartist government, which devours the freedoms so precious to Florent and the "Thin" of the 1848 revolution. The plight of these Republicans was echoed in the ill-fated 1871 Paris Commune, whose bloody repression Zola witnessed shortly before he began his novel.

Michel Tournier: *The Ogre*

> He was a monstrous creature with something of genius and something of magic about him. Was he a grown-up dwarf, whose development was arrested while he still had the stature of a child, or was he a baby giant, as his shape suggested? I couldn't say. (Tournier 1997b, 18)

With these words, Tournier's protagonist Abel Tiffauges describes the enigmatic Nestor, his friend and protector at St. Christopher's school in Beauvais (Picardy). Many ogres populate Tournier's novel, but it is Nestor who best illustrates the ogre's alimentary proclivity. An obese schoolboy with an enormous appetite, Nestor, the son of the concierge and thus privy to the secrets of the school, reigns over his peers with "absolute despotism" (1997b, 21). At the lunch table, students give him portions of their meal, "surround[ing] him, like an antique god, with offerings of food" (1997b, 20). Abel reports that Nestor eats "seriously" (1997b, 20), as if partaking in a sacred ritual. Years later, when Abel is no longer a puny and weak child, but becoming a man of imposing size and strength, his appetite becomes insatiable, and he believes this is Nestor's doing: "[M]y teeth, as Nestor had prophesied, began to grow: every day my stomach was gnawed by the most voracious appetite" (1997b, 66), especially for raw food. Oysters are his first obsession: "The gluttonous delight I felt when I sank my teeth in the glaucous mucosity, cool, salty and pungent as spray, of the soft shapeless little bodies abandoning themselves to oral possession, was one of the revelations of my vocation as an ogre" (1997b, 66). He goes on to steak tartare, which he consumes without the condiments, which "only mask the frank nudity of the flesh itself" (1997b, 67). Thanks to endless eating, Abel's weight finally grows in proportion to his height, and he notes that his body begins to resemble that of a horse, "because all my strength is massed in my wide hips and my rippling back" (1997b, 68). If Abel, with his massive torso and myopic vision, physically resembles the ogre or giant of fairy tales, he is in fact an anti-ogre of sorts. He drinks only unpasteurized and unhomogenized milk, "this liquid synonymous with life and tenderness and infancy" (1997b, 68), and he has a loving relationship with the flesh he consumes. So it seems, at least, in the following passage, in which Tournier happily broaches the paradox of love and tender consumption: "When I say I love meat and blood and flesh the only thing that matters is the word love. I am all love. I love eating meat because I love animals. I think I could even slaughter with my own hands an animal I'd raised as a pet, and eat it with affectionate appetite" (1997b, 67).

An abnormal interest in excrement is another characteristic that Abel "inherits" from Nestor. Late one night Nestor takes his protégé to the lavatory where he delivers a lecture on the nobility of the act of defecation. Climbing onto "his throne," Nestor is solemn, "as if performing some ritual" (1997b, 55); his folds of flesh veiling a tiny penis remind Abel of "a Hindu sage or a benevolent, meditative Buddha" (1997b, 56). Nestor names the anus omega, and like other "refined souls," he takes a "regal pleasure" (1997b, 56) in examining the sculptural or architectural wonders it can create on the toilet: "Tonight, . . . omega has been in medieval mood. Look, pretty Fauges[7]—towers and turrets surrounded by a double rampart" (1997b, 57). When he bids Abel to perform his "office," ordinary toilet paper will not do; he has Abel use a paper inscribed with the sacred signs of one of Father Superior's best sermons.

Abel never forgets this night, which turns out to be Nestor's last. The next day he perishes in a fire that has the happy consequence of closing the school and saving Abel from a severe punishment for a prank of which he is innocent. Abel is persuaded that Nestor died for him, and, more importantly, that his personal destiny is secretly linked to events in ways that no one can imagine. Nestor, "microgenitomorphous" like Abel (1997b, 65), is his savior, and the spiritual progenitor of the ogre that Abel is destined to become.

Thanks to Nestor's influence, omega and anality will be a great force in Abel's life, to the detriment of alpha, the phallus, for which he feels no kinship. Constipation approaches art for him. When suffering from this malady, he describes himself as "a bust of human flesh standing on a plinth of feces" (1997b, 120). Although he does not yet understand why, he feels an affinity for the earth, perhaps recalling Nestor's remark that there is a certain "magnetism" (1997b, 56) between the anus and the earth, that element full of the decomposing matter so necessary for life.

Drafted into the French army in 1939 and taken prisoner in Alsace, Abel will journey eastward and northward to a camp in the mysterious land of East Prussia, "[a] black and white country, . . . not much gray, not much color—a white page covered with black signs" (1997b, 167). It is here that Abel will encounter the multiple ogres—a monstrous blind elk, a two thousand-year-old cadaver exhumed from the peat bog, and Field Marshal Hermann Goering—who will explain the significance of his existence.

As a prisoner of war in East Prussia, he digs trenches with energetic enthusiasm, because "foraging in the earth seemed a way of expediting a message addressed to him alone" (1997b, 167). But his greatest joy is the "fecal felicity" [*béatitude fécale*] he experiences at the end of the day in the latrines: "Perhaps it was something to do with all the rich black earth he shifted day after day . . . It was perhaps the best moment of the day and brought back vividly the years in Beauvais. It was an interlude of solitude, calm and meditation during an act of defecation performed generously and without excessive effort, by a regular descent of the turd into the lubricated sheath of the mucous membranes" (1997b, 168). For Abel the act is a spiritual beatitude; a "rite of meditation" (1997b, 168) that recalls the yogic and ritualistic atmosphere of Nestor's last night.

Abel is a hard worker, and his captors grant him a good amount of freedom; thus he manages to escape from time to time to the solitude of a cabin he has discovered in the woods. He calls the cabin his "Canada," remembering Jack London's and James Curwood's stories of the great North American forests, tales that thrilled him (and Tournier as well) as a boy. Here he feeds and befriends a great blind elk, an ungainly monster for whom he feels a strong affinity: "The elk of Canada was blind. Now Tiffauges understood the begging demeanor, the awkward gait, the somnambulistic slowness; and because of his own awful myopia he felt close to the dark giant" (1997b, 177). He learns from the chief forester that the locals call the elk "Monster,"[8] believing that he is "a sorcerer, a devil" (1997b, 182), foreshadowing the reputation that Abel himself will later have as the "Ogre of Kaltenborn" (1997b, 294), kidnapping young Prussian boys to serve in the Nazi military school.

Shortly thereafter, a second fantastic creature bearing an uncanny resemblance to Abel appears. A perfectly preserved corpse is exhumed from the acidic peat bogs near the prison camp, and it is first thought to be Abel, because of its large build. The archeologist in charge of the excavation theorizes that it was a king of some ancient German tribe, who was perhaps killed in a ritualistic sacrifice. He is wearing a band over his eyes featuring a six-pointed golden star. Buried next to him is a small figure—probably a child—of whom only the head remains. The archeologist triumphantly declares that the man will be called "The Erl-King," after the mysterious king of the dark forest who frightens a young boy to death in Goethe's famous ballad.[9]

The forester, who appreciates Abel's love for "Monster," eventually assigns him as a mechanic to the hunting lodge of the Rominten Wildlife Reserve, presided over by "the ogre of Rominten" (1997b, 196), Hitler's second-in-command, Field Marshal Hermann Goering. A man of enormous size and appetite, cruel toward man and beast, keenly interested in excrement, the two hundred and eighty pound Goering is shockingly similar to his pet lion. As Abel watches them dine, Goering teases the lion, waving a boar's leg in front of it: "Finally the Master of the Hunt sank his teeth into it, and for a few moments his face disappeared completely behind the monstrous joint. Then, with his mouth full, he held the leg out to the lion, who bit into it in his turn. From then on the leg passed regularly back and forth between the two ogres, who gazed at each other affectionately as they chewed the lumps of black, musky flesh" (1997b, 206).

As Master of the Hunt, Goering regards stag hunting as "a cult at once amorous, sacrificial and culinary" (1997b, 204), centered around the size, span, weight, and color of the antlers. For Abel, always searching for symbols, the antlers are the sublimation of the animals genitals, always severed after the kill: "The fact that the antlers were so literally phallic lent hunting and the art of venery a disturbingly profound meaning. To bring a stag to bay, kill it, emasculate it, eat its flesh, and steal its antlers to glorify himself with them as a trophy—this was the procedure in five acts of the ogre of Rominten, official sacrificer of the Phallophoric Angel" (1997b, 212). The ogre of Rominten—Goering—is thus the high priest of the hunt. His "enormous white rump" (1997b, 211) and his "coprological gifts" (1997b, 212)—no one could surpass him in the knowledge and interpretation of animal droppings—make him moreover a man of omega (the anus), annihilating alpha (the phallus) from the Rominten game reserve. Goering constantly reminds Abel of Nestor, and he is thrilled to be "the servant and secret pupil of the second most important person in the German Reich, an expert in phallology and coprology" (1997b, 213). He is equally elated when he has the opportunity to learn about horses, who serve in the massacres of the stags. The forester gives him an enormous black gelding—an appropriate choice for the "microgenitomorphous" Abel—which he decides to name Bluebeard. Fascinated by the animal's hindquarters and especially by its impressive ability to defecate, Abel declares that "the crupper makes the horse the Spirit of Defecation, the Anal Angel, and makes Omega the key of its essence" (1997b, 226). In Abel's world of symbols, then, since the horse is used by the hunter to pursue the stag, the hunt is "the persecution of the Phallophoric Angel by the Anal Angel, the pursuit and putting to death of Alpha by Omega" (1997b, 226).

If the ogres of fairy tales are normally slow-witted, those of Tournier's novel are distinguished by their "intellectual" activities, namely, an interest in semiotics. For Goering, this is limited to his interpretations of the droppings of forest animals. Nestor, however, described through the admiring eyes of Abel, seems wise and serious beyond his years. He walks with a "majestic slowness" (1997b, 19) and talks with a "professorial solemnity" (1997b, 19) that earn him the uneasy respect of students and teachers alike. For Nestor is a sage, like his venerable namesake in Greek mythology, a veteran of the Argonauts' quest and hero of the Trojan War. But for Abel it is especially Dionysus's old teacher whom Nestor resembles: "There was something of Silenus about him, with his pendent cheeks, round belly and large rump. His life's rhythm was the trilogy ingestion-digestion-defecation, and these three operations were surrounded by general respect. But this was only Nestor's visible face. His hidden face, which only I suspected, was signs, the deciphering of signs" (1997b, 20). Physically, Nestor is a monstrous paradox: a large dwarf or a baby giant (1997b, 18), recalling images of Silenus. Grotesque like the great satyr, Nestor appears—at least in Abel's eyes—to be just as wise as Silenus, in antiquity (most famously in Alcibiades's encomium to Socrates in Plato's *Symposium*) often identified with Socrates. As Silenus taught Dionysus, so does Nestor instruct Abel, imparting to him the ability to understand the deep meanings beyond ordinary events.

Reading signs and symbols becomes Abel's obsession. The major events of current history—most notably the war—are all invested with meanings that he is sure connect to his personal destiny. In September 1939 Abel is unjustly accused of having molested a young girl, Martine, whom he sometimes drove home from school. His collection of photographs of school children is considered damning evidence, and he is certain to be given a severe jail sentence. But war is brewing, France is mobilizing. The judge drops the case because he knows Abel will be drafted. Abel is convinced that war has broken out for no reason other than to save him from jail, just as the fire in which Nestor perished was fate's way of sparing him punishment: "Fate was on the march and had taken in charge my poor little personal destiny. . . . The great stewpot of history has started to simmer, and nothing can stop it, and no one knows who will come out of it or who will be thrown in. The school is going to burn down, as it did twenty years ago in Beauvais. But this time the conflagration will be in proportion to Tiffauges the giant, and to the terrible threat that hung over him" (1997b, 125).

After meeting the blind elk, Abel believes that East Prussia has sent the creature to him as a "representative: a half-fabulous beast that seemed to emerge from the great Hercynian forests of prehistory" (1997b, 176). Lying awake at night, he has "the strange conviction he'd always had of possessing immemorial origins, of having roots that went back into the deepest mists of time" (1997b, 176). Likewise he believes that the "Erl-King" and his young companion, buried for centuries in the peat bogs, also have a special, but as yet unknown message for him. His journey as a soldier and prisoner of war is a passage through time as well as space, which will reveal to him both his origins and his destiny:

> He was thinking that his long migration toward the east, into which he had been plunged by the Martine affair and the war it had caused, was accompanied by a pilgrimage into the past, marked from the reflective point of view

by the appearance of the Monster and the peat-bog man. . . . He suspected with a delicious anguish that his journey would take him still farther, still deeper, into the most venerable shades, and that he might finally arrive at the immemorial darkness of the Erl-King. (1997b, 200–1)

Prussia itself is a country "studded with allegories and hieroglyphs" he yearns to read. In its "cold and penetrating hyperborean light, all symbols shone with unparalleled brilliance" (1997b, 179). With its "totemic signs" and "emblematic fauna," this land is a "constellation of allegories" awaiting "a Tiffaugian interpretation" (1997b, 180). He believes that he can decipher it with what he calls his "prophetic eye" (1997b, 178), which excels where his myopic physical eyes fail him. Later on, while working at the Kaltenborn Nazi military school, he is not particularly surprised when a doctor he works with insists that his surname, Tiffauges, must be a derivation of the German *Tiefauge,* or deep eye (1997b, 261).

After Abel has spent some time at his next assignment, innocently "recruiting" (kidnapping, in fact) young boys for Kaltenborn, he begins to learn from the commandant of Kaltenborn castle, a Prussian aristocrat immersed in heraldry, about the corruption, or "malign inversion" (1997b, 302) of signs, for which the Nazis have been responsible: "Signs are strong, Tiffauges—it is they that brought you here. Signs are irritable, and the symbol thwarted becomes a diabol. From being a center of light and concord it becomes a power of darkness and division" (1997b, 302). Abel's supreme passion is what he calls "phoria," the simple act of tenderly carrying a child. But Abel's recruiting activities have turned him into the feared and hated "ogre of Kaltenborn" (1997b, 294), and an innocent deed into a crime. After Jesus carried his cross, the situation was inverted and the cross carried him: "When the symbol devours the thing symbolized, when the cross-bearer becomes the crucified, when a malign inversion overthrows phoria, then the end of the world is at hand" (1997b, 303). Indeed, fulfilling the commandant's prophecy, the novel soon ends in an apocalyptic vision of destruction. Shortly after Abel learns of the horrors of Auschwitz from a young refugee named Ephraim, the Russians destroy Kaltenborn and its boys in a hail of bullets and rain of blood. In the final scene, Abel, fleeing the conflagration, becomes a modern Christ—or Christophoros—succumbing to the weight of his cross, as he sinks slowly into the swamp, Ephraim clinging to his shoulders. Like the archaic "Erl-King" and his small companion, they descend into, and become one with, the enigmatic land that held Abel's destiny and death.

Daniel Zimmermann: *Le Dixième Cercle: L'Anus du monde*
[The tenth circle: The anus of the world]

Near the end of *The Ogre*, Tournier's narrator refers to Auschwitz as "the Anus Mundi, the great metropolis of degradation, suffering and death" (1997b, 353). This cynical nickname for the extermination camp was coined by an SS doctor at Auschwitz, Heinz Thilo, whom Daniel Zimmermann quotes in one of the epigraphs to his shocking novel: "Here we are in the *anus mundi*" (Zimmermann 1997, 11). The central role of excrement in *Le Dixième Cercle: L'Anus du monde* is underscored by this and the two other epigraphs on the same page. Zimmermann first recalls a scene from the eighth circle of Dante's *Inferno*:

> We went there; and in the moat I saw people plunged in a filth that seemed to have come from human latrines.
> And as I looked closely I saw one with his head so soiled with excrement that one could not tell if he was a layman or a cleric.

And finally there is this reflection from *Tseenah Ureenab*, by Jacob ben Isaax Achkenazi, on the miraculous manna that fed the Israelites for forty years during their exile in the desert (Exodus 16): "People's bodies absorbed the manna and they never had to defecate."

Le Dixième Cercle is the excruciating story of twenty-one-year-old François Katz, first in his class at the *Ecole Normale Supérieure*, class of 1939, whose two passions are the violin and the dissertation he is just beginning on Dante's *Inferno*. Little does he realize how similar France in the 1940s will be to Dante's thirteenth-century Florence: "The Guelphs and Ghibellines tear each other to pieces in Florence, the barbarism of this time, massacres, prohibitions, loss of citizenship, imprisonments, tortures and executions" (Zimmermann 1997, 34). Indeed, the French police of the Vichy Regime, collaborating with the Nazi occupiers, soon arrest him as a Jew.[10] He is interred at Drancy, in the northeast Paris suburbs, then deported to Auschwitz and Treblinka. What was merely an intellectual fascination for Dante becomes François's life, an abominable journey through the hellish circles of the Nazi system of labor and death camps. The novel, dedicated to Zimmermann's thirty-seven relatives "gassed and burned by the Nazis at Auschwitz and Treblinka" (1997, 9), tells the story of a young man who desperately wants to survive, and in so doing must perform unspeakable tasks and sometimes betray his fellow prisoners in order to save his own life. His situation and that of his comrades is hopelessly obscene: perhaps the only apt description of it is in fact through Zimmermann's disturbing scatological metaphor.

Before his arrest in the fall of 1940, François has had an easy life. He is a brilliant student, spoiled by his mother (a doctor) and his father (an accountant and decorated World War I veteran). His family is atheistic, and his only attachment to his Jewishness seems to be a weakness for certain dishes, like chopped liver with onions (1997, 28). François quickly forgets his interest in eating at Drancy, where the daily menu is "famine organized around two soups and two hundred twenty grams of bread" (1997, 56); here the fundamental task is how to maintain one's dignity when the privacy of defecation is suddenly lost. But as the head of his prison cell, he does have one advantage: "In fact, he has the right to be the first to go to the toilet. More appalling than he had foreseen: a pit dug outside, impossible to be alone, sixty men urinate and defecate side by side, no toilet paper, not even a piece of newspaper" (1997, 53–54). As the prisoners are overcome by weakness and illness, the entire prison resembles the latrines, nicknamed the "Château." François's private toilet paper—his notebook full of notes for his dissertation—is soon used up: "The steps, the courtyard are covered with excrement. . . . Now, when he must go to the foul stench of the Château, he has to walk through the excrement strewn all around it. With one hand, he holds back his trousers and underwear, with the other he wipes himself" (1997, 57–58). More than once he sees men faint with hunger who, after having cleaned themselves with their finger, unthinkingly scratch their head with the same finger. Once again François thinks of the *Inferno*, recalling the scene quoted above of the man "with his head so soiled with excrement," and resolves not to let himself fall into such degradation.

This "river of shit" (1997, 104) that is the eighth circle of hell is a leitmotiv of the novel, whose subtitle Zimmermann never lets the reader forget. Deported to Auschwitz, François becomes the "feces inspector" [*inspecteur des selles*] (1997, 175–97), and later, at Treblinka, the "master of shit" [*maître de la merde*] (1997, 222–42). As feces inspector, he helps the SS doctors determine the fate of prisoners in the infirmary. They are given one minute to defecate, and François must examine the results: "More or less solid feces result in an immediate assignment to a work unit. If the excrement is liquid, without any other anomaly, the patient stays in the infirmary. The third category is that of bloody stools. In this case the secretary writes down Death from diarrhea on his register, even if the patient in question must wait until the evening or the next day to be gassed or injected" (1997, 191). At Treblinka, the SS give him a similar task. He must dress up as a rabbi, sit in the latrine and regulate bowel movements, limiting each prisoner to two minutes. As master of the "asshole of the world" (1997, 238), he carries on some interestingly cynical theo-scatological discussions with another intellectual of the camp: Since the Hebrews who were nourished by manna during their exile had no need to defecate, "did they have anuses or not?" (1997, 239). Did Adam and Eve possess anuses, since they ate a divinely vegetarian diet in the Garden, and would thus totally absorb this perfect food (1997, 240)? If they did have anuses, does that mean that God does too, since he created the first humans in his image? What use would an anus be to the Perfect Being (1997, 240–41)? These discussions provide the reader with some needed, albeit cynical comic relief, without straying from the repulsive and insistent extended metaphor of the novel. Defecation is a fundamental need as well as a fundamental right, the abuse of which is a principal tool of the SS in the death camps, where Jews, whether French, German or any other nationality, are but "sows of shit to exterminate, trash to burn" (1997, 206).

The cover of the "Folio" edition of *Le Dixième Cercle* features a detail of Goya's famous *Saturn Devouring His Child*. This depiction of the wild-eyed cannibal god, hands clutching the torso of a decapitated figure, mouth encircling a blood-drenched stump that was once a left arm, serves to introduce a secondary ogre theme of the novel: cannibalism. Marina Warner notes the "saturnine humour" in the possibility that Goya's *Saturn* may have hung in the painter's dining room (Warner 1999, 48). Nevertheless, this work of art suggests a serious link between cannibalism, infanticide, and eroticism. Warner points out that the "almost voluptuously painted buttocks" (1999, 50) suggest that the figure being devoured is not a newborn baby as in the Greek myth.[11] Perhaps it is not even a son, as the usual title given to the painting implies, but a "nubile young woman" (1999, 50), one of the god's daughters. She goes on to explain that before its restoration (1874–78), the painting may have depicted Saturn with an erect penis. She interprets the erotic charge of the work as follows: "The artist perhaps intuited that Saturn's famished assault on the body of one of his children would have excited him. Or, he may be showing that his sexual appetite stimulated his murderous violence. In either case, the ogre's drive to incorporate has erotic force for him" (1999, 51).

Warner remarks that the "motif of cannibalism, in its earliest mythological expression, enfolds a threat to children above all" (1999, 53). Indeed, some of the more horrific scenes in *Le Dixième Cercle* concern children being abused, both by the SS and by other prisoners. At Drancy, François enters a room full of children waiting to be deported to Auschwitz: "He discovers, bewildered, the horror of the scene. The room has no furniture. Just straw mats scattered on the ground, disgustingly filthy, soaked with urine, stained with semi-solid excrement or liquid feces.... What upsets François the most is the resigned look of the kids, their motionless features, their staring eyes.... What are they doing here . . . in the river of shit in the second *bolgia*[12] of the eighth circle?" (Zimmermann 1997, 104).

In Auschwitz, some of Dr. Mengele's lethal experiments concern twins, and persons with heterochromia (eyes of two different colors). François, forced to be the doctor's "supplier of fresh flesh" (1997, 155), spares baby twins from the gas chamber and brings them to Mengele. Some days later, Mengele asks him to play Gabriel Fauré's *Lullaby* for the twins. As he plays the air—his mother's favorite—on the violin, thinking he is lulling them to sleep, he is sickened to see two nurses plunging syringes into the babies' chests (1997, 174).

In another scene, François is forced to betray his friend Hans—one of the highest ranking kapos[13]—by some of Hans's rivals. In order to show what will happen if he does not obey, they tie up a young boy and put him on a white-hot stove, where he quickly burns to death. One of the rival kapos, Mietek the Bloody, throws the corpse on the floor, "disembowels it with a slice of his knife, and eviscerates it with his bare hands, groaning with pleasure" (1997, 177). Later, a young boy is "forced to bend to the vile demands of the adult monster" (1997, 218–19); when he bites the SS who is raping him, he is hanged.

A young boy is also victimized in the final pages, when the famished prisoners turn to cannibalism, which is the culmination of the Saturnian themes in the novel. The crime takes place at Treblinka, but already in Auschwitz Franz has his first realization that such abominations are happening in the death camps. He witnesses the arrival of a convoy of Greek Jews from Salonica; hundreds died of hunger or asphyxiation during the twenty-two day trip, and the seventeen survivors apparently stayed alive by eating human flesh. One of François's fellow prisoners remarks ironically: "Hunger is when a human being looks at another human being, saying to himself that it is something edible" (1997, 152); and "the human brain is truly so delicate that one can eat it without cooking it" (1997, 153). Later, when François is being punished with three others in a minuscule cell, without food and water, he remembers in his delirium a cannibalistic scene from Dante: "The Poet saw two frozen men in the same hole; the one's head covered the other's; and as one eats bread when one is hungry, the one on top planted his teeth in the second one, where the brain joins the nape of the neck. No, even if he were desperately hungry, he could never resolve to endure in this way, like the young Jewish cannibals from Salonica" (1997, 185).

But he does succumb to this unthinkable temptation in Treblinka. One evening, what seems to be "a true miracle" (1997, 231) comes to pass: a thick, delicious soup, full of meat. François's good friend Rudy, a young teenager, becomes hysterical when in his bowl he discovers a human jawbone, "bristling with teeth" (1997, 232). "I ate a man and I want to die" (1997, 232), cries Rudy, and, with François's reluctant help, hangs himself. The senior prisoner of the camp, afraid that anthropophagy may become rampant among the starving prisoners, declares to François: "Better to die than to return to the dawn of prehistory. Thus, in the name of the committee [group of prisoners planning an insurrection] I order you to personally execute all the cannibals" (1997, 234). Which François does: the months spent in the "anus of the world" have turned the scholar-musician into an efficient killer with only one goal: to survive.

The final pages of the book recount in gruesome, rapid prose the burning of thousands of corpses by the prisoners. The end of the war is in sight, and the SS, fearing that the camp may soon be liberated, is attempting to conceal the horror of what took place there. François, utterly exhausted, is counting the days to the insurrection. With one day left, he is about to burn a particularly plump corpse that has just been unloaded from the train. A fellow prisoner—a pious Jew who used to perform circumcisions—declares that the body cannot be burned because it contains several tattoos of the sacred tetragrammaton IHWH ("Yahweh," or "Lord"). Invoking Freud, another prisoner suggests that by eating the man, they would ingest his "physical and moral qualities" (1997, 251) and thus become strong for the insurrection.[14] The novel ends with this macabre scene the night before the revolt. François—the confirmed atheist—asks his friend to circumcise him as the group prepares to roast and eat the dead man:

> The big tattooed man was not burned, but roasted. François wondered if he would participate in the cannibalistic feast or not. . . .
> "Am I too old to be circumcised?" . . .
> While Moshe severed his foreskin, François looked at the stars; they shone more brightly. Moshe stopped the bleeding with his mouth,[15] then he wrapped the glans in a filthy rag. Next they ate. Moshe and François shared the liver.
> "I used to like it finely chopped with onions," dreamed Moshe.
> "And me, I liked it better browned in butter with a bit of lemon juice," remembered François.
> The next day, the insurrection erupted. (1997, 251–52)

"The ogre is a distant descendant of Saturn," writes the poet and essayist Gérard Macé in *Le Goût de l'homme* (Macé 2002, 11) [The taste of man]. The cannibalistic scene with which Zimmermann closes *Le Dixième Cercle* is worthy of the fearsome god; however, the cruelty evident in Goya's painting is absent here. For cruelty is not necessarily the foremost element of cannibalism; it can be a desperate act of survival, or a ritual of homage to a respected enemy or friend, as in the Freud text in which the father to be devoured is "feared and envied" by his sons. Both aspects exist in this scene.

We have seen how, earlier in the novel, seventeen Jews survive the harrowing voyage from Salonica to Auschwitz in a boxcar by eating their dead companions. This extreme response to a hopeless situation brings to mind the Jewish mother who, according to the historian Flavius Josephus's *The Wars of the Jews,* kills and eats her baby during the siege of Jerusalem in the first century AD. She commits infanticide not just to feed herself, but also to save her infant from "the calamities of us Jews" (Josephus 1987, 737).

This act stuns the modern reader who cannot help but see a disturbing similarity between the "calamities" of the Jewish people of the first century—enslavement and starvation—and those of the twentieth century. Marina Warner writes that the "callous motives" of the mother, whose infanticide "nullifies the meaning of maternity" (Warner 1999, 56) hardened Caesar against the Jews. Furthermore, stories of eating the flesh and drinking the blood of newborns, whether real or fictitious, will contribute to anti-Semitic propaganda over the centuries (Warner 1999, 56; Detienne 1998, 59).

The cannibalistic feast of the Treblinka insurgents is a ritualistic meal by which the men hope to incorporate the spiritual and physical traits of the victim, in order to carry out their desperate revolt against the SS. The victim is the perfect sacrifice, both physically (given his plumpness) and spiritually (given his sacred tattoos). The scene, lyrically recounted, is tinged with a liturgical, cultic spirituality. While François is being circumcised, his companions are "singing joyously" (Zimmermann 1997, 252). François, apparently renouncing his fervent atheism, hopes that the circumcision ceremony will give him the spiritual fortitude necessary to succeed. Moreover, the cooking of their meal is ritualistically correct, following the strict sacrificial rules of the ancient cults of Dionysus.

In *Dionysos*[16] *Slain,* Marcel Detienne examines the Orphic myth of Dionysus, in which the child god is killed and eaten by the Titans. Of fundamental importance is the fact that Dionysus is not consumed raw: he is boiled, then roasted. Even though the accepted Greek sacrificial practice was the opposite—the victim should be roasted before it is boiled—still the act is not a crazed, bloodthirsty murder, like Saturn eating his children, but a sacrificial ritual (Detienne 1998, 72). Detienne, the great French Hellenist, studies in detail the cultural and religious significance of roasting (a primitive cooking method) and boiling (a more modern, thus more refined culinary technique, leading to well-seasoned stews, and eventually to such French favorites as *coq au vin* and *pot au feu*). Citing Aristotle's *On the Parts of Animals* (350 BC), he reveals that the Greeks required the internal organs (liver, heart, etc.) of sacrificial animals to be roasted. These are "vital parts" (1998, 75), full of blood, and thus the most important food of the sacrificial meal.[17] Consumed first, without wine, without salt, they are reputed to confer power on the person who eats them (1998, 75).[18] When shared with others, viscera (*splánkhna* in Greek, meaning the heart, lungs, liver, and kidneys) bestow a kind of solidarity on the group. As an example, Detienne cites Book Three of the *Odyssey*, in which Nestor and his sons share with Telemakhos the splánkhna of a solemn sacrifice to Poseidon: "In this way, Telemakhos and his comrades are fully associated with the sacrifice. By receiving their share of the viscera, they take their place in the circle of those the Greeks called 'eaters of *splánkhna*'" (1998, 77).

The Greeks did not limit their sacrifices to animals. Detienne describes the fascinating tradition of human sacrifice and cannibalism in ancient Greece, which occurs most notably among the devotees of Dionysus. While not in the mainstream of Greek culture, these practices deserve attention, since to understand a society is "to map out its transgressions, interrogate its deviants" (1998, ix). Effervescent Dionysus, "mirror of the Other, the Savage," is also "the god of inspiration, of the enthusiasm that knows no limits imposed by the social order" (Caillaud 2000, 9). Detienne writes that he is the incarnation of man's bestial, instinctual, and savage appetites: "Dionysos the savage hunter is not simply the 'eater of raw flesh' . . . ; the omophagy he requires of his devotees leads them, like true wild beasts, to indulge in the most cruel allelophagy" (Detienne 1998, 62). In other words, Dionysus's worshipers were required to eat raw animal flesh (omophagy; often thought of as eating the god), and so developed a taste for human flesh (allelophagy), and began to practice cannibalism. Detienne goes on to cite various Dionysian rituals in which cannibalism was practiced, and concludes that Dioysianism was at once savage and sacred: "Tasting human flesh and surrendering oneself totally to allelophagy both belong to a set of behaviors designed to make man a wild creature and allow the establishment, through possession, of more direct contact with the superhuman, in this case Dionysos eater of men" (1998, 63).

Thus François and his companions at Treblinka are not bloodthirsty barbarians. Their act, though born of desperation, is also steeped in history and cultic spirituality. Ingesting the tattooed man is a way to incorporate his spiritual and physical health. No allusion is made to the consumption of non-vital parts of the victim. Only the roasted liver is mentioned and, although Moshe and François dream of spices and sauces, it is served plain, as Aristotle reports was the law of the ancient Greeks.

A reader of Zimmermann's novel can profit from a perusal of Gérard Macé's *Le Goût de l'homme,* a collection of three essays touching on anthropology, anthropophagy, and anti-Semitism. Macé too finds links between the Jews, Nazism, and cannibalism. The title of the book is quite literal: "the taste of man," according to those who have experienced it, is actually quite delicious. The recently vanished Guayaki tribe of Paraguay, studied by Pierre Clastres in the 1960s (*Chronicle of the Guayaki Indians,* 1973), used to eat its dead. The only taboo connected with this practice is that one did not eat close relatives. Thus the prohibition of incest applied to the cannibalistic practice of the Guayaki: "one does not eat those with whom one would not make love.... For them, as for we who 'consummate' marriage, love is a sublimated form of devouring" (Macé 2002, 60). As for the taste of man, the Guayaki claimed that it is very close to that of the pig (2002, 61).

Promoters of anti-Semitism have long assimilated the Jewish interdiction of pork to an identification of Jews with pigs, and with the practice of cannibalism. The bizarre logic was: "if they don't eat pork, they eat humans" (2002, 64). Macé reports that for the Roman poet Juvenal (first century), Jews make "no distinction between human and pork flesh" (2002, 64). He also recounts some European folktales where Jesus turned Jews into pigs and vice versa. The Gospels[19] recount how Jesus drove the demons out of a possessed man and caused them to enter a herd of swine, which then rushed into the sea and drowned. The "unclean spirit" (Luke 8:29) is thus diverted into the unclean beast, demonizing not only the pig, but also, for the anti-Semitic reader, the Jew with whom it is identified.

Pork, writes Macé, is "the Christian meat par excellence." The pig is thus "the closest Other, and ... it thus allows us to trace a dividing line between Christians and Jews, and then to assimilate the latter to the foul beast" (2002, 67). "The closest Other" is also how one can consider the monstrous, the ogre that is both strange and familiar, in the way the Freudian "uncanny" is at once *heimlich* and *unheimlich.* Jean Burgos entitles one of his essays "Le Monstre, même et autre" ("The Monster, Same and Other"). So that even if the monster is that which is incalculably different from how we like to see ourselves (neither Goya's Saturn nor Frankenstein's creation resembles me in the least ...), it is nevertheless part of us, a creature of our imagination and a scion of our distant past: "The Imaginary [l'Imaginaire], this crossroads of the constant exchanges between the dark forces gushing forth from the deepest part of our being and the forces emanating from the natural and social milieu, meeting place of instinctual drives seeking to take form and objective temptations that never stop modifying our most secret desires; it is also the place of all creation. That is where the monster is born" (Burgos 1975, 14). The ogre is other, the ogre is self: "The fear that the ogre inspires signifies the fear of the Other. But it also reveals the fear of the Ego: the primordial forbidden, transgressed by the barbarian, exhibits everyone's buried desire" (Caillaud 2000, 7).

Anti-Semitic reasoning holds that the Jewish people, so much like Christians in appearance, were nevertheless "killers of God" (Macé 2002, 68), as different from non-Jews as pigs, and that they could never be forgiven. The barbaric Nazism described in *Le Dixième Cercle* was not, according to Macé, "an accident of history" (2002, 68): "For the murder—so well prepared—to be accomplished on such a large scale, an insanity unknowingly had to assume two thousand years of Christianity, and at the same time detach itself from it to identify with the pagan world" (2002, 68–69).

Gustave Doré, p. xiii, "Le Petit Chaperon rouge," by Charles Perrault. Bibliothèque Nationale de France, Paris, France.

2
The Ogre as Sexual Predator

Love is an ogre; only he who is devoured by love understands.
—Clot 1987

I didn't want to kill her. I loved her. I only wanted to eat her.
—Issey Sagawa, a student at the Sorbonne,
after eating a Dutch woman; quoted in Tournier 2002b

Paedophiles are our late millenial ogres, and they bring the bogeyman very much closer to home than aliens or medieval devils.
—Warner 1998

IN HER ARTICLE "L'OGRE DANS LA LITTÉRATURE" [THE OGRE IN LITERAture] (1988b, 1081), Arlette Bouloumié reminds us that Charles Perrault's moral to "Little Red Riding Hood" warns the reader that of all wolves "the most dangerous" ones are the "gentle wolves" who "follow young girls into their houses, even into their bedrooms" (Perrault 1999, 73). The ravenous wolf—metaphorically the brazen seducer in legends like Don Juan and Bluebeard—is a double of the ogre, who can be as hungry for sex as he is for meat. Thinking back to *Le Goût de l'homme*, where Macé remarks that the pig is "at once tender, gluttonous, and disgusting" (2002, 61), and that it therefore has always occupied a place close to man,[1] it should perhaps be no surprise to see an author like Tournier meditating on the connection between food and eroticism and mentioning the pig in the same breath as feminine beauty. Observing two teenage girls at the beach, he writes: "Piglike with their thick and sensual muzzles, but triumphantly carnal, they are the negation of the skeleton-like models sought after by the fashion industry. This is what traditional painting from Rubens to Renoir wanted woman to be. This is the appetite for food and erotic desire fused in one unique drive" (2002b, 153).

Indeed, Claude Lévi-Strauss remarks on the vocabulary many languages share between carnal and culinary pleasure: "All over the world, human thought seems to conceive a deep analogy between the act of copulation and the act of eating, to the point that a great number of languages designate them by the same word" (*The Savage Mind;* quoted in Bouloumié 1988a, 97). Lévi-Strauss is referring here to the word *consommer,* which can be translated as either "to consume" or "to consummate." Other examples of French sexual expressions borrowing from the culinary arts are *passer à la casserole* ("to get laid"), *mignon(ne) à croquer, on en mangerait* ("good [cute] enough to eat"), *dévorer quelqu'un des yeux* ("to eat someone up with one's eyes").

In this section I will examine works where the ogre metaphor waxes erotic. For the most part, I will not be dealing with intellectual erotic musings, as in Tournier's seaside observation. More often, the ogre is a symbol of dangerous excess: he is the violent and aggressive sexual predator.

MICHEL TOURNIER: *THE OGRE*

In the opening sentence of Tournier's novel, the protagonist Abel Tiffauges, writing in the left-hand journal he calls his "Sinister Writings," recalls the troubling words his lover Rachel used to repeat: "You're an ogre" (Tournier 1997b, 3). Later, she points out that his monstrousness precludes his ability to love: "You're not a lover, you're an ogre" (1997b, 9), she complains, stressing that he cares little about her pleasure. He could solve his problem of *ejaculatio praecox* (1997b, 8), she theorizes, nicely reversing roles, if he imagined that she was a wolf who would eat him up when he stopped making love to her.

The ogre does not love; he devours the object of his desire. Rachel complains to Abel, who is a mechanic: "You sate yourself with raw flesh and go straight back to your car bodies. . . . You reduce me to the level of a steak" (1997b, 8–9). Abel does not disagree, and, noting that a man eating bread does not worry about the bread's satisfaction, concludes that the acts of loving and eating are not that different. The parallel between the two can rise to sacred heights, in fact, in the Christian celebration of the Eucharist. Later on, after receiving communion one day, he ponders the delicious similarity: "Reviving freshness of the panting flesh of the Infant Jesus, beneath the transparent veil of the dry little host. What words can describe the infamy of the Roman priests who refuse the faithful communion in both kinds, reserving for themselves the succulence the flesh must gain from being moistened in its own warm blood" (1997b, 129–30). Abel is perhaps aware of the traditionally sacred nature of cannibalism, in which the eater has enormous respect for the eaten, and hopes to assume his or her virtues. But at this point Abel does not yet seem to equate holy love and sacramental eating, as he will elsewhere and later. His choice of words seems to evoke an epicurean murder rather than a devout sacrificial act of love.

Abel is anything but a great lover, yet a night at the opera *Don Giovanni* convinces him that he is just like Don Juan. Abel is impressed by the famous scene in which Leporello reads the long catalog of his master's numerous conquests across Europe ("Ma in Ispagna son già mille e tre."). This "is a good example of the *desire for exhaustiveness* that I'm only too familiar with. Rachel might have said to Don Giovanni as she said to me, 'You're not a lover, you're an ogre!'" (1997b, 91–92). The ogre is insatiable, and like the absurd hero described by Camus in *The Myth of Sisyphus*, he lives for the moment with little thought for the future. We will discuss this desire for exhaustiveness in the next chapter: it is related to the "density of atmosphere" (1997b, 327) that Tournier links to totality and totalitarianism.

Abel foresees that his death will be similar to Don Juan's. But unlike Mozart's hero, he will not be carried off to hell by the statue of another man. His death will come when his other self—his ogre self—fulfills its phoric destiny: "It will be the final victory of the man of stone that is in me over what remains to me of flesh and blood" (1997b, 92). As his destiny is to carry children, so will destiny carry him away, "and my last cry, my last sigh, will die away on lips of stone" (1997b, 92). As we have seen, Abel will die with a child on his shoulders, literally becoming a "man of stone"—a fossil in the making or a statue of St. Christopher—as he sinks into the peat bog like the ancient "Erl-King."

Pierrette Fleutiaux: "La femme de l'Ogre" [The ogre's wife]

Pierrette Fleutiaux's adaptation of "Le Petit Poucet" ("Little Tom Thumb") is the opening story of *Métamorphoses de la reine* [Metamorphoses of the queen], which was awarded the Goncourt Prize for short stories in 1984. The book is a feminist rewriting of selections from Charles Perrault's 1697 *Contes de ma mère l'Oye* [*Tales of Mother Goose*]. In her preface the author explains the book's genesis: "So the idea came to me that these tales were children's tales and I was not a child; more specifically that they were little girls' tales and I was a woman; still more specifically that when they spoke of women (and of men too, of course), I didn't like them at all" (Fleutiaux 1984, 10). In an interview with Bettina Knapp, Fleutiaux cites her admiration for another author we will examine in this chapter: Sylvie Germain. *Métamorphoses de la reine* differs from Germain's novels in that its fictional universe is the fantasy world of the fairy tale, as opposed to Germain's bleakly realistic settings. Nevertheless, Fleutiaux acknowledges the influence of Germain, whose naturalism, like Zola's, does not preclude a close affinity with myth and legend: "Her *fleuve* style, her writing and her vision. An epic, mystic, and visionary writer, whatever that means. Death, war, evil, history, time . . . A powerful writing and vision, rare among French writers. Perhaps her first book helped me unjam something within me, helped open the dike" (Knapp 1997, 144).

What flows out of the "dike" in this collection of tales is a complete reversal of the patriarchal viewpoint that dominates Perrault's stories. Thus Cinderella ("Cendrillon") becomes the shy, hard-working boy Cendron; and Little Red Riding Hood is transformed into an athletic tomboy called Little Red Trousers. In "La femme de l'Ogre," the minor figure of the ogre's wife from "Little Tom Thumb" becomes the protagonist: a diminutive, kind woman who contrasts sharply with her cruel husband who, like Alfred Jarry's Ubu (Knapp 1997, 116), is a pure creature of instinct, dominated by his penis and his belly. He incarnates all the prototypical traits of the ogre in Western folklore. Fleutiaux explains why she was more intrigued by the ogre's wife than the ogre: "In "Little Tom Thumb," the character of the Ogre's wife haunted me. She appears only in a few lines, she is at the same time so unassuming and so bold, and her situation is so strange because it is through her that the cruelest and the most innocent worlds come into contact" (Fleutiaux 1984, 11).

The ogre's existence is limited to three concerns: he wants to raise his seven little *ogrelettes* to be as bloodthirsty as he is; he "chews, crunches and gulps" (1984, 17) vast quantities of raw meat; and he fornicates violently and insatiably, sometimes with his wife, who barely survives his aggressions, sometimes with animal carcasses, before he and his daughters devour them.

His wife, by contrast, is a gentle soul, a vegetarian nauseated by the excesses of her husband, and devoted to her daughters, despite their ogreish behavior. When her husband is in bed, exhausted after one of his orgies, the "other life of the Ogre's wife" (1984, 18) begins. As a "soft hunger awakens in her" (1984, 18), she uncovers the vegetables she has hidden in the forest, and takes strength from a forbidden meal in the balmy night air, far away from the stench of meat.

One cold night, Little Tom Thumb and his six brothers, abandoned in the forest by their parents, seek shelter at the ogre's house, preferring to take their chances with the monster rather than risk being eaten by wolves. They cleverly avoid the ogre and the little ogrillons; the father and his daughters, crazed by the smell of raw flesh, but failing to find the boys, eventually devour one another.

Finally liberated, the ogre's wife is at first content to live a peaceful, meatless existence. However, another hunger arises in her: a desire for cunning Little Tom Thumb, who disappeared the night of her husband's death. She dons the ogre's seven-league boots and flies until she finds Tom and his brothers, and with a terse "It's you that I want, not them" (1984, 46), gives the brothers the supplies they need to survive, and flies off with Tom.

The characters of myth and folklore often have ambivalent personalities, and the ogre's wife is no exception. After her husband's death, the self-effacing and sexually timorous woman boldly seeks out Tom, the little man of her dreams, whom she feels had always been speaking to her through a "tiny noise" (1984, 19, 38, 45, 48) that seemed to be emanating from the dark night of the forest. Tom notices the transformation, and remarks: "How she has changed" (1984, 46), as he happily jumps into the pocket of her blouse. As they speed through the country with the seven-league boots, Tom, hopping from pocket to pocket, "visits" the various parts of her body. Overcome by desire, she finally climaxes one night as Tom lies sleeping on the "little pillow" (1984, 48) between her legs: "Tom began to move. . . . In the dark undergrowth of her body, the Ogre's wife heard that tiny noise like leaves and branches brushing together; she followed it, and all the force contained in her body rose up in the vibrating cone and suddenly burst out, carrying away her troubles, her memories, her fears, carrying away all the vines and brambles and dead bark, flowing like the great river outside, shimmering and rippling in the middle of the city" (1984, 49).

Now it is Tom's turn to change. Lying against his lover, he feels himself growing taller and taller, until he is the same size as she. A mosquito slips into the room, dons the seven-league boots and flies away, and we can assume that the now quite "normal" lovers live happily ever after.

Gilbert Durand's *Structures anthropologiques de l'imaginaire* inspires an interesting interpretation of Fleutiaux's rewriting of Perrault. The most important revision Fleutiaux makes to the original story is her substitution of the ogre's wife for the ogre as the second main character; indeed, the ogre's wife—who remains nameless but whose character Fleutiaux carefully develops—becomes the protagonist, while Tom remains a secondary, rather static personage. Thus the importance of the "villain" is reduced, and that of the "helper" (to use Vladimir Propp's terminology in *Morphology of the Folktale*) is enhanced. One might say then that Fleutiaux's modification euphemizes the horror of the ogre—a common strategy, according to Durand, by which the imagination deals with the terrors of violence and mortality.

Durand separates the imaginary into two regimes, the diurnal and the nocturnal. The diurnal regime resides in the Platonic—or Platonistic—tradition of antitheses, where typical images are unambiguous oppositions between archetypes such as light and darkness, intelligible and sensible, ascending and falling. Images of darkness reveal a deep fear of mortality and death. Durand classifies these as 1) "theriomorphic" symbols (devouring animals or monsters, like the ogre or the wolf; chthonian animals, like spiders and snakes); 2) "nyctomorphic" symbols (creatures or objects of the night, such as the moon, the bat, the witch); and 3) "catamorphic" symbols (fear of falling, as depicted, for example, in the myth of Icarus; the downward movement of food through the intestines; and images of the sewer). Our desperate attempt to overcome time is an incessant theme of art and literature, and the typical diurnal hero accomplishes this symbolically through the violent action of severing the head of a monster: Apollo, Saint George, and Tristan all gained fame as dragon slayers. For this reason, Durand summarizes the diurnal regime by the sword arcanum of the Tarot deck.[2]

The nocturnal regime of the imaginary is divided into two parts. First, the Tarot arcana of the coin and the wand represent alternative ways to deal with time. The round shape of the coin suggests a placid view of time as a cycle where ideas of reincarnation or seasonal rebirth offer us rays of hope. The straight line of the wand evokes the belief in time as progress toward a better world in the future, as we see in teleological ideologies like Marxism and Christianity.

The second part of the nocturnal regime is symbolized by the cup of the Tarot. The gradual slope of the inside of the cup hints at yet another defense against mortality: the abrupt fall of a character like Icarus—of the diurnal regime—is euphemized into a gentle descent, as into the hollow of a cup. Symbols of intimacy (the tomb, the cave, the womb) abound in this domain of the imaginary, as do symbols of inversion ("gulliverisation," "embedding" [*emboîtement*], and the romantic cult of woman).

It is this "cup" of the nocturnal regime that "La femme de l'Ogre" illustrates. Images of this regime are largely feminine, writes Durand, centered on earth goddesses as opposed to solar gods: "[T]he Great Goddesses who, in these constellations, will replace the Great male Sovereign . . . will be at once beneficent, protectresses of the home, givers of maternity, but they might also contain a remnant of the fearsome side of femininity and so will also be at the same time terrible goddesses, warlike and bloodthirsty" (1984, 226).

Thus it is the woman who takes center stage in Fleutiaux's story; her function is to soften the ogre's bite, easing the terror that the latter inspires, transforming it into a less fearsome erotic tryst between her and Tom. This is a common phenomenon in the nocturnal regime. Durand explains that the ogre is an avatar of Cronus/Chronos, and thus a figure of time. There is "a progressive tendency to euphemize the brutal and fatal terrors [of time] into simple erotic and carnal fears . . . . And psychoanalysis has brilliantly shown that Chronos[3] and Thanatos are conjugated in Eros" (1984, 220).

Which symbols of inversion and intimacy, hallmarks of the nocturnal regime, appear in "La femme de l'Ogre"? First, the feeding frenzy in which the seven ogrillons devour each other and their father is an example of what Durand names "double negation" (1984, 230), in which "by a negative action the positive is reconstituted, by a negation or a negative act the effect of a first negativity is destroyed" (1984, 230). The killer is killed. This allows Tom to invert the fatal course of time, incarnated by the ogre, and find intimacy with the ogre's wife. Before being sexual, the intimacy is that of a child with his mother, what Freud, in his 1905 essay on "Infantile Sexuality," called "the 'affectionate current' of sexual life" (Freud 1953–74, 7:200): tiny Tom lays his head on the woman's breasts, and, like an infant emerging from the womb, rests between her legs, "lying in the center, in the moist and fragrant bed" (Fleutiaux 1984, 48). Symbolically, he turns back the hands of time, inverting its destructive nature "to find once more prenatal quietude" (Durand 1984, 230).

The ogre evokes the horror, not of being swallowed, but of being torn apart by a mouth full of teeth. Durand, and Bachelard before him, analyze the "Jonas complex" (Durand 1984, 233; Bachelard 1948, 129–82), by which the imagination "transfigures the tearing action of dental voracity into a soft and harmless sucking" (Durand 1984, 233). Biting and devouring are violent verbs of the diurnal regime;[4] swallowing belongs to the gentler night: "*Swallowed and not devoured:* that is a distinction to be made between the day myths and those of the night" (Bachelard 1948, 156–57). Even if Tom Thumb is not swallowed by the ogre's wife as Jonas was by the whale, his actions—from riding in her pockets to lying in her "center"—certainly suggest a desire to return to the intimacy of the womb, to be "embedded" in the woman like Jonas in the whale.

The theme of embedding brings to mind "the dialectic of the contained and the container" (Durand 1984, 238), where the "contained" must often be miniaturized, or "gulliverized," in order to fit in the container. Durand explains that "gulliverization" is a type of nocturnal inversion "where we see the reversal of solar values symbolized by virility and gigantism" (1984, 239). In "La femme de l'Ogre," the ogre is sexually frustrated, and he certainly cannot satisfy his wife: "[His] penis, which fortunately is not too big . . . moves inside her without her feeling it, like an absence. . . . What he is doing is so far removed from what could be good for her!" (Fleutiaux 1984, 35–36). Tom Thumb, on the other hand, brings her to unopposable orgasm, and then literally grows erect into a man. Size matters—by inversion. Thus the miniature is maximized, while the gigantic is minimized. The large is largely impotent, while the small is immensely potent, recalling the conceptive power of the homunculus—the microscopic man thought to live in sperm, growing to an adult in the womb—in the alchemical literature of Paracelsus and in Goethe's *Faust II:* "The Lilliputians and the Tom Thumbs of our legends are no more than the folkloric vulgarization of an eternal theme that the Paracelsian doctrine of the homunculus had widely diffused in cultivated milieux, homunculus embedded in the spermatic fluid, then embedded in the philosophical egg of the alchemists" (Durand 1984, 239).[5]

Sylvie Germain: *Days of Anger*

Days of Anger, Sylvie Germain's third book, won the Prix Fémina in 1989. The novel takes place in the wooded and mountainous department of Nièvre, Burgundy, populated by what the local priest calls "those semi-barbarians of the forests" (Germain 1993, 14). Ambroise Mauperthuis is an angry man; anger is the source of both his love and his madness, and leads him to murder the only being he ever cared about, his granddaughter Camille.

Mauperthuis's madness results from his obsession with a dead woman. He witnesses the murder of Catherine Corvol by her jealous husband, a bad match for this woman who embodied the wild beauty of her surroundings, but who, like Emma Bovary, was stifled by the boredom of her monotonous, provincial life: "[S]he was possessed by the devil: the devil of desire, movement, and joy. And her beauty had the sharp, luminous brilliance kindled by that enjoyment of living in those whose hearts are enamoured of space and speed" (1993, 32).

Mauperthuis falls in love with a corpse—he had never seen the woman alive—and thus his encounter with beauty has "the tang of anger" (1993, 23). Catherine possessed a strange, troubling beauty; her green eyes were thought by the local peasants to be evil and bewitching: "Eyes the colour of mythical serpent's skin that glistens in the waters of streams. A green river-snake" (1993, 36). Before burying her near the bank of the river Yonne where she died, Mauperthuis licks the blood of her wound: "He licked the blood of beauty and desire. He licked the blood of anger. He buried his head in the hollow of her shoulder, and his hands in her hair—blonde hair that still retained life's warmth and smell. He kissed her temples and eyelids, he sucked her parted lips" (1993, 37). Catherine's blood will make him an instrument of revenge: "Catherine Corvol's blood was now mingled with his own, carrying a mute cry through his veins, a persistent clamour for revenge. The blood that had blackened on the grassy bank had become a macabre incantation in Ambroise Mauperthuis's heart" (1993, 40).[6]

In order to buy Mauperthuis's silence, the murderer gives him his valuable forest land, and promises to marry his daughter Claude to Mauperthuis's son. Years pass, the marriage takes place, and soon Camille is born. As she grows older, Mauperthuis is mesmerized by this green-eyed girl who so resembles her dead grandmother. The villagers are wary of the young beauty: "And already [Mauperthuis] bore the child a passionate love full of pride, the love of an insanely jealous lover. Look at that child with her serpent eyes,[7] everyone said, she already has the old man infatuated with her! . . . And the prediction for when she was older was . . . that she would be capable of bewitching even the trees of the forest, by the sole charm of her serpent-green gaze" (1993, 61).

Both Catherine and Camille are closely tied to nature, especially the traditional "feminine" elements of water and earth.[8] The narrator continually identifies them with snakes, which are for Gaston Bachelard the prototypical animals of the earth, living underground like some darting, sinuous roots of the animal kingdom (Bachelard 1948, 262). The Vouivre, on the other hand, is more closely associated with water: she always lives near water and is protected by water snakes. The lidless eyes of snakes have always fascinated, and so it is that the green gaze of Catherine and later Camille is both beautiful and unsettling.

Catherine's husband, lying on his deathbed, is haunted by her spirit, which seems to belong to the earth:

> And his consciousness, at its most sharply attentive, had soared over this vast expanse like a very high-flying bird winging above an immensity of fields, towns and forests. . . . He had seen Catherine, the young, fair-haired girl, with green, almond-shaped eyes, and the young woman whose breasts had the bright roundedness and warmth of day, and of the earth, in the hollow of his hands, and whose mouth had the redness of dark roses, and the brilliance of day, and whose body had the day's depth and heat. Earth, roses, earth, day. Roses, fires of the earth, freshness of day. (Germain 1993, 121)

It is when Camille takes on a lover that Mauperthuis's ogreish qualities become unmistakable. He had long been a mad, angry man, jealously protecting Camille, the double of her grandmother: "this much-desired body, this glorious body: Catherine-Camille. His Spark of Life" (1993, 154). Now his jealousy turns to violence. He imprisons Camille in the attic while he seeks revenge on her lover, Simon: "He would hunt out this dog, this thief of beauty, this debauchee who had dared to lay his filthy hands on the Spark of Life, and strip him of these monstrous rights that he had treacherously usurped" (1993, 162–63).

The chapter detailing Camille's imprisonment is entitled "In the Attic" (*Sous le comble*), the same expression Muriel Cerf will use repeatedly in *Le Verrou* to describe the room where Massimo Cuori engages in frenzied sexual activity with his young lover Nora Neumann. Two young girls abused in the attic—one sexually humiliated, the other dragged by the hair and abandoned—by men who love them too much. Both girls rebel against the disproportionate love of their "protectors": Nora disappears after robbing Cuori, Camille sets fire to the house and escapes from her grandfather, whom she had grown to hate, hoping "that he would die, freeing her from the burden and menaces of the too-possessive love of this grandfather who ruled as all-powerful lord and master" (1993, 159). In the end, though, it is Camille and Simon who die by the hand of Mauperthuis, just as Catherine had been killed by her husband more out of jealous love than of hate. And so the ogre lives on, "desperately chewing on those sharp and bitter seeds of his madness" (1993, 238).

Pascal Bruckner, in the interview reprinted in the appendix, insists that perhaps the most treacherous kind of ogre is the one who harms a defenseless person by a stifling excess of love. The psychoanalyst Christiane Olivier corroborates Bruckner's opinion, observing that excessive love can be the result of a parent or lover failing to recognize that all beings have separate identities. The ogre craves an impossible symbiotic relationship with the Other: "No one is more vicious towards the Other than the person who loves passionately, since passion is born in those who are looking for symbiosis and who, refusing to accept difference, are living in an ALL or NOTHING world, as during the first year of our life with our parents, characterized either by the presence or the lack of object love" (Olivier 1998, 42).

The ogre Mauperthuis inhabits the all or nothing world of primary narcissism, focused entirely on his own desires, needs, and anxieties. He feels wholly entitled to possess the object of his love, because he imagines he incorporated Camille when he intermingled his blood with that of her dead grandmother. His love is the ogre's bite: possessive, destructive, all-consuming.

Sylvie Germain: *The Medusa Child*

Like *Days of Anger, The Medusa Child* takes place in *la France profonde,* this time in an unnamed region with extensive wetlands. Eight-year-old Lucie Daubigné lives in a small village with her mother, father, and half-brother. She is drawn to the creatures and odors of the marshes, while her close friend Félix, interested in astronomy, is always looking up to the stars. Life seems idyllic in their tiny village, until, at the beginning of summer, the body of nine-year-old Anne-Lise Limbourg, strangled and sexually assaulted, is found lying in a ditch: "From this time on the paths round about, however peaceful they may appear, are haunted by the footsteps of the Ogre. The children no longer go out except in groups" (Germain 1994, 52).

At about the same time, Lucie's ordeal begins. One night, her handsome half-brother Ferdinand, twenty-six years old and her hero, climbs into her bedroom window and rapes her. He repeats the horrible crime most nights for about three years, threatening to kill her if she tells their parents. One night, however, he falls from her windowsill, lands on his back and is unable to move, his paralysis confounding all the doctors. Lucie can at last exact her revenge.

This highly visual novel is divided into thirteen sections, each of which is composed of a scene described as a type of "drawing" (illumination, red chalk, sepia, charcoal, fresco), followed by a "legend." Germain's writing has been described as "spectacular" and "visionary" (Narjoux 2005, 74). Nowhere is this truer than in *The Medusa Child*, where each of the "drawings" is a superb example of *ecphrasis*, the detailed description of a work of art in literature. These passages of the novel are essentially spatial: brief interruptions of the plot, which then resumes its temporal flow in the "legends." The first two "illuminations," representing, respectively, a solar eclipse and a rainbow, symbolize the happy childhood of Lucie and Félix, absorbed in their admiration of the earth and sky. Cécile Narjoux observes that this is an ecphrastic period, a timeless enjoyment of a space "full of enchantment" (Germain 1994, 15). Their world is "a great book of pictures" (1994, 17), in which Félix sees "galactic visions" (1994, 109) in the sky, and Lucie glimpses "fairies and wizards" (1994, 24) in the meadows, forests, and marshes. The children's eyes, writes Narjoux, mirror their universe, and are "always open on a vast *ecphrasis*" (Narjoux 2005, 74) of their pictorial world.

Nevertheless, the first illumination of the novel combines images of beauty and terror, fragility and force, setting the stage for the struggle between Lucie and the ogre who will try to devour her. It is the total solar eclipse of 1961, and the awe-struck children in the schoolyard are witnessing the swallowing of the sun by the moon:

The celestial wolf is devouring the light.
  Yet the sky is beautiful. The moon has engulfed the sun's body. . . .
  It is neither day nor night. It is another time altogether, a fragile tangential point between passing time and eternity, wonder and terror. The heart of the world is laying itself bare: a dark heart encircled with glory.

Suddenly there is doubt in men's souls about their destiny in the wind of time, in the flesh of the world: will their death be like that flashing image up there above their heads? (Germain 1994, 13–14)

Solar eclipses have always been harbingers of catastrophes. Omens of death, they are considered in some mythologies to be the death of the sun, devoured by some monster or wild animal, such as a wildcat, a serpent, or the "celestial wolf" that Germain describes above (Chevalier 1982, 389–90; Durand 1984, 92). Eclipses are manifestations of the "black sun," which illuminates another world during its nocturnal voyage, and heralds great change, such as the beginning of a new age, or the fiery end of the world (what the Stoics called *ekpyrosis*).

Shortly before his suicide in January 1855, Gérard de Nerval published his sonnet "The Disinherited" ("El Desdichado"), in which the black sun conveys a personal feeling of melancholy:

> I am saturnine—bereft—disconsolate,
> The Prince of Aquitaine whose tower has crumbled;
> My lone star is dead—and my bespangled lute
> Bears the *Black Sun* of *Melancholia*. (Quoted in Kristeva 1989, 141).

This poem inspired Julia Kristeva's extended essay on depression and melancholy, *Black Sun*. In a close reading of "The Disinherited," she wonders if—given Nerval's interest in esoterica—"saturnine"[9] could refer to the fifteenth Tarot card, the devil, which is ruled by the planet Saturn. Kristeva's observation sheds light on the troubling oxymoron of the black sun, which is not unlike the double face of Lucifer, at once the "Bearer of Light" and the "Prince of Darkness":

> The qualifier "saturnine" . . . is consonant with the Prince of Darkness already suggested by the tarot pack as well as with night deprived of light. It conjures up the melancholy person's complicity with the world of darkness and despair.
> The "black sun" . . . again takes up the semantic field of "saturnine," but pulls it inside out, like a glove: darkness flashes as a solar light, which nevertheless remains dazzling with black invisibility.[10] (Kristeva 1989, 147)

The stunning eclipse that opens *The Medusa Child* foreshadows the tragedy that is about to befall Lucie. A new age will soon begin for her: the age of the ogre and the end of innocence. As the celestial monster swallows the sun, so will the ogre Ferdinand, driven by hunger for "the pretty, forbidden fruit," for the "frail child's body" (Germain 1994, 75) ripe with the "delicious sweetness of childhood" (1994, 153), devour Lucie each night, transforming a carefree child into a sullen creature consumed by terror, guilt, and hate. She will in effect take on an ogreish, saturnine personality, full of anger and melancholy, like Saturn (Cronus), the prototypical ogre from classical mythology who, as we noted in chapter 1, devoured his children one by one.[11]

While the novel opens with an evocation of the eclipse, a celestial spectacle, it quickly becomes clear that, like Camille in the previous novel, Lucie is a child of the earth rather than the sky. She loves to wander through the fields, forests, and especially the marshes, where water and earth meet, "their gentle mirrors of grey water" (1994, 25) providing shelter for countless plants and animals. The smells and sounds of the marshlands stimulate her sense of adventure, while bringing her the peace that comes from the awareness that she is where she belongs. Lucie "draws her strength from the vigorous odours of the earth and the grass, the flowers, the trees, the sleeping waters. For her, joy is to be found in this visible world at hand" (1994, 59). She loves to hear the chant of Melchior, the ancient toad[12] that has lived near her house for years: "She listens to the raucous, syncopated song of Melchior, that benign genius of the place who watches over the night, over memory, over the peace of the earth. . . . She is inheriting a voice of the earth, humble and deep, which sings from age to age and links the living to their earth, to their parents, and further beyond, unknown to them, to their departed ancestors" (1994, 59).

The Earth-Mother provides Lucie the love and security that her own mother, who favors Ferdinand, does not. However, like the ancient earth goddess Gaea, who embodied all forces of nature, the earth is not only benevolent and life-giving, but also malevolent and murderous. Lucie will become a victim of this dark side of Gaea, like innumerable humans in Greek mythology. For the Earth's lineage includes such fearsome creatures as the Titans—notably Cronus—the Giants, and numerous reptilian monsters like Typhon, Echidna, the Lernean Hydra, Python, Erichthonius, and finally, the namesake of the novel, Medusa.

Gilbert Durand has demonstrated the family resemblance between the ogre, the black sun, and Medusa, also called Gorgon, since she is the most well known of the three Gorgon sisters: "This animal devouring the sun, this devouring and shadowy sun seems to us to be a close relative of the Greek Cronus, symbol of the instability of destructive time, prototype of all the ogres of European folklore. . . . This ogre is the negative valorization, black, . . . of Gargan-Gargantua, the Celtic sun. It is the active sense of swallowing up, of eating: the father of all the Gorgons living in the western Gorgades" (Durand 1984, 94–95).

Lucie, who loves the smell of the earth, contends with a new earthy but sickening smell, that of fear, and of the ogre outside her window:

> It is fear that keeps her whole being alert. It is hatred and dread.
> Her dread has a nauseating smell, like damp straw mouldering at the back of a cowshed. It is the smell of the blond Ogre who is coming to take possession of her. (Germain 1994, 77)

Lucie has lost sight of the sky that Félix had brought into her life, and the earth has become a sterile mudhole. She feels alone, like the many incest victims studied by Olivier in *L'Ogre intérieur,* who report that their guilt turns them into loners; they shun not only the company of adults but that of children as well (Olivier 1998, 146–47). One could say that Lucie suffers from the "cannibalistic solitude" that Kristeva has discerned in her patients (Kristeva 1989, 71); a feeling of "absence" (1989, 72), of "cadaverization" (1989, 73) that consumes one's life. Lucie feels like Crusoe marooned on an inhospitable island:

> Her brother's cruelty had forced her eyes downward, rooted her to the ground, buried her in the mud. . . .
> She had found herself shipwrecked on a desert island—the Ogre's island—completely alone, without even a Man Friday to keep her company. . . .
> [I]t was now the season for earthly visions, moulded in mud, flesh and roots, and for opening and inventing new picture-books, with images no longer gathered from the sky like wondrous fruits of light, but torn from the belly of the earth like entrails or flints, pulled out by the root from the arid soil of the Ogre's island. (Germain 1994, 106, 109)

Nerval's celestial metaphor for melancholy—the black sun—is inadequate for this girl of the earth. "Black blood" will henceforth be her image of the despair that overwhelms her. The mud of the "Ogre's island" reminds her of the blood that binds her to her vicious brother and her indifferent mother. She cannot imagine this criminal blood as red: "For all this blood was black: the blood from the mother's belly, that of the obscene, grotesque unions between the murderous older brother and the little sister who had not yet reached puberty" (1994, 117).

Lucie feels certain that Ferdinand murdered Anne-Lise Limbourg and that he sexually abused a second little girl, Irène, driving her to suicide. Victims of Ferdinand's madness, Anne-Lise and Irène are like sisters to Lucie, and thus share the black family blood of vice. As she pedals past the cemetery and the fields dotted with poppies, Lucie realizes that Anne-Lise and Irène died in 1961, the year of the black sun. The dead little girls, once dazzling, are now dark, like the night sun that lies buried beneath the horizon: "Sun, little sun, pretty sun! These words had long rung in her head. Sun-Irène, eclipsed for ever, only to reappear all the brighter in the fields in summer, in thousands of crimson suns with black hearts" (1994, 171). Lucie vows to avenge Irène and Anne-Lise.

Lucie's first form of vengeance is her self-imposed anorexia. Much like Sonia, Vania, and Lisa—three victims of incest we will meet in Cerf's "Trois soeurs"—Lucie wants to be skinny and unattractive, in order to dissuade her abuser. Her body has been assaulted, and she wishes it could melt away and disappear:

> She would like to become so thin as to be impalpable, invisible, so that the wolf would lose his desire, the Ogre his insatiable appetite. . . .
> [T]here was only one solution left to her: to become as thin and dry as a dead branch, and so ugly as to discourage all desire. (1994, 81, 88)

Sullied by the ogre, she dreams of his death: "The wolf dead! . . . Dead, the handsome fair-haired ogre, dead at last!" (1994, 94). Her reaction is similar to the actual experiences of child victims of incest reported by Christiane Olivier in *L'Ogre intérieur*. In half of these cases, the perpetrator is an alcoholic; so is Ferdinand, who creeps through her window "stinking of alcohol and sweat" (1994, 86). Lucie is obsessed with removing his scent from her body: "If she could, she would wash herself in bleach, scrub herself with wire wool, rub herself with sulphur and ether, in order to repel her brother with his ogre's nose" (1994, 87). This recalls Olivier's report of an interview with "Angélique," who says of her abusive father: "I wanted to kill him, to slit his throat, I wanted him to kill himself in his truck, and to hear from someone that he was dead! I felt dirty and I washed myself three times a day!" (Olivier 1998, 151).

Ferdinand corresponds to Olivier's portrait of many adult rapists of a preteen daughter, niece, or sister: a neurotic disappointed in love who, needing unconditional, symbiotic love, thinks he can find it in the "pure heart" of his young relative (1998, 150). Ferdinand is listless, unambitious and unemployed, and his chief interest is alcohol. The handsomest man in the village, the image of his dead father, people wonder why "lovely Ferdinand," as admiring women call him, hasn't married (Germain 1994, 67). The root of his indifference is his failure to create his own identity: he is merely the double of his father, the martyred war hero, as his doting mother continually reminds him. Thus "[h]is body is full of torment and darkness. Ferdinand grew up as an outsider in the shadow of his own body, estranged from himself and others" (1994, 73). He seems indifferent to his own life, until the ghost of his father, blown to bits on the battlefield, stirs within him: "It was as if his father's body, of which he was the double, was awakening and moving about restlessly inside him. For the dead man had never received a burial" (1994, 73).

Like Mauperthuis in *Days of Anger,* Ferdinand metaphorically carries another being inside himself. We have noted that Freudian "incorporation" is characteristic of the oral stage, and is one way the ogre seeks to satisfy his hunger. Again like Mauperthuis, Ferdinand never matures psychologically, and turns to little girls for love: "Little children: but he loved them. Ferdinand was not a bad fellow. He never wished any harm to those little girls he grabbed now and again. All he was looking for each time was a little relief from the torments of the love that burned in him. He was the victim of a diseased love, a sick desire. And because he was weak, he succumbed" (1994, 154).

Ferdinand will finally fall victim to Lucie's second scheme for vengeance: the paralyzing fear triggered by the Medusa's gaze of her too-large eyes that, with imaginative makeup, become nightmarishly ugly. Lucie is ecstatic when she realizes that Ferdinand, sprawled on his back after falling from her bedroom window one night, is seriously hurt and cannot move. Half-conscious, Ferdinand is confused and terrified by the creature crouching above him on the windowsill, the monster with horrific eyes who used to be his little sister. Like one of the Erinyes—avengers of blood-guilt—Lucie stalks her brother, a modern and perverted Orestes:

> The little girl remains perfectly still, as if sculpted in this leaning posture like a chimera, or a gargoyle with eyes of burning lava, dishevelled hair, thin, protruding knees, and grimacing mouth. For her mouth is hideously distorted, with puckered lips and bared teeth. And her grimaces have both colour and sound. She has daubed her mouth dark red and blackened her teeth. . . . And she uses her eyes also, rolling them upwards, dilating them, half-closing them: so that each time she can afterwards pierce all the harder again into the recumbent man's face with her straight gaze. (1994, 99–100)

One can read *The Medusa Child* in part as a reenactment of a version of the Medusa myth, which recounts how Medusa, like Lucie, was a beautiful young girl raped by a powerful ogre. In the myth, the rapist is Poseidon, and the act is done in a temple dedicated to Athena, whom the victim rivaled in beauty. Furious at Poseidon's crime, Athena could do little to her rival god, but she punished the mortal Gorgon by transforming her beautiful hair into a nest of snakes and her eyes into two penetrating orbs that would turn all who beheld them into stone. Thus Medusa, granddaughter of Gaea, will always be associated with the snake, chthonian animal par excellence. We have seen how Lucie belongs so intimately to the earth, and feels a particular affinity with grass snakes and their disconcerting stare, from "tiny, unblinking, often glassy eyes" (1994, 110).

Ferdinand finally dies after months of lying immobile in his bed.

Lucie credits herself with his death, because every day she tortures him, creeping into his bedroom, hissing like a snake, and staring with those "stinging eyes" that "spit poison" (1994, 156).[13] She is aided in her revenge by her slimy allies of the earth: she places slugs and earthworms on Ferdinand's handsome face and watches them slither. Yet Ferdinand's death does not bring Lucie the joy that disappeared the day she became tainted "with the mark of the ogre" (1994, 224). As she looks in the mirror, she fears that her life will never regain the lost luster of childhood:

> She no longer had any enemy to challenge and transfix with her piercing Medusa gaze. Suddenly her Medusa eyes lost their brilliance and grew heavy and opaque. Mirrors, which had once been magic lanterns that showed Lucie multiple, warlike images of herself slaying the ogre-dragon, now had no depth in them at all any more. . . .
> There was no joy for Lucie wherever she turned. (1994, 220)

It is only thirty years afterwards, following many travels and the death of her parents, that Lucie's life regains a semblance of normalcy. She begins to forgive, and realizes that she must "learn afresh how to look, how to see. Not only the sky, but the trees, the paths in the fields, the shadows that slide over walls and objects, and of course faces" (1994, 243). Helping her forget the ogre, monster of the earth, is a new-found love for the sky, which she learns from her old friend Félix's mother, who possesses the wisdom and sensitivity so tragically lacking in Lucie's own mother. She tells Lucie: "I look with all the concentration I can possibly muster, until I feel that my eyes are completely at one with the visible world . . . with the sky, the light, the clouds . . . and then, I almost become a cloud! I mean that I feel as if I am being carried away into the swirl of the clouds and dissolved in the light and the mist, as if I am the rain and the wind . . . Then I don't suffer any more; I forget my pain, my loneliness" (1994, 242). Inspired by the old woman, Lucie finally escapes the ogre, and at age forty at long last begins to live, recapturing the joy of her lost childhood.

MURIEL CERF: *OGRES ET AUTRES CONTES*
[OGRES AND OTHER TALES]

Ogres et autres contes is a collection of nine stories in which the author analyzes relationships, some between lovers, some between parents and children. What these relationships have in common is their ugliness, and, as the editors write in their synopsis on the back cover, it is their very hatefulness that makes them fertile ground for Cerf's remarkable imagination: "There where love becomes a prison, where desire turns into obsession, where the father finds his daughters so beautiful, and the mother her own too attractive, there where only black magic can bring back the unfaithful spouse: there we find the ogres" (Cerf 1997a).

Immense appetites for food arouse the sexual appetites of the protagonists in several stories. "Corps amoureux" [Bodies in love] is written mostly in stream of consciousness, with page-long sentences, typical of Cerf's style, which one might describe as a seven-course meal shared by Marcel Proust and Henry Miller: she has inherited the hypotactic structure and transatlantic sentences of the former and the gluttonous, erotic obsessions of the latter.[14] A first-person female narrator, sitting in her fenced-in garden, reflects on her obsession with her lover; their relationship seems to be one extended sex act, punctuated by sumptuous meals. They are "addicts" (1997a, 19), fixated on the "physical ideal" (1997a, 17) that each represents for the other. The story concludes with a third-person narrator who observes the couple:

> And tonight they will dine outdoors in the blue garden, and will cut up and zealously devour a whole chicken, they will suck the bones and the cartilage and the blond sauce on their fingers, leaving none of the elastic and buttered skin, they will dig with their fingers under the carcass to find the exquisite and brown dressing, and the wine will flow black in the crystal glasses, and in the shadow of the arborvitae shine the cutting edges of their strong teeth and their pungent knees will meet under the table and the man's hand will grab the sparkling pareu[15] on her smooth belly, wrinkling its golden threads between her hot thighs, the odor of honeysuckle is sickeningly heavy, the black wine flows now in their loving bodies; beyond the fence the world is over. (1997a, 19–20)

In "A Fès" [At Fez], a man's passion for the beautiful young dancer Lalla threatens his marriage, tenuously held together by the grains of couscous that his wife Latifa can cook like no other. Before he met Lalla, Azziz's life and love were contentedly centered on couscous and dinner:

> Aziz would eye her ardently as he attacked the pyramid . . . of couscous; he would hold a chickpea or a raisin delicately in the hollow of his right hand, then take a handful of semolina, and with a flick of his thumb as skillful as it was elegant and without ever taking his loving eyes off her, the smoking snow would jump into his mouth and each grain of semolina thus tasted was a grain of love, and their love had the sweetness of the raisin and the brutality of the spices, that's the way it had always been. (1997a, 76)

In two of her tales, "La Passion selon Rose Mouret" [The Passion according to Rose Mouret] and "Ogres," Cerf tells of women in bad relationships: their abusive partners have pushed them to the brink of insanity, and divorce or suicide seem likely escape routes. Rose Mouret contemplates leaving her husband, whose vampirish and ogreish ways contrast with the pure and noble Alpine scenery that, like a guardian angel, protects her from him. As she stands on the balcony of her chalet, her body, reinvigorated by the temporary absence of her husband, reaches out to the mountains: "Her sumptuous breasts, . . . drunk with purity, stood erect in good faith" (1997a, 104). Snowy Mount Blanc and crystal blue Lake Bourget, symbols of perfect love for the Romantic poet Lamartine, form an ironic backdrop to the gory recollection of her husband's bloody tastes, so far from the courtly love she has read about in Denis de Rougemont's *Love in the Western World.* Her husband's predilection for lamb brains "bathing in their blood" (1997a, 118) nauseates her, as do his sexual tastes. His anal-erotic inclination leads her to question his masculinity, and he is slightly necrophilic, she thinks, since he likes to take her while she is "asleep like Sleeping Beauty" (1997a, 109). But it is especially blood that he craves: "[V]ictim of his obsession, Nathan should have lived during the time of Nero, or of Assurbanipal, who poked out the eyes of captive kings, or of the Aztecs (this typically Aztec taste he had for kissing her down there while she was menstruating), or of the Tibetan disciples of Kali, drinking blood out of cranial cavities, for which that most delicious part of herself was obviously a substitute)" (1997a, 115–16).[16] In the end, Rose decides not to divorce this man who reminds her of a "vampire" (1997a, 104), a "wolf," and a "bogeyman" (1997a, 108). As she turns away from the pristine Alps and goes back into the chalet, she remarks to herself: "Dirty guy and dirty love and my husband forever" (1997a, 130).

"Ogres" is a monologue by an old woman wise in the ways of the seductive ogre. She is warning her neighbor Diane, about to enter her apartment, to beware of her (Diane's) companion, whose talent for love cannot conceal his violent nature. Diane's life has become a prison, which the narrator describes in Foucauldian terms: "Disciplined and punished, seduced and imprisoned, stripped of all your rights, especially the right to say that you suffer, that you are a victim, if you say that, he'll have your hide. You see, this guy drinks, and alcohol is evil in the blood" (1997a, 88). Alcohol awakens the ogre in Diane's lover, eager to consume his exquisite victim, as the old woman seems to know from her own experience:

But you, or me yesterday, the same contemplative eyes, the same delicious curled up toes, cheeks as sweet as almond cakes from Aix, and everything that ogres adore, lips of orange jam, flesh of sugared almond, breasts of nougat, fresh as cream, the same mouth-watering innocence in peril, and, on the horizon, no knight in armor with sword and steed to save you: here you can only hear the panting breath of the monster who will pounce on the sweet one—footsteps in the hall. . . .

Do not open the door to the ogre, Mademoiselle Diane. (1997a, 94–95)

The mysterious old neighbor is a sort of guardian angel or anima, exhorting Diana not to be as she herself was: a weak and loving creature, dominated like a docile pet dog, and at times tempted by suicide, a last desperate effort to escape the "law of the ogres" (1997a, 96).

The women in these last two stories—Rose and Diane—suffer from what has been called the "Bluebeard animus" (Kast, in Jacoby, Kast, Riedel 1992, 86). Named after the tale of the rich and cruel nobleman who makes a habit of murdering his wives, the Bluebeard animus describes "a sadomasochistic pattern of relationship: a dominating, destructive man stands in relationship to a woman who identifies herself with his apparent power until she realizes that her femininity must inevitably be destroyed by this relationship" (1992, 86).

Bluebeard has become one of the prototypes for the ogre figure; Kast describes him as "a god of death for women only" (1992, 93). Neither Rose nor Diane is able to overcome this destructive animus and free herself from his power. Indeed, we have seen that Rose associates Nathan with various symbols of death: Assurbanipal, Kali, vampires, wolves, and bogeymen. Likewise, Diane accepts, like a submissive pet, the prison that her lover has constructed around her. Both are enthralled by the ogre: their own personalities have been mortified, buried like Bluebeard's dead wives in the secret room.

The most disturbing tale of Cerf's collection is "Trois soeurs" [Three sisters]. The narration shifts between two first-person voices: first Sonia, the eldest of three Croatian sisters, and then an unnamed confidant. Narrative time alternates as well, between the present, when Sonia is almost twenty, and nightmarish memories of her past, when she was eleven.

Because she has constantly had to defend herself and her little sisters against the advances of their father, Sonia is disconcertingly aware of her sexuality even as a child of eleven: "The sheet lifts up over my golden sex; I am eleven years old. No one but me will touch this golden sex. No one" (Cerf 1997a, 61). We learn later what her father has done:

> The father lifts up the sheet that covers Sonia's body, pulls back the nightgown from her genitals. Lifts the nightgown a little further. Fondles her breasts. Fondles her genitals, rapes her with his finger. There is some blood on the sheet. Otherwise, she has not yet bled. He does the same with Vania,

but there is no blood; he didn't penetrate her as deeply. Vania screams. The father and his stooges leave quickly, laughing. Vania will scream until morning. (1997a, 66)

Suddenly time shifts and we are nine years in the future. We learn that Sonia's defense against her father has been to make herself unappealing to him by refusing to eat: "Now I flaunt my thinness, which means: I am almost consumed, so you have nothing to consume here. I am taboo and sterile, erased, I lift up my skirt to my golden sex, I'm almost twenty" (1997a, 61). Her anorexia, a mirroring of the ogre's desire to consume, uses her to the point that the disease becomes a prophylaxis of a greater malady: the ogre's bite. Sonia's sisters use the same technique to discourage their father and his drunken friends:

> Vania cries. She doesn't want to eat anymore. Sonia and Lisa will refuse to eat a little later in their lives. Vania screams that she doesn't want to eat so that the ogres won't eat her, so that there is nothing to eat on her. Sonia will do the same thing, until they take her to the hospital, until she wants to die. For Lazar's daughters, men crazed by hunger and alcohol will always be at the door. It is the flesh on the girls that they want. The girls want no flesh on themselves. (1997a, 67)

Sonia and her sisters are victims of what Christiane Olivier calls "the inner ogre." The subtitle of her *Ogre intérieur* is "De la violence personnelle et familiale" [On personal and family violence]. Olivier examines the potential for violence that is in each one of us. Building on the theories of Freud, Karl Abraham, and Melanie Klein, which define the earliest form of infantile violence as "cannibalistic," that is, the desire "to incorporate the Other in order to use him to satisfy one's own needs, or own hunger" (Olivier 1998, 20–21), she analyses manifestations of the Freudian death instincts that result in destructive violence toward others or oneself. Violence toward others includes incest and rape ("family violence"), violence toward oneself bulimia, anorexia, alcoholism, and depression ("personal violence"). Olivier studies above all the most helpless victims of personal and family violence, children: "Since antiquity . . . we have killed and battered babies, exploited the weak, shut away the unruly, bound, beaten, and raped children, deprived them of food, burned them with cigarettes . . . Don't we hear almost every day of adults, outwardly calm—social workers, educators, medical practitioners—who have abused their authority, forcing, raping, humiliating a child?" (1998, 8–9).

Cerf's "Trois soeurs" reads almost like one of Olivier's case studies. "Patricia," for example, lived in mortal fear of her abusive father: "As soon as my father came close, I was terrorized, I wanted to crawl underground, to me he looked like an ogre" (Olivier 1998, 148). The fictional Sonia is robbed of her childhood in Cerf's story, as the transitionless shifts between the little girl of eleven and the young woman of twenty suggest. Paradoxically, her refusal to eat, while making herself "unappetizing" to her brutal father and his vicious companions, increases her sex appeal to boys her own age, and although she does not like these boys, she nevertheless likes to enhance her slender fashion-model looks with provocative clothing. Using a curious antithesis, Cerf describes the perverse pleasure she derives from flaunting her thin body, frigid like the sun: "This sex is something colder than winter, it burns the hands of men, and now that she is almost twenty, grown up, it blinds them, it is a sun that shines below her stomach, between her soft and hollow thighs, hollow because she does not eat" (Cerf 1997a, 63).

Olivier's research shows that girls abused by their father often relinquish the idea that they may ever have a loving relationship, and they tend to objectify their bodies. Although Sonia does not prostitute herself, the narrator describes her as a "whore," whose body is like a painting of inestimable worth, too valuable to sell (1997a, 62). Sonia herself, admiring the various parts of her body in a mirror, calls them a "treasure" that she will greedily keep to herself: "Yes, look at them, my breasts too, you will never touch them. I will show them to you as if it were the treasure of the earth, guarded deep in a cavern by giants or dragons" (1997a, 61).

Sonia's anorexia eventually leads her to be hospitalized, in a state of depression so deep that she wants to die. Her anorexia is not atypical. According to Olivier, this disorder is often deeply rooted in a girl's relationship with one or both of her parents. She might see her mother as a more successful rival for the father; anorexia will transform her almost literally into the "shadow"[17] of her mother that she feels she is. Or conversely, as in Sonia's case, anorexia "serves as a rampart against the desire of the father, who does not find her beautiful as she is, guaranteeing a barrier between them" (Olivier 1998, 118–19).

Muriel Cerf's *Ogres et autres contes* are fictional illustrations of the "inner ogre" observed by Olivier. At the center of each tale is a cannibalistic desire to devour, to consume: violent reenactments of the baby's desire to ingest the breast, and so arrive at a symbiosis between it and its mother. Possession of the loved one is the goal of each protagonist, and this is accomplished in myriad ways: carnal possession accompanied by gastronomical pleasure, alcohol-induced sexual violence toward a partner, or a disturbed father's rape of his daughter, the horror of which she eventually turns against herself, as incest breeds anorexia, and family violence brings on personal violence.

Muriel Cerf: *Le Verrou* [The bolt]

Le Verrou is a monumental novel of ogreish passion; published in the same year as *Ogres et autres contes* (1997), it develops many of the same themes. To summarize the novel's plot, I can do no better than to translate Cerf herself, who provides this précis on the back cover:

> The bolt is what locked the attic door of the villa where, long ago, Massimo Cuori led Nora Neumann to celebrate, fanatically and religiously, the body of his young mistress. Now the patriarch of a scrupulously respectable family, he undertakes the narration of the sole transgression of his adult life.
>
> With unnerving precision, his memory restores each shimmering flame of that summer he held his lover captive in an idolatrous, corrupt, and secretly criminal passion. In effect, Massimo Cuori could never forget the first instant he had laid eyes on the girl who would become the object of his desire, a young Austrian prostituted by her mother; he could never forget the moment he had met her again in a Viennese hotel, a sixteen-year-old waitress he seduced and took away to Milan, where, in the rich family mansion, he presented her as his fiancée. (Cerf 1997b, back cover)

The bolt represents the twenty-seven-year-old Cuori's power over Nora, his unquestioned right—bought with his family's money—to do with the sixteen-year-old as he pleases. Fragonard's famous rococo painting, *Le Verrou* (1777), depicting the struggle in a lavish bedroom between a woman and a man, the latter reaching up to bolt the door, provides an erotic, luxurious, and decadent backdrop to the novel. The relationship between the couple in the painting, as well as the one in the book, is ambiguous. What is going on behind that closed door, bolted from the outside world? Are we witnessing a tussle between lovers or a rape? For Cerf's narrator Cuori, the act he perceives in the painting is tinged with violence and perversion, just like his liaison with Nora. Blood is the color of the sheet in the bedroom, in sharp contrast to the pale white of the light that shines on the bolt and on the face of the woman: "In the Fragonard copy, the bedsheet is blood red, and pale is the light shining on the bolt that the man's hand is going to shut, and towards which flies the woman's hand in a last defense, and I always thought that the guy was going to rape and murder this woman, not engulf her in sweet caresses; I never thought that there was any libertinism in this painting" (1997b, 299). The cover of the novel depicts a detail from Fragonard's painting in which neither the bolt nor the characters appear, only the bed and a night table. The dominant impression is red: a red apple on the table, red curtains, and red sheets cascading over the round white corner of the bed. The image conveys the two colors of the altar upon which Cuori worships the divine Nora, who becomes his goddess, his "daily wine and bread" (1997b, 590).

Massimo expresses his oral obsession with Nora in endless metaphors of food and especially drink. The old narrator remembers that summer long ago, as he watched her drink in a Milan café. In Nora's presence, the mundane café is filled with the exotic smells and tastes of magical brews: "I might as well say it crudely. Given all that I drank from the swollen little lips of her pussy after that, if I had been abstemious, I wouldn't have stayed so; it was like drinking ancient brews filtered through the alembics of her body: hippocras with cinnamon and clove, claret with honey and spices, and all those heady wines of the Orient distilled in her veins, her blood, flowing through her body, coating her sex" (1997b, 135).

Cuori often refers to Nora as Ondine,[18] the sweetly seductive divinity of rivers. But after she has robbed his house, then left him, he realizes that inside this watery Ondine was a hard, hateful Fury. The victim becomes the victimizer:

> This Ondine at whose sex I quenched my thirst, as at a river of paradise, she from whom I had drunk so many balms, and the water of her eyes and the tears that gave them so much brilliance, tears that never flowed, which lay beneath her eyelids like hard bits of gravel, the gravel of her hate; . . . this passion of hate that had undoubtedly vanquished me as much as her beauty, had something admirable about it like all wild things that only obey the laws of nature, such as the flight of migratory birds or the awakening of a volcano. (1997b, 551)

As in Cerf's short stories, the essence of the ogre in *Le Verrou* lies in his need to devour. Food, drink, and lover become one in a religious ritual of consuming. We have seen Abel's fascination with the "panting flesh of the Infant Jesus" (Tournier 1997b, 129) in the sacrament of the Eucharist. In Cuori's case, making love to Nora evokes the Last Supper "'This is my body, said the guy from Nazareth, and it was the body of my spouse, the only one forever and the bread of my life, and this source of my river was as holy to me as was the heart of Jesus to others, and I write this in memory of her as Christ said Do this in memory of me'" (Cerf 1997b, 422). Nora's body is a "benediction chalice," he writes, and he yearns to pour her bodily fluids into precious flasks, since such fluids surely "could work miracles" (1997b, 424–25).

Finally, Cuori analyzes the cannibalistic nature of his love. We have noted the sacred aspect of cannibalism, whereby the cannibal hopes to transform himself by incorporating the admired traits of his victim (Zimmermann 1997, 251). Cuori's love has none of this altruistic quality, despite his religious allusions. In a remarkable, delirious monologue toward the end of the novel—worth quoting at length—Cuori sounds first like Freud's "polymorphous pervert," hungry to devour a mother's breast, and then like a Catholic vampiric visionary, intermingling erotic and spiritual ecstasy:

> Wanting to drink and eat her, to sit down at the table of this small and slender body, to make a feast and communion of her, was doubtlessly just one of the expressions that love can assume; yet it is the very expression of love, that it always wants to lick, to kiss, to touch, to steal with one's fingers or mouth a bit of mana from the idol; this love is such that one wants to swallow the object and never give it back to the world—but we are forced to be satisfied with pretending. Love is such that in its puerile, avid cannibalism, it brings tears to your eyes, your lips open in a pout, you are a child once again, tottering, arms stretched out and truly crucified against the sky, giving crazily and crazily wanting to receive. . . . I dreamed as much of devouring her whole and drinking the marrow of her bones as of holding her in my belly, where she would feel neither cold nor hurt nor fear; may she never again escape, may her blood become mine, transfuse every bit of her in me, that was my way to love her; in effect, I wanted her to dwell in me as Christ dwells in he who eats his flesh and drinks his blood, and the mystery of my way of loving this little girl was no less sublime than the mystery of the bread consecrated in the ciborium and the wine in the chalice. (Cerf, 1997b, 590–91)

Cerf's *verrou* metaphor signifies more than the metal latch that allows the ogre to feast privately on the body of the teenager. Reflecting on his affair of long ago, the old narrator, a writer, turns to fairy tales to understand the workings of his psyche. The *verrou* is the bolt that forever closes childhood, and forever corrupts the innocence of the fairy tale. Cuori laments the passing of those early days when he devoured not young girls but stories: "It doesn't matter how many bolts you push or pull, it's all the same, it's the one that closes and closed out once and for all in my existence the enchanted world where Hansel and Gretel eat a house of marzipan" (1997b, 39). It is perhaps the solace he found in fairy tales that, at age twenty-three, first attracted him to a scrawny girl of twelve. Nora seems to have stepped out of a tale, a poor Beauty who fell—or pretended to fall—in love with a well-to-do Beast. Cuori remains under her spell for the rest of his life, like the luckless victim of a fairy-tale witch. Writing forty-two years after his affair, at age sixty-nine, he still dreams of "her legs that are like those spindles that pierce your fingers and send you into a bewitching sleep, and it is from this world of fairy tales that she comes" (1997b, 45–46).

Four decades have metamorphosed Nora into a fairy tale character. Like all creatures of myths and tales, she embodies both positive and negative values.[19] Physically, she is the frail heroine of *Beauty and the*

Beast, but her character is that of a ravenous Gretel turned evil, a sweet tooth without the sweetness: "this Gretel with teeth of a marten was not a bit sweet" (1997b, 46). As for Cuori, rewriting the tales in his mind, he finds only evil in his own character. He is the ferocious Beast, not the generous and gentle prince inside. He is not the Hansel who comforts his sister in their distress, he is a Hansel who longs to devour Gretel. Speaking to his psychoanalyst about his relationship with Nora, he characterizes himself as an insanely jealous Beast, "that monster with the bushy spine, voracious, naive, and blind, . . . who is none other, in the hinterland of symbols, than the fetid ogre who swallows his own children, and in the entertaining country of psychoanalysis, 'the perverted image of the father'" (1997b, 381). Finally, he is an incestuous Hansel, whose appetite is merely whetted by the witch's house: "[T]he strong, spotless teeth allow him to eat the witch's house with Gretel (for me the gingerbread roof, for you the window of candied sugar) . . . Then he will drink and eat the body of Gretel that is all gingerbread and candied sugar, and he will have his way with her at night" (1997b, 382).

It is not surprising that Cuori's favorite fairy tale (1997b, 39) is "Hansel and Gretel," a tale that is meant to help children overcome oral anxieties and fixations they might retain after being separated from the mother's breast (Bettelheim 1989, 159–66). We have seen that the fundamental nature of Cuori's desire for Nora is oral possession, an overwhelming desire he expresses in dizzying metaphors of devouring, blending food, drink, and sex. Cuori has not learned the lessons of his favorite tale. His hunger and thirst are never quenched and, unlike Hansel and Gretel, he does not mature from his encounter with the witch, and he certainly does not live happily ever after.

In summary, *Le Verrou* is an astounding discourse on evil, in which an ogre's obsession is recounted with an inspired lyricism. For Massimo Cuori—"maximum heart(s)"—is not totally evil. He is the *porte-parole* of the author, and it may not be too far-fetched to say he is "all heart." Muriel Cerf told me in an interview (May 24, 2002) that in this novel "the ogre, unlike Saturn, can appear to us as kind. That was my intention." And indeed, at the end of the novel, as Cuori ponders the approach of the "monster" of death (Cerf 1997b, 621), the reader does feel sorry for the pathetic ogre who prays for forgiveness because what he thought was love was in reality a criminal passion: "[H]ave pity too on those who have passion *without heart,* and that is the majority of people, who think they love but instead kill, take pity on those who see the victim and say that it's not their fault" (1997b, 626–27; my emphasis). "All heart" but "without heart": Massimo Cuori embodies the hopelessly paradoxical nature of erotic passion.

The ogre is all teeth and belly. His teeth, a synecdoche for the monster of time in Durand's diurnal regime, tear and kill victims, and embody the "dental sadism" (Durand 1984, 89) of many giants and ogres in folklore. The ogre and his seven daughters in Fleutiaux's tale are such creatures, and they end up tearing one another apart. The pitiless ogres of Germain's novels—Mauperthuis and Ferdinand—work their mischief in the same sadistic way, metaphorically consuming their victims before killing them.

The belly is a much more complicated body part. Word usage shows us that belly, bowels, stomach, womb, uterus, and vulva overlap in meaning; indeed, Freud's notion that the "digestive belly" and the "sexual belly" are symbolically close is a key to understanding the soft descent into the hollow of the cup—assimilated by the psychoanalyst to the female sex organs (Durand 1984, 275)—that is a crucial image in the nocturnal regime of the imaginary: "The imagination of the descent verifies the Freudian intuition that makes the digestive tube the descending axis of the libido before its sexual fixation . . . , and psychoanalysts will always be free to see, when this buccal or anal digestive imagery appears, a symptom of regression to the narcissistic stage" (1984, 228).[20]

Durand reminds us that both the digestive and the sexual belly can carry negative connotations tinged with the guilt of gluttony or lasciviousness; indeed, vegetarianism, sobriety, and chastity have always held the moral high ground (1984, 129), even among the most formidable ogres of the political arena. Yet "the belly is the first cavity positively valorized by both hygiene and dietetics"; it is "the hedonist symbol of the happy descent, libidinously sexual and digestive at the same time" (1984, 229).

It is no wonder then that the works we have studied in this chapter present ambivalent attitudes toward the ogre. Let us revisit several passages we have already quoted. In Muriel Cerf's "Corps amoureux" and "À Fès," the digestive and sexual bellies of the couples are inseparable. Chicken, wine, and couscous constitute culinary foreplay: in the first story, "black wine flows now in their loving bodies" (Cerf 1997a, 20); in the second their love has "the sweetness of the raisin and the brutality of the spices" (1997a, 76). In *Le Verrou,* Cerf's imagination of "embedding" is evident in Massimo Cuori's euphemism of his desire to feast on Nora. He pictures himself not merely eating her but protecting her in the ultimate shelter—his belly: "I dreamed as much of devouring [*croquer*] her whole and drinking the marrow of her bones as of holding her in my belly, where she would feel neither cold nor hurt nor fear" (Cerf 1997b, 590–91). Cuori summarizes eloquently the paradox of the "loving" ogre, who wants both to devour his victim (*croquer* suggests biting, not the more passive swallowing) and drink her blood, while nonetheless offering her the most intimate protection imaginable—the protection of the womb.

Kindlifresserbrunnen (Ogre Fountain), Bern, Switzerland. Photograph provided by Andrew Bossi, cc-by-sa-2.5.

3

Avatars of Cronus: Time, Totalitarianism, and the Scapegoat

> "Germany, mother of us all!" cried Gérard de Nerval on the banks of the Rhine. Yes, I suppose so, but an ogress mother, a mother with great teeth, menacing and dangerous.
> —Tournier 2004

> At a certain age, we are in the presence of time rather than life. We cease to see life live. We see time devouring life raw.
> —Quignard 2000

IN THE PREVIOUS CHAPTER WE NOTED THAT GILBERT DURAND ASSIMIlates the "black sun"—symbol of melancholy and also the ogreish animal that devours the sun each night—to the Greek Titan Cronus, known to the Romans as Saturn. He also reminds us of Goya's terrifying *Saturn Devouring His Child,* which firmly fixed the Titan in the Western imagination as the prototypical ogre: a gigantic, cruel, and ravenous supernatural being. Since—as we have already seen in chapter 2—Cronus has forever been confused with Chronos,[1] the Greek guardian of time, we find in literature countless associations between the ogre and the destructive aspect of time. Marina Warner comments on the connection: "Hence, in traditional zodiac imagery, on calendars and in numerous astronomy and astrological treatises, the complex figure of Kronos/Saturn, presiding genius of Melancholy, holds a scythe and an hourglass as he rides in his chariot round the wheel of the heavens. Sometimes he is shown devouring his children, who are allegorized as the Hours. He comes to represent the unrelenting passage of Father Time, who devours all" (Warner 1999, 59).

The wings of Chronos have given way to the scythe and hourglass of Cronus. Cronus wields supreme power over life and death, inspiring the authors we will analyze in this chapter, authors for whom the ogre is a metaphor for the tyrant and the many faces of totalitarianism. Indeed, in most of the stories, Germany—at once Nerval's cultural "mother" and Tournier's Nazi "ogress"—casts an immense shadow that darkens and chills all it touches.

Yet an ogre can also be a victim vanquished by a person or group more powerful, more intelligent, more resourceful or crueler than he. According to René Girard, even the ghastly Cronus, betrayed as we know by his son Zeus, may have also been a casualty of mythological deformation—a scapegoat for a founding collective murder too scandalous to accept, hence erased from the mythology. Girard recounts the tale of how the baby Zeus is saved from Cronus's wrath by menacing warriors who actually seem to want to kill him:

> The Curetes, fierce warriors, hide the baby by forming a circle around him. The cries of the terrified baby Zeus could lead his father to his hiding place. To drown out his crying and deceive the devouring monster, the Curetes clash their weapons and behave in as noisy and threatening a way as possible. . . . The more actual reassurance and protection they provide, the more frightening they appear. It looks as if they are forming a circle around the baby to kill him, whereas they are actually saving his life. (Girard 1986, 70–71)

What interests Girard is the *absence* of collective violence in this myth whose characters (terrifying armed warriors, a defenseless potential victim) and structure (the hunted encircled by the hunters) bear all the marks of the archetypal collective murder, of the kind that Freud describes in *Totem and Taboo* (Freud 1953–74, 13:141–42; see above in chapter 1, n14). It is in fact almost identical to another Greek myth, in which this time the son of Zeus, the baby Dionysus, is lured into a circle of Titans, whereupon the ending is not so happy: "In order to attract the young Dionysus into their circle, the Titans shake a kind of rattle. Fascinated by the brilliant objects, the child advances toward them, and the monstrous circle closes around him. Altogether, the Titans assassinate Dionysus; after which they roast and eat him. Zeus, father of Dionysus, destroys the Titans and revives his son" (Girard 1986, 72–73).

The two myths are clearly transformations of one another, but which is more authentic? Roberto Calasso claims that they are actually one and the same myth. For Zeus had a "secret," "his having been killed, as an infant, in the Cretan cave" (Calasso 1993, 304). This secret he transferred to his son Dionysus, and thus not Zeus, but "the baby Zagreus[2] was killed by the Titans" (1993, 304). This confusion of the divine father and son is reasonable given the etymology of Zeus and Zagreus, both of which can mean "the Great Hunter" (1993, 307).

For Girard, the murder of Dionysus is without a doubt the more genuine story, for there is something missing in the tale of baby Zeus and the Curetes: the collective murder. Girard believes that there is most likely an older myth that actually gave an account of the murder of Zeus, but since "[t]he dignity of Zeus is incompatible with his death at the hands of the Curetes" (Girard 1986, 71), it had to be suppressed or, as Calasso maintains, transferred to Dionysus-Zagreus. So Zeus and the Olympians replaced Cronus and the Titans in the Greek pantheon, the former symbolizing good and the latter evil: "There is to be found in [the myth of the Titans], always to Zeus's advantage, the same division between *good* and *evil* as in the myth of the Curetes. Collective violence persists but is declared evil akin to cannibalism. As in the myth of the Curetes violence is attributed to an older mythological generation and to a religious system now seen to be' barbarous' and 'primitive'" (1986, 74).

Zeus's murder would have been unthinkable, especially at the hands of the sacred Curetes—part priests, part warriors—revered and deified as the god's protectors (*Larousse* 1996, 91). The scapegoat for the ills of a discredited past age thus became the king of that age: Cronus, the Titan cannibal father.

Sometimes the victim status given an ogre is quite dubious. A case in point is Gilles de Rais, fifteenth-century nobleman and a French historical prototype of the ogre. A marshal general who fought alongside Joan of Arc,[3] Gilles de Rais eventually descended into madness and crime, and in 1440 he was condemned to hang. He had been found guilty by an episcopal court for "heresy, evocation of demons, practice of magic, and sodomy," and by a ducal court for "felony against his suzerain, kidnappings and murders of children" (Heers 1994, 8). It is believed that he tortured and murdered hundreds of young boys. Jacques Heers recounts that after a historical novel appeared in 1992 and suggested that Gilles de Rais was innocent, some historians decided to "reopen" the case, and concluded that this ogre in fact was not guilty: the guilty verdict had been reached because greedy nobles and church officials were anxious to acquire Gilles's considerable property. Heers, a distinguished medievalist, rebukes the "revisionists" (1994, 12) who call Gilles de Rais's 1440 trial "the first Stalinian trial in Europe" (1994, 11). This bizarre "pardon" of Gilles corroborates Pascal Bruckner's argument—which we will consider in more detail later in this chapter—that a "victimist competition" permeates our culture (Bruckner 2000, 231), and prevents the voices of real victims from being heard. Bruckner cites certain perpetrators of genocide, who declare that it is the ones they have murdered who are actually the murderous ones. This type of false victimization is "the active negation of the concept of humanity, the open call to murder" (2000, 239).

In the novels considered below we will see several examples of transformations and inversions between the persecutor and the persecuted.

Northrop Frye identifies these two figures as the two poles of demonic imagery, the first representing pure evil, the second pure innocence, the archetype of which is Christ: "In the sinister human world one individual pole is the tyrant-leader, inscrutable, ruthless, melancholy, and with an insatiable will, who commands loyalty only if he is egocentric enough to represent the collective ego of his followers. The other pole is represented by the *pharmakos* or sacrificed victim, who has to be killed to strengthen the others" (Frye 1957, 148).

These two characters are normally polar opposites, and remain separate. We will see, for instance, in Pennac's *The Scapegoat*, a clear opposition between the victim (Malaussène) and his persecutor (the Nazi "ogre"). But "polarize" can also have an opposite meaning: to concentrate. So, as Frye observes, persecutor and persecuted are sometimes one and the same person: "In the most concentrated form of the demonic parody, the two become the same" (1957, 148). Kings in a number of primitive societies used to fulfill this role. Having reached a certain age or fallen out of favor with their people, once powerful rulers were ritually killed or made to commit suicide.[4] Similarly, Abel in Tournier's *The Ogre* and Jean in Chessex's *A Father's Love* exert power but in the end are powerless: they die as victims or as scapegoats, *pharmakoi*, but not before exhibiting ogreish tendencies of their own.[5]

Michel Tournier: *The Ogre*

On the first page of *The Ogre*, Michel Tournier transports the reader back to a mythical time of ogres and fairies. Abel Tiffauges is composing the first lines of his "Sinister Writings," a journal he writes with his left hand—ostensibly because he recently injured his right hand in a work accident. He feels a strong affinity with "the mists of time," hearkening back to a primeval age imbued with what Mircea Eliade calls the "magical prestige of the beginning" (Eliade 1963, 35): "*January 3, 1938.* You're an ogre, Rachel used to say to me sometimes. An ogre? A fabulous monster emerging from the mists of time? Well, yes, I do think there's something magical about me. . . . And I do believe I issued from the mists of time. . . . I was already there a thousand, a hundred thousand years ago. When the earth was still only a ball of fire spinning around in a helium sky the soul that lit it and made it spin was mine" (Tournier 1997b, 3). The author refuses to let the reader bask in the comfort of the historical time that he had so clearly delineated in the opening line of the novel, where the exact date is highlighted in italics. For historicism, Gilbert Durand reminds us, "completely devalues the imaginary, symbolic thought, reasoning by analogy, and thus, the metaphor" (Durand 1994, 9). And it is precisely in the poetic register of the symbol, or the "diabol" (Tournier 1997b, 302), and in the metaphor of the ogre, rather than in historical events, that the greatness of this novel resides. Symbols, continually shifting between positive and negative, weave the plot and determine the protagonist's fate.

Allow me to remind the reader of material already presented in chapter 1. Abel Tiffauges, an awkward, anti-social garage mechanic in pre–World War II Paris, believes he has a higher calling. His "vocation as an ogre" (1997b, 66) was conferred on him in junior high school by his mysterious friend and mentor, Nestor, who predicted: "M'Abel[6] will have formidable fangs" (1997b, 35). Here the ogre's teeth are not mere instruments of destruction. Indeed, Tiffauges's vocation is to be a lover and formidable protector, rather than a killer, of children. He becomes a bizarre and childlike prophet or magus, an ominous yet innocent ogre, in contrast to the two murderous monsters of *The Ogre*, Hitler and Goering.

Throughout the novel, Abel reminds the reader of his origins in the "mists of time," believing that his timelessness confers on him a superior destiny and power over ordinary human beings. The first pages of his "Sinister Writings" continue: "What's more, the dizzying antiquity of my origins explains my supernatural power" (1997b, 3). He is as old as Being, he claims, and thus understands the human soul as few can.

The illusion of antiquity was a gift of his schoolmate Nestor, whom Abel also considered to be a timeless being—something like his namesake in Homer's *Iliad*. "Intemporal" is the word that comes to Abel's mind as he attempts to describe his monstrous and magical friend. He writes: "I have spoken of eternity with reference to myself. So it is not surprising that Nestor, from whom I undoubtedly derive, should, like me, escape the measure of time" (1997b, 18–19).

Although the reader might find them more grotesque than numinous, Nestor and Abel claim to share an ageless dignity that the latter identifies with art. Wandering through the Louvre one day, Abel is mesmerized by an ancient statue of Apollo that, like him, originated in antiquity and has traveled through multiple centuries to come to rest in a museum. Art's "essential function," he says, is to comfort a humanity sick with mortality: "[T]o our hearts made sick by time—by its erosion, by the universal work of death, by the inexorable annihilation hanging over all we love—the work of art brings a little eternity. It is the sovereign remedy, the haven of peace for which we all long, a drop of cool water on our fevered lips (1997b, 84).

It is precisely this timelessness that Abel seeks by other means. A social misfit, Abel rebels against society in small ways that constitute epiphanies and allow him to escape from the pain of mortality. Writing with his left hand, for instance, he becomes *gauche,* as befits his awkward and *maladroit* body. Moreover, he turns into an eternal child, imitating children, who, he claims, will naturally extend their left rather than their right hand to greet someone. The right comes to represent all that is conventional in a society Abel rejects, whereas the left is the realm of innocence, of genius, of eternity: "I thus have two sets of writing: one that is "adroit," pleasant, social, commercial, reflecting the masked character I pretend to be in the eyes of society; and one that is "sinister,"[7] distorted by all the "gaucheness" of genius, full of flashes and cries—in short, inhabited by the spirit of Nestor" (1997b, 30).

His left hand traces words that will cause society to brand him as a fool, or even demented, but which will set him apart from, and above, he believes, the mediocre norm. Abel will strive to overcome historical time by emulating his dubious "personal Pantheon" (1997b, 10) of great—but misunderstood, according to him—figures: Alcibiades, Pontius Pilate, Caligula, Hadrian, Frederick William I, Paul Barras, Talleyrand, and Rasputin.[8]

But it is undoubtedly "phoric ecstasy" ("extase phorique") that most allows Abel Tiffauges briefly to escape the sad lot of human mortality. For Tournier, "phoria" ("la phorie") refers to a man carrying a child on his shoulders, a seemingly banal act, which, like all important symbols, incorporates complex and ambivalent connotations. In his autobiography *The Wind Spirit,* Tournier reveals that "[t]he word comes from the Greek *phoreō* (to carry), a root that can be found in such words as doryphorus (spear carrier), euphoric (literally, bearing well), and Christopher (bearer of Christ)" (Tournier 1988, 101). Phoria is "Tiffauge's specific perversion and the ogre's primary act" (1988, 101), and contains the potential for both good and evil:

> The exemplar of the good phoric hero, Saint Christopher, humbles himself by ferrying travelers across a river upon his back, as though he were a beast of burden. For there is abnegation in phoria, but of an equivocal sort, secretly possessed by the inversion of malign and benign, a mysterious operation which, without causing any apparent change in the nature of a person or thing, alters its *value,* putting less where there was more and more where there was less. Thus, the good giant who becomes a beast in order to save a small child is not so far from the predatory hunter who devours children. He who carries the child carries him away. He who serves him humbly embraces him criminally. In other words, the ghost of Saint Christopher, bearer and saver of children, is the erlking, abductor and murderer of children. (1988, 102)

The legend[9] of Saint Christopher, the Christ-Bearer, who became the patron saint of travelers, recounts how this third-century martyr, renouncing his master Satan, became a ferryman, hoisting travelers on his shoulders to cross a dangerous stream. One day he was carrying a small child to safety when, despite his prodigious strength, he was almost crushed by the weight of the boy. The child, of course, was Christ, heavy with the burden of humanity's sins.

For Tournier, the malignant inversion or "ghost" of St. Christopher is the Alder King (or Erl King), from Goethe's famous ballad about a young boy who succumbs to a mysterious supernatural being while being borne on horseback through a dark forest with his father. It is this ballad, which "has always been *the* German poem par excellence for every French schoolchild embarking upon the study of German literature, a symbol of Germany herself" (1988, 97), that inspired Tournier with the title of his novel.[10]

Gilbert Durand's research lends credence to Tournier's intuition that there is a shadowy side to St. Christopher. He mentions a seventeenth-century painting called *St. Christopher the Dog-Headed* (or "Cynocephalus") in the Byzantine Museum of Athens; this work is a fascinating example of how "inversion" or "negation" of mythological symbols helps us deal with our mortality. Durand (1984, 231) explains how two opposite myths converge in the painting. The haloed, cross-bearing figure, clearly labeled "Christophoros," is obviously a saint. But his dog head points toward a negative version of the myth, perhaps a reference to the Egyptian Anubis, the jackal-headed god who ferries dead souls across the infernal river, or to Cerberus, the three-headed (or, by some accounts, fifty-headed) dog who guards the gates of Hades. These fearsome figures of the underworld recall the origin of St. Christopher, who was from North Africa, beyond what the Romans considered the civilized world, a land they thought inhabited by a cannibalistic, dog-headed people (Woods 1999). Christopher was the name he took at his baptism; his name originally was Reprobus, meaning "reprobate," or "wicked." Thus this huge, powerful man was originally a "cruel, man-eating giant" (Durand 1984, 231). The myth is inverted and he is converted into a saint, and at the same time, death is tamed, euphemized by the Christian belief in eternal salvation: "It is Christ "carried" by death [i.e. Reprobus] who transforms and inverts the meaning of death itself. Christ accompanies souls on their voyage, forces himself to make the same perilous passage, and the image of the cynocephalus tamed, transformed into christophore, inverts its meaning and becomes a protector, a talisman against the violence of death" (1984, 231).

Abel Tiffauges is captivated by the story of Christopher. Like the legendary saint, he feels destined to bear children, an oddly "maternal vocation" that one critic feels is the most scandalous aspect of the novel because it upsets all that Freud has taught us about family relationships:

Abel is "the man-mother, the child-bearer who by his tenderness pulverizes the Oedipal trilogy" (Monès, in Tournier 1970, 587).[11] Tiffauges realizes that he incarnates the duality of Christopher, "huge as a giant and terrible of aspect" (Tournier 1997b, 39), who at one time served the devil yet was destined to carry the Christ-child. Abel's "huge clumsy hands" (1997b, 320) belie their sensitivity to "all the quiverings of [the boys'] muscles" (1997b, 321) as he carries them off to serve in the Nazi military school. He is oblivious to the violence he is doing, caught up in the simple joy of his child-bearing vocation:

> The first thing I do with a new boy is put my hand on his neck, a little below the nape. . . .
> My hands are made for carrying, lifting, bearing off. . . . Phoric hands, indeed! And it's not only the hands but the whole body, from my inordinate height, my porter's back, my Herculean strength—all things that correspond to the small light bodies of children. My bigness and their littleness are two elements perfectly adapted to one another by nature. All of it is preordained, willed, prepared from all eternity; and so, venerable, adorable. (1997b, 321)

Tiffauges's phoric epiphanies constitute high points of the novel, from the first instance, when he picks up the young Jeannot, injured at the garage (1997b, 78–79), to the last, when he carries a young Estonian refugee away from the bloody battle and disappears into the marsh (1997b, 366–70).[12] Phoria entails euphoria, a feeling Tiffauges describes variously as an "unbearable and heart-rending sweetness" (1997b, 78), "a wave of beatitude" (1997b, 79), an "intoxication" (1997b, 351). In part erotic pleasure, phoria cannot, however, be equated with sexual desire. Genital sexuality is a poor, crass second to Abel's phoric ecstasy: "It was not a lewd and limited titillation, but a total joy of all my being" (1997b, 79). His attraction to children is not sexual: "My vocation is higher and more general" (1997b, 87). "Higher" here means less transitory, in proximity to the eternal.

The relationship between phoria and time can best be examined in a passage in which Abel is engaged in his favorite occupation: taking photographs of children. The boys are roller skating, when one of them falls and cuts his knee. Rather than help the boy, Abel, fascinated by the wound, first takes pictures of it, and as he does so he is overwhelmed by "a kind of drunken happiness beyond [his] control" (1997b, 107). He lifts the boy onto his shoulders, and immediately seems to step out of human time:

> I stood up, and my shoulders touched the sky, my head was encircled by archangels singing anthems in my praise. Mystic roses poured forth their sweetest perfume. For the second time in a few months I'd lifted a wounded

3: AVATARS OF CRONUS: TIME, TOTALITARIANISM, AND THE SCAPEGOAT

child in my arms and been enfolded in phoric ecstasy. That alone was enough to prove I'd entered upon a new era.

The children around me could not understand the light transverberating my face. (1997b, 107)

Like Atlas, one of the "phoric heroes" (1997b, 82) who in his view hold the key to his destiny, Abel feels he is touching the sky as he lifts the child. He hears the music of the angels, and shares in their divine glory. The "new era" he seems to enter is timeless, beyond the confines of human history.

But the epiphany must end, and Abel returns to human time as he lifts the boy into his car and takes him to the pharmacy: "I must step back into time, take up the thread of ordinary events again, pretend to be just one more of the great human family" (1997b, 107).

This passage reveals the affinities between phoria and photography. Photography is the ogre's hobby par excellence. When Abel observes children behind a schoolyard fence, they seem to be in a cage, helpless and vulnerable, exciting his "ogre's soul" (1997b, 93). He takes a rapid series of shots, "with the intense and guilty joy of a hunter shooting zoo animals in their cages" (1997b, 93). Photography for him is a sublimation of sexual aggression, the camera symbolizing at the same time the pleasure of the glans-lens and the power of Polyphemus, the one-eyed Cyclops who devoured several of Odysseus's men when they were cast ashore on Sicily: "I enjoy being equipped with a huge leather-clad sex whose Cyclopean eye opens like lightning when I command it to look, and closes again inexorably on what it has seen. It is a marvelous organ, seer and remembrancer, a tireless hawk that swoops on its prey to steal from it and bring back to its master that which is profoundest in it and most deceptive—appearance!" (1997b, 103).

The photographer, stealing images and developing them in the obscurity and privacy of his darkroom, mesmerizes his subject, takes possession of it. Photography provides a means of consuming the unattainable. Thus the photographer is "miserly, greedy, avid and centripetal," the opposite of the painter, whose nature is "expansive, generous, centrifugal" (1997b, 103). Photography is an ambivalent art, in keeping with Abel's ogre character. It is a sort of witchcraft, involving "the half-amorous, half-murderous possession of the photographed by the photographer" (1997b, 104). Abel's neighbor articulates the occult nature of his obsession when she sees him returning from a session photographing school children: "There goes Monsieur Tiffauges back from the market with supplies of raw meat. Now he'll shut himself up in the dark to eat it. There are some things one can't do in broad daylight, aren't there?" (1997b, 111).[13]

Phoria, then, is the first method that Abel uses to escape from human time, dominate children, and fulfill his ogreish desires. A second method is what he calls "atmospheric density," an idea inherited from Nestor, who could control "the closed world of St. Christopher's, the school life in the center of which he crouched like a spider in his web" (1997b, 88), because, thanks to his father the concierge, he held the keys to every room. Abel measures atmospheric density by the number of children occupying an enclosed space: thus in the outside playground it is relatively weak, whereas it is "at its very richest in the dormitories in the middle of the night" (1997b, 88).

Atmospheric density, or "saturation" (1997b, 85), procures for Abel a pleasure that rivals phoric ecstasy. Walking down an alley as school happens to be letting out, Abel is jostled by the rushing crowd of children; he is "shoved and elbowed but deliciously happy too, with the happiness of a little flower braving with all its stamens the assault of a pollen-laden squall" (1997b, 89). He is symbolically fertilized by the swarm of rowdy children, and realizes that atmospheric density is actually superior to phoric ecstasy because it bears "the definitive seal of *totality*" (1997b, 90).

Taking pictures of children helps Abel experience the joy of total immersion in childhood. Sifting through the images at home amounts to possessing the children, who have become supernatural, abstract beings in his personal mythology: "The lens is the narrow gate through which the elect, those called to become gods and heroes *possessed,* make their secret entry into my inner Pantheon" (1997b, 104). The photographed children lose their individuality, and each focused image becomes part of a blurred collectivity, thus satisfying Abel's "need for exhaustiveness": "For each photograph raises its subject to a degree of abstraction that automatically confers on it a certain generality, so that every child photographed is a thousand children possessed" (1997b, 104).

Atmospheric density is a factor of two variables: numbers (the mass of undifferentiated children) and claustration, which can be abstract (children being "trapped" in the eye of the camera), or concrete (children confined to the various rooms of the boarding school or, later, to the Kaltenborn military school where Abel works). In the following passage Abel is joyfully stifled and half-blinded by steam rising from the showers: "Bodies merged into and emerged out of it suddenly, as in a dream, only to vanish again. All these children were being boiled in a giant cauldron before being eaten, but I had thrown myself in through love and was cooking with them" (1997b, 328). Always the loving ogre, Abel is a happy claustrophile, eager to share in the cramped space of his victims.

His acute sense of smell—always highly developed in the flesh-eating ogre—also leads Abel to experience the rapture of atmospheric density. As a French prisoner working in East Prussia, Abel has to renew his German pass once a month at the local town hall. One fine April day, he is captivated by "an exquisite, fresh, springlike smell, redolent of pepper and seed" (1997b, 235) emanating from one of the rooms of the edifice. Following his nose, Abel enters a room filled with "a whole swarm of completely naked little girls" (1997b, 235). In order to conserve the "nascent purity" of the scent rising from the girls' flesh, he quietly shuts the door "so as to restore the atmospheric density that only completely hermetic closure could supply" (1997b, 235).[14] He later learns that there was a similar assembly of little boys across town; the reason for these gatherings is that every April 19 (the eve of Hitler's birthday), all children ten years of age must appear before a board to be drafted into the Hitler Youth.

Returning to Rominten, where he is still working for Goering, Abel's reflections show us the link between the ogre and totality (or "exhaustiveness"). The most dangerous ogre of all is the totalitarian ruler—Hitler in this case—who controls masses of innocents for his single-minded end. By comparison, the fearsome, enormous Goering is pitiful: "[Goering] had dwindled to the rank of a little, imaginary, picturesque ogre out of an old wives' tale. He was eclipsed now by the other, the ogre of Rastenburg,[15] who demanded of his subjects the exhaustive birthday gift of five hundred thousand little girls and five hundred thousand little boys, ten years old, dressed for the sacrifice, or in other words naked, out of whose flesh he kneaded his cannon fodder." (1997b, 236).

So far we have been concerned with Abel Tiffauges and the relationship between time and his personal ogreish destiny. Yet *The Ogre* also contains fascinating insights into the importance of time in Nazi ideology, firmly rooted in the past, both in Teutonic mythology and in the mythologized history of National Socialism. Tournier recounts how important the calendar is for the Nazi "liturgy," whose pageantry seduces the young boys of the Hitler Youth, who celebrate with flags, fire, and fanfare the anniversaries of Nazi martyrs (1997b, 266–67, 278–79 305), the winter solstice (1997b, 264–65), and the summer solstice (1997b, 282–84). Abel Tiffauges witnesses many of these events, and comes to realize that Hitlerism is essentially regressive, focused on the past, espousing a cyclical, rather than linear, view of time:

> It took me some time to jump on this great flagged merry-go-round, noisy and gaudy, with its cargo of children and handful of adults. Now that I'm on it I understand better what makes it work. It is clear that the trajectory of time here is not linear but circular. You live not in history but in the calendar. So it's the undisputed reign of the eternal return—the merry-go-round

image is exact. Hitlerism is resistant to any idea of progress, creation, discovery, or imagination of an unknown future. Its virtue is not rupture but restoration: hence the cult of race, ancestors, the dead, the soil. . . . (1997b, 265–66)

One cannot help but notice the role of fire in the rituals celebrated by the young pupils of the Kaltenborn military school—the *Jungmannen*. Lighting candles on a fir tree at the winter solstice symbolizes "the death of the sun god . . . lamented as an impending cosmic fatality" (1997b, 264). Likewise, the feast of the summer solstice bears a "secret sadness" because the sun is already beginning its decline: "[t]hus the child at his zenith of health and beauty already carries the seed of decrepitude" (1997b, 282). The boys end the summer celebration by jumping through the pyre, foreshadowing their imminent fiery deaths at the hands of the Russians: "This ceremony, obstinately mingling the future and death, and throwing the boys one after the other into the live coals, is the clear evocation, the diabolic invocation, of the massacre of the innocents toward which we march, singing" (1997b, 284).

The Jungmannen celebrate a past rendered magnificent, but their future will be bleak and brief. They will be consumed by flames, as befits these students of Teutonic mythology, whose world also ends in a fiery "Twilight of the Gods."

Jacques Chessex: *A Father's Love*

Jacques Chessex's novel *A Father's Love* (*L'Ogre*), which won France's *Prix Goncourt* in 1973, is the story of the unfortunate Jean Calmet, continually bullied by a series of ogreish characters. Jean's colossal, domineering father, a doctor well respected by the community, has just died, but his memory continues to haunt Jean. A thirty-eight-year-old high school Latin teacher in Switzerland's Vaud canton, Jean is also terrorized by his powerful and sadistic principal and to a lesser extent by a fanatical neo-Nazi acquaintance. Shy, dominated by others, including the nineteen-year-old woman he has fallen in love with, Jean reacts to his humiliation by becoming an ogre himself, seeking strength from the youth and vigor of his students: "Saps were seething in the boys. The girls secreted marvels. Jean Calmet gorged himself on both, fed, drank, strengthened himself" (Chessex 1975, 59). His girl friend Thérèse soon leaves him, frustrated by his jealousy and his impotence. Jean's suicide, described in gruesome detail in the final pages, is induced by his inability to stand up to the various ogres and ogresses who oppress him, especially Thérèse and his deceased father, who still seems to be mocking him from the crematory urn.

3: AVATARS OF CRONUS: TIME, TOTALITARIANISM, AND THE SCAPEGOAT 89

In the opening scene, Jean thinks back to the many dinners he suffered through as a child, sitting at the table with his parents and his four older brothers and sisters. Although he loved his father, he feared him and was jealous of his strength and appetite. He remembers the doctor, immense and powerful, "hissing" and "sucking" as he gobbled down his food, lit by the setting sun that seemed his equal. He appears to Jean as "that other sun, infallible and detestable, which turned red, which shone, which illuminated itself with all its power" (1975, 4).

Anne Marie Jaton observes that "the Father" and "Time" are the primary figures of the novel: "The image of Cronus, this castrating father, playing with knives and razors to scare his child (whom he often pretends to eat as well), reminds us that the passing of the hours and the days devours us little by little" (Jaton 2001, 82). This echoes Marina Warner's observation that "the onward march of time" (Warner 1999, 58) is the central issue in myths and fairy tales about ogres and cannibals. The ogre is often a father figure, and the child is his natural enemy and victim. Since "[c]hildren bear away the future with them" (1999, 58), Warner writes, they constitute a threat to the ogre's permanence.

Indeed, Jean metonymically associates his father with time, as symbolized by the large clock directly behind the doctor's place at the dinner table. The narrator introduces the recurring image of the clock—clearly associated with death—early in the novel:

> The doctor sat with his back a few centimeters from the solemn pendulum clock, a *morbier*[16] tall as a coffin....
>
> Jean Calmet marveled at the fact that his father had gone on sitting for years in front of this machine that stood like a monument behind him: as if he had wanted to warn all of them of his irrevocable domination. (Chessex 1975, 19)

If the mythical Cronus castrated his father Uranus at his mother's bidding, this new avatar of Cronus metaphorically castrates his son, who will always feel inadequate, especially with women. At age nineteen, Jean loves seventeen-year-old Liliane, who works in his father's office. One day he discovers the two of them locked in a tight embrace in the office, Liliane naked from the waist up. Jean is horrified, but concedes that the tyrant has a sort of *droit du seigneur* to possess this working class girl: "He was the father! The man of vigor, the owner, the law! Fifty-eight years of age. Seventeen years old. But the law . . . Jean Calmet immediately discarded the idea of the abduction of a minor; the doctor had not led this girl astray, had not seduced her. He had exercised a right" (1975, 52).

Jean never gets over this humiliation, and when he meets Thérèse, nineteen years later, the image of his father pursues him. He repeatedly pictures the good doctor, ashamed of his impotent son, taking his place in her bed, satisfying her as only he can. One day, in a café, a simple cane in an umbrella stand conjures up visions of his father's terrible penis: erect, aggressive, powerful. Troubled, momentarily paralyzed with fear, Jean must touch "the hard organ, let his fingers run over its knots" (1975, 71). Ashamed, he wonders if it is an act of exorcism, but it is in fact an attempt to incorporate his father's potency—not unlike the cannibal who devours his enemy out of respect for his force.

When Jean takes his students on an outing to Bern, Thérèse goes along with her new lover, a boy in Jean's class. Despondent, Jean is consumed by shame and jealousy. Suddenly, the group comes upon the remarkable *Kindlifresserbrunnen,* a colorful fountain depicting, at the top of a column, a grinning ogre devouring a child, while he carries off others in a sack.[17] The students are delighted and laugh at the ogre—after all, it is meant to be a carnival figure—but Jean is revolted, struck by the resemblance between the bloody statue and his father, who, red like the setting sun, used to terrorize him at the dinner table:

> The Ogre's mirth! . . . Could the Ogre be his father, a new image of his father risen up from the Crematorium to warn him again and persecute him? . . . Jean Calmet remembered the evening ritual, the hissing of the sharpened knives one against the other: "That child is so cute I'd eat him. I'm going to gobble him up raw!"
>
> And the grunts, the drools, the mimicry of impatience and appetite accompanied the sharpening ferociously, and the doctor's big hand squeezed Jean Calmet's throat, immobilizing him on knees as hard as those of the dirty statue. (1975, 156–57)

Late in the novel, he sees Thérèse one last time. He is drying her after her bath, and is distressed by his lack of desire for this beautiful woman who wants to make love with him. He imagines that he sees his father "considering him with an ironic look": "You're trying to arouse yourself, Jean Calmet. You know very well that it's impossible. They're for me, those dainty morsels. Leave that girl alone. You know you'll never be able to have her" (1975, 181). Four days later, Jean slits his wrists in his bathtub, as befits this son of Cronus for whom the razor was a "sacred object" (1975, 62), emblem of his father, doctor and castrator.

A Father's Love is ogreish and Oedipal, a bleak story of "intergenerational strife" (Warner 1999, 71), which was also the central issue in both Sophocles' *Oedipus the King* and Hesiod's recounting of the power struggles between Uranus (the Sky), Cronus (the Titan son of Uranus and Gaea, the Earth), and Zeus (an Olympian god, son of Cronus and Rhea). Uranus was horrified by his hideous offspring—the monstrous

Titans, Cyclopes and Hecatoncheires—and banished them far underground. The last-born, Cronus, avenged his siblings by castrating Uranus with a sickle; this bloody act gave birth to Aphrodite, the Furies, and various monsters (Hesiod 1993, *Theogony* I. 137–455; *Larousse* 1996, 88). As we have already seen, Zeus (another last-born child) ended the reign of his cannibal father by slipping him a drug that made him vomit up the children he had swallowed; together with Zeus they defeated Cronus, who, according to Homer, "was driven from the sky and cast to the very depths of the universe and there enchained in the region which stretches beneath the earth and the fruitless sea" (*Larousse* 1996, 91).

The subject of castration has continued to fascinate, for storytellers have often confused the fates of the two punished fathers, and attributed to Zeus the same cutting edge as Cronus. Marina Warner recounts three examples. First, an Orphic tradition has Zeus repeating his father's act, castrating Cronus, as Cronus had done to Uranus (Warner 1999, 57). Second, an illustration of *La Bible des poètes* (1507) shows the difficulty authors have had separating Cronus's and Uranus's fates at the hands of their sons. The two stories merge into one, as Uranus—instead of Cronus—is pictured holding the scythe of Father Time, and eating one of his children (1999, 52). Third, Freud, in his *Interpretation of Dreams*, mistakenly writes that Zeus castrated Cronus, perhaps wanting to emphasize the violence inherent in a son's aggression toward his father and rival(1999, 68–69).[18]

Castration is certainly a fundamental theme of Chessex's novel. Jean is both attracted to and repulsed by the razor. As a boy, he longed to have a razor just like his father's, but the instrument also frightened him, because the doctor used it to tease him in repeated "tragi-comic" rituals (Chessex 1975, 62), making the boy touch the blood that oozed from small shaving cuts. The adult Jean prefers the razor to his electric shaver, but he can only use it when he feels strong (1975, 61). Conversely, Jean loves to visit a little neighborhood barbershop where, in the hands of his adroit Italian barber, the razor brings him "a deep, light peace," "a special joy," and "new confidence" (1975, 38–40).

This love-hate bond with the razor reflects his ambivalent attitude towards his father, and the psychological violence at the heart of their relationship. In the myth, Zeus gets the better of Cronus; the ogre-father becomes the victim—banished or emasculated—of his youngest and much cleverer son. For Marina Warner, this is the normal order of things, and the lesson to be drawn from similar myths and tales: "The ogre who eats babies . . . embodies a monstrous and anomalous paternal response to the anxiety that his offspring would supplant him; his wicked folly makes plain the social and human imperative that the young must be allowed to thrive and grow. . . . In this sense, fairy tales do offer allegories of time and resignation: the future belongs to the young giant-killer" (Warner 1999, 77).

In Chessex's tragic novel, however, there is no "young giant-killer." Hesiod's Cronus-Zeus myth is reversed, and the metaphorical castration is wrought by the father on the youngest child, Jean. Such an outcome would be unthinkable in the Greek myth, in which Cronus and his Titan siblings symbolize "a barbarous history," while Zeus and the Olympians signal "the glorious arrival of a new, human-scale, civilized, political and religious order" (Warner 1999, 96). Chessex has turned the myth on its head, declaring that the ogre, far from being a creature of the past, is undoubtedly the present and the future of a brutal world.

Daniel Pennac: *The Scapegoat*

The Scapegoat (*Au Bonheur des ogres*) is a detective novel, a brilliant parody of *The Ladies' Paradise* (*Au Bonheur des dames*), Zola's novel about the rise of the department store in 1860s Paris. Benjamin Malaussène officially works as a quality controller for a Parisian department store in the 1980s, but his real job is that of a scapegoat: that is, he takes the blame when dissatisfied customers return defective purchases. He cuts such a pitiful figure that, more often than not, the customers feel sorry for him and withdraw their complaints. When there is a succession of bomb attacks in the store, killing several people, Malaussène becomes a scapegoat for these events as well. He and his colorful family—along with friends from the Belleville district of Paris—help him prove his innocence and find the real killer.

The ogres who figure in the French title are a cult of six Nazis who haunted the same department store in 1942, while it was closed during the Occupation. Purporting to run an underground railroad to help Jews escape to Spain or the United States, they lured children into the shuttered store. Needless to say, the children would never leave: the six ogres raped, killed, and ate them as a part of their demonic ceremonies.[19]

Forty years after these unspeakable crimes, the six members of "The Chapel of 111" (so named because $6 \times 111 = 666$, the number of the "Beast" or "Antichrist" who will rule the world at its end) are killed in the mysterious explosions, implicating the luckless Malaussène, who inadvertently always finds himself at the scene.

What is the relationship between time and this novel of scapegoats and Nazi ogres? At the core of National Socialism, writes Mircea Eliade in *Aspects du mythe*, was an "eschatological and millenarian mythology" that announced "the End of this world and the beginning of an era of abundance and beatitude" (Eliade 1963, 91). Toward the end of *The Scapegoat,* the perpetrator of the explosions—a little old man who was a member of the cult—explains to Malaussène the critical importance of the millennium to believers in the Nazi ideology: "They spoke about it as if it were tomorrow, young fellow, convinced that by gobbling up Europe they had annexed Time itself" (Pennac 1999, 186).

The millenarian aspect of Nazism accentuates its fundamentally pessimistic character. "The racist myth of 'Aryanism,'" notes Eliade, shares the "passion for 'noble origins'" (1963, 224) common to many European societies. As we have seen in the rituals of the Hitler Youth in Tournier's novel, it seeks to recapture the glorious past of Teutonic mythology. Eliade points out elsewhere that besides conferring upon the German race the nobility and strength of its divine ancestors, this obsession with Germanic mythology serves "to abolish Christian values and recover the source of the 'race'" (Eliade 1957, 25). Eliade calls the Nazi myth "strangely awkward" and pessimistic (1957, 25), especially when compared to the other totalitarian mythology of the twentieth century: the optimistic Marxist-Leninist eschatology that predicts the final victory of the proletariat. For the Nazi myth claims that before humans are born anew in the Nazi millennium, the present world must end in a cataclysmic battle similar to the Teutonic *ragna rök,* often translated as the "Twilight of the Gods," a gigantic catastrophe in which gods, giants, monsters and men annihilate one another. *The Larousse Encyclopedia of Mythology* recounts in bloody detail the final conflagration in Teutonic mythology, and then describes what is left of the earth:

> All the great gods were dead. And now that Thor, protector of mankind, had disappeared, men were abandoned. They were driven from their hearths and the human race was swept from the surface of the earth. The earth itself was beginning to lose its shape. . . . The giant Surt set the entire earth on fire; the universe was no longer more than an immense furnace. Flames spurted from fissures in the rocks; everywhere there was the hissing of steam. All living things, all plant life, were blotted out. (*Larousse* 1996, 276)

It is perplexing, concludes Eliade, that such a mythology, which amounts to embracing "collective suicide" (Eliade 1957, 25), should have captured the imagination of so many of the German people. Perplexing—until, perhaps, one contemplates the various forms of Christian millenarianism that are still widespread today.

The Nazi myth is based on a magnificent mythological past; its adherents, however, face a catastrophic future, which leads Pennac's cult members to pursue reckless pleasure in the present. After the murders have finally been solved, the chief superintendent explains to Malaussène that the raison d'être of the 1940s Nazi "orgiastic and murderous" sects was "a radical critique of materialism"—which explained why they chose a department store for their orgies—along with a "mystical belief in the Moment," which coincided with their hate of commerce and its encouragement to forgo instant profits in order to save for the future. "Death to tomorrow! Long live the moment! And glory be to orgasmic Mammon, the Prince of the Eternal Moment!" (Pennac 1999, 210). Moreover, the final moment of each of the six ogres is "a last dose of pleasure" (1999, 211), the perfect fusion of sex and death: the explosions in fact were not murders but suicides, and each victim died with an "orgasmic expression" (1999, 210) on his face, dying on the day he believed appointed by the stars.

The totalitarian ogre desires to stop or to "eat" time; his crime is to feed on the freedom of his victims. Reduce the future to the instant, abolish waiting in favor of immediate gratification: this is the meaning of the necrophagous and pederastic orgies of Pennac's novel. His ogres believed they could appropriate infinity: "So, during that period, imaginations ran rife over the infinite field of legendary possibilities. Within a few months, a millennium had actually passed by in everyone's memory. It was at that time of vibrant eternity that the six ogres of 'The Chapel of 111' lived" (1999, 186).

The French sociologist Michel Maffesoli names this "moment" or "vibrant eternity" revered by Pennac's Nazis "vertical time" (Maffesoli 1984, 51; 1993, 64), as opposed to historical or "horizontal time." It is a key concept of both *Essais sur la violence banale et fondatrice* [Essays on common and original violence] and *The Shadow of Dionysus*. For Maffesoli violence is a necessary social structure whose effects are not solely negative. Dissidence and disorder can be constructive and useful, foundations of a new and better society. The carnivalesque chaos of Mardi Gras celebrations is an annual salutary channeling of innate social violence. Such festivals are an antidote to boredom and contribute to the vitality of a culture. We must accept the "dark destruction" of our Dionysian side, writes Maffesoli, remembering that classicists have shown a parallel "between the exuberance of the orgiastic practices of the Dionysian cult and the blossoming of urban civilization" (1984, 26). Moreover, following Freud and René Girard,[20] Maffesoli reminds us in his two studies that societies are often founded by an act of violence:

> From the Phoenix to Dionysus, by way of Osiris, all mythologies show us how destruction is the foundation of structuration, but although one can say this *a posteriori*, it is felt at the time to be an intolerable aggression.

It is in this sense that one can speak of the fundamentally ambivalent nature of violence. (Maffesoli 1984, 48)

National, religious, or popular festivals recall a crime, an act of disobedience, a revolt or the death of a god or celebrated personage. It is always a matter of a *founding* crime. Of course, it is instituted, legalized, but all the same, the commemoration is logically the object of similar excesses. (1993, 81)

"Vertical time" is the triumph of the present, a "totality" (1984, 61) in which one lives completely in the here and now, without a care for the past or future. It is the supreme form of cyclical time, in which the cycle has shortened to a point, an instant. Tournier's Robinson Crusoe explains it eloquently. As the years pass, and he realizes he will never leave his island, he senses that historical time no longer holds any meaning for him. Why count the hours, the days, the years, when nothing will ever change? "For me the cycle has now shrunk until it is merged in the moment. The circular movement has become so swift that it cannot be distinguished from immobility. And it is as though, in consequence, my days had rearranged themselves. No longer do they jostle on each other's heels. Each stands separate and upright, proudly affirming its own worth.... Are we not now living in eternity, Friday and I?" (Tournier 1997a, 204).

"Vertical time," according to Maffesoli, denotes a kind of "eternal present" (1984, 53), an escape from the often dismal past and the always unknown future that define our mortality. It is the moment of Dionysian excess, exuberance, and *jouissance,* where passion and the spirit of carpe diem prevail over economic, political, or moral virtue (1993, 8). In short, it is the time of the orgy:[21] "Beyond linear or catastrophic time, outside quantitative order, there exists a vertical time where lives the banal intensity of the present. This notion which might appear abstract refers in fact to the crystallization of all the little nothings that macroscopic vision does not take into account but which constitute the vital force, the power of social structuration, the dynamic of the orgy" (1993, 64).

For Gilbert Durand the orgy is "the negative epiphany of the vegetal and lunar cycle" (Durand 1984, 358), one of the fundamental symbols of the attempt to conquer mortality through a conception of time as cyclical. It is a return to primitive chaos, "a negative moment where norms are abolished, and at the same time a joyful future promise of order reborn" (1984, 358–59). Durand notes the close functional relationship between the orgy and the sacrifice, the latter also being an attempt to master time, in this case by "bartering" (1984, 356) with the divinity.

In his two essays, Maffesoli shows that the Dionysian orgy and the Nazi myth are inextricably linked. Each is based on the effacement of the individual for the sake of the community. Ecstatic religious practices build a strong communal bond. In spiritual eroticism, writes Maffesoli in *The Shadow of Dionysus*,

> Drunkenness, excess, prostitution, debauchery: all refer to the matricial fusion, the community and, by way of consequence, to social fecundity. "Being everything to everyone," the paradigm of which is the deity, is the efficient sign of a cosmic union where one sees the creation/destruction of love and fear. . . . The orgiastic religion . . . is a carnal copulation, a bodily blending which unites the individual and that which goes beyond, the divine, the world of the gods—that is to say, the sociality. . . . This cruel or tender eroticism that one finds in vastly different cultural fields is thus the necessary route, or the necessary initiation, which founds the human community. (Maffesoli 1993, 36–37)

In *Essais sur la violence banale et fondatrice*, Maffesoli cites Nazism as one of the "perverse forms" of the "return of the communitarian system" (1984, 103), which often rests on a leader's charisma. The sociologist could be describing Tournier's Jungmannen in *The Ogre*, when he recalls "the collective emotions, the celebrations of the fatherland, of the earth" (1984, 104) that characterize National Socialism. Nazi ideology, despite its "deplorable perversity," nonetheless has this in common with acceptable social organisms: "violence plays fully its role in the founding or the regeneration of the community" (1984, 104).

This then is the world of Pennac's ogres, as they celebrate their cannibalistic orgies in the closed department store, "in the secrecy of that dimly lit world crammed with fossilized merchandise" (Pennac 1999, 186). The constricted indoor space recalls Abel Tiffauges's heightened pleasure when he could enjoy children in crowded places, where "atmospheric density" (Tournier 1997b, 88) was maximal. The innocent Abel—an ogre in spite of himself—contrasts with the perverse ogres of *The Scapegoat* and the cruel father of *A Father's Love*, both loved and hated by his son Jean. The three novels illustrate the "organic ambivalence of violence," which can "attract and repel" (Maffesoli 1984, 93) like Dionysus himself. Dionysian effervescence is inherently violent, and violence of course is not generally healthy. Obviously, the murderous ceremonies of Pennac's ogres possess all of the negative and none of the positive aspects of Dionysian excess. Although they hope to be at the dawn of a new order—the Nazi millennium—hindsight will justify neither their acts nor the new society they aspire to create.

Pascal Bruckner: "Les Ogres anonymes"
[*Ogres Anonymous*]

Pascal Bruckner is best known for his novels Lunes de fiel (1981; adapted for Roman Polanski's 1992 film *Bitter Moon*) and *Les Voleurs de beauté* [The beauty robbers] (1997; Prix Renaudot). He is also the author of many philosophical essays, notably *La Tentation de l'innocence* (1995; Prix Médicis), translated as *The Temptation of Innocence: Living in the Age of Entitlement*. In this book, described by *Le Monde* as "ferocious" (quoted on the back cover), he reveals the ogreish character of modern Western society, seduced by the gluttony of consumerism; he also excoriates our curious and perverse tendency to glorify victimhood.

"Les Ogres anonymes" is also ferocious, but very funny: a dark children's tale about a Parisian ogre who is trying to quit. Deceptively simple, it started out as a story for Bruckner's young daughter, which he wrote as a respite after the two prize-winning "serious" works that he had just published. Descended from a distinguished and wealthy line of Polish ogres, Balthus Zaminski, apart from his razor-sharp teeth and oversized hands, is nothing like the stereotypical repulsive ogre of folktales. A young, stylish attorney by day, he commits his awful deeds at night, snatching children, then grilling, roasting, or sautéing them according to his favorite gourmet recipes. His vegetarian servant, Carciofi (Italian for "artichokes"), tries in vain to cure him of his ogreish ways, by subjecting him to yoga, a vegetarian diet, psychotherapy, tranquilizers, electroshock, etc. Nothing works: unfortunately it appears that Balthus's ogreism is incurable.

Like Abel Tiffauges, Balthus claims to love the children he preys on. After Carciofi manages to "wean" (Bruckner 1998, 68) him off children by attaching him to his bed and starving him for a month, Balthus feels remorse, and decides to make amends for his life of crime by staging a spectacular suicide at the circus where he is now employed, having been fired by his law firm. On Christmas day, before hundreds of children, Balthus dresses up in a Santa costume and a chef's hat, and walks to the center of the ring, where a huge cauldron of hot broth is bubbling. He publicly confesses his countless murders, and encourages all the children in the audience to avenge their dead comrades: "I propose that you take collective vengeance on me. I am going to jump into this simmering bouillon, and I'll be cooked in about half an hour. . . . When I'm done, all of you come up, one after the other, and eat a part of my body, any part you like" (1998, 74). The children, shockingly bloodthirsty, are only too glad to oblige.

The "ferocious" nature of Bruckner's short story lies in this troubling dénouement. Balthus gives the ultimate and even Christlike "gift of himself" (1998, 70) to the children of Paris in reparation for his sins. The roles of ogre and victim have once again been reversed, and the persecutor has become the persecuted. We have seen several examples of this inversion. The mild-mannered Abel Tiffauges, for example, is ultimately fodder for far more powerful ogres: Hitler, Stalin, and the monstrous war. Jean Calmet, a victim in the end, is nevertheless at times an ogre himself. He "feeds" on his students, he wishes that Thérèse and her lover could be devoured by the *Kindlifresser* of Bern. The six ogres of Pennac's novel all become victims, suicides like Balthus and Jean Calmet. Finally, the sexual predators in Cerf's and Germain's novels are all vanquished in various ways. Impoverished or remorseful, dead or insane, most are, in the end, victims of their immoderate desires.

In these works, the moral is clear: the ogre is bad and receives his just dues. But Bruckner's lesson is less conventional. Before jumping to his death into the boiling soup, Balthus winks at his distraught servant. Carciofi, after much research into ogre lore, eventually discovers the meaning of the mysterious signal—a wink to the reader as much as to the servant: "His master had winked at him because he who eats of the ogre, even just a scrap of skin, a bit of a nail, becomes an ogre himself . . . And today hundreds of Paris street kids, released into the world, are developing impressive jaws and beginning to lick their chops as they eye their little friends" (1998, 78). What can we conclude from this closing wink? The author's *Temptation of Innocence,* published three years earlier, provides one possible interpretation. What Bruckner means by "innocence" in this essay is failure to accept responsibility, or "the consequences of our own acts" (Bruckner 2000, 9). Innocence manifests itself in two ways: first, by "infantilism" (2000, 9), in which an adult possesses the "boundless greed" of childhood, continuously fed by "consumerism and entertainment" (2000, 9); second, by "victimization," "the tendency of the citizen coddled by the capitalist 'paradise' to think of himself in terms of the model of a persecuted people" (2000, 10).

The ogre metaphor abounds in Bruckner's critique of consumerism. The typical consumer acts like a child: he wants "everything, and right away!" (2000, 60). He obeys a "cannibal logic" (2000, 83), a gluttonous desire for immediate gratification. Consumerism is an ogre: "[e]verything that is not it (history, ethics, rites, beliefs) it voraciously swallows up. It is a stomach that can digest anything" (2000, 83).

Balthus Zaminski is such a consumer. He eats children, and seems to have ingested their childishness; he is immature, a "big adolescent" (Bruckner 1998, 42) who still can't resist buying toys. He is Bruckner's typical consumer of material goods, craving "pretty things and comfort to an unimaginable degree" (1998, 25). He indulges in expensive shoes, suits, and restaurants, lives in a large apartment in the Tuileries neighborhood of Paris, and owns a house on the coast and a chalet in the mountains. The suicidal act of feeding himself to children symbolizes the "cannibal logic" of *The Temptation of Innocence*. By infecting all who partake of his flesh in this bizarre communion, Balthus ensures that the childish greed of consumerism will perpetuate itself . . . at least in and around Paris.

Balthus embodies not only the infantilism of contemporary humanity, but also the penchant of social groups—in his case the ogre race—to claim themselves as victims. The narrator sketches the history of ogres, all descended from the Titan Cronus. After enjoying a period of power, they were in turn persecuted and driven from their lands. In a description that calls to mind another ill-treated minority—the twelfth- and thirteenth-century Cathari ("the pure") in southern France—the ogres were banished to "the mountains, to harsh lands, immense impenetrable forests," and took refuge in impregnable castles and dark fortresses" (1998, 13–14) in order to survive. Such is the hatred that humans have for ogres, that the modern association of Ogres Anonymous, formed by ogres who have admitted their weakness for eating children and sincerely want to renounce this vice, must operate in total secrecy: "Their destiny is to cure themselves without declaring their existence; if they did they would be spotted and eliminated by those normal people they want to become like. They must reconquer—against themselves and against others—the right to exist" (1998, 60).

Part three of *The Temptation of Innocence* is called "Victimist Competition" (Bruckner 2000, 213). Written during the genocidal Yugoslav Wars of the 1990s, Chapter 6 ("The Innocence of the Torturer") is a sharp critique of the Serbian leadership of that time. Bruckner remarks how the Serbs' aggression toward Croatia, Bosnia, and Kosovo grew out of their self-perception as eternal victims. Most recently they endured atrocities at the hands of Nazi Germany's Balkan allies during World War II. Their suffering only served to validate the victim status conferred on them long ago, when the Christian Prince Lazar was defeated by the Islamic Ottomans in 1389, thus thwarting the "great destiny" of which they believed themselves worthy: "The Serbs appear to be intoxicated with the wrongs that have been inflicted on them and they cultivate, especially in their epic poetry, the exaltation of the trials endured, the rock-hard belief in their martyrdom" (2000, 220).

The "persecutor persecuted" is a cliché of history. Bruckner cites the example of Nazism, which pronounced a belligerent discourse of the "rough blond thug," yet at the same time it also perceived itself as "a Germany humiliated by the Treaty of Versailles and the Judeo-Masonic conspiracy" (2000, 252n4). Tyrants compete to see who can be "more

Jewish than the Jews" (2000, 231), and thus perversely share in the aura of the "victims of Auschwitz," who are, in the words of Paul Ricoeur, "the quintessential representatives in our memory of all the victims of history" (Quoted in Bruckner, 2000, 231). Like an "obscene Christ" (2000, 242), the oppressor declares himself the victim of his victim, whom he kills and then asks the world for sympathy: "An archangel covered in blood, the torturer can then cry over himself in all good conscience, even in the midst of a heap of corpses!" (2000, 243).

This is the lesson of "Les Ogres anonymes." Balthus the hunter is eaten by his prey. But like the countless political aggressors that Bruckner analyzes in his essay—Serbs, Nazis, and others—he is a false victim. His mask of generosity and self-abnegation is betrayed by an ironic wink; he knows that his death—far from being a victory for the innocent—will on the contrary merely serve to perpetuate the timeless cruelty of his ogreish kind, a metaphor for the infinite monstrosity of the human race.

Pierre Péju: *Le Rire de l'ogre* [The ogre's laugh]

Like *A Father's Love* and "Les Ogres anonymes," Pierre Péju's *Le Rire de l'ogre* is a meditation on the permanence of human barbarity. Péju's fourth novel, awarded the Prix FNAC (chosen by a jury of readers) in 2005, follows the life of Paul Marleau from teenager to old man of ninety. Part 1 alternates between two story lines. First, a homodiegetic narrator (the sixteen-year-old Frenchman Paul) recounts the decisive summer of 1963, during which he visits a pen pal in the Bavarian village of Kehlstein. Then we flash back to the Ukraine, in the summer of 1941, and a heterodiegetic narrator relates the excruciating experiences of two men from Kehlstein serving in the German *Wehrmacht*—Dr. Lafontaine and Lieutenant Moritz—during the beginning of Germany's invasion of the Soviet Union.

In 1963, Paul meets in Kehlstein the strange, enigmatic Clara Lafontaine, daughter of the doctor and war veteran. She is a dark-haired, blue-eyed beauty, atypical of the region. Clara observes the world through the eye of her movie camera, which she constantly has with her, just as Paul always carries a notebook, in which he draws monstrous, tortured figures. Two marginal adolescents, they are naturally drawn together. Through Clara Paul learns about a local tragedy that everyone knows about but dares not speak of: one day, during a family outing near Kehlstein's Black Lake, friends noticed that Moritz, the veteran of the Russian Front, was missing with his little boy and girl. After a long search, he was found in the thick forest, seated at the base of a tree with a bizarre, insane grin on his face, his two strangled children locked tightly in his arms.

The 1941 chapters describe Lieutenant Moritz's and Dr. Lafontaine's reactions to the appalling brutality of the German army and the Ukrainian militia. Both men are intelligent and sensitive, but the war turns them into monsters, and they become unlikely participants in the atrocities inflicted on the Ukrainian Jews.[22] Moritz forsakes his idea of saving a group of children, and instead leads them off into a clearing in the woods to be shot. Prefiguring his murder of his own children, a trusting boy and girl cling to his hands as if they think he is leading them to safety, but instead he delivers them to Ukrainian militiamen to be shot and buried in a mass grave. As for Lafontaine, he betrays his interpreter Klara—a Jew—and turns her over to the SS to be executed.

Part 2 begins in 1964 and ends in 2037. Paul meets Jeanne, his future wife, during the 1968 student uprisings in Paris. Clara—apparently named after the murdered interpreter—reappears from time to time, a troubling memory from Paul's youth—tinged with eroticism and also with the horror of her village's dark secret. The ogre of Péju's novel is war, and the author is especially interested in its lingering effects: the secondhand damage done to those who were not its immediate victims. Paul and Clara have both been permanently affected by the viciousness of a war they never witnessed. For them it has been like a fatal disease incubating for years and finally erupting in events that cast a permanent shadow over their lives: Moritz's infanticide, the murder in Paris of Paul's father, a former resistant, and the unspoken sadness of Clara's father, still practicing medicine in Kehlstein. The ogre of war shapes their careers, as they relive the terror through their art. Paul becomes a sculptor, and chisels cruel works with titles like *Summary Execution, Belly of the Beast,* and, most significantly, *The Ogre's Laugh.* Living in an idyllic valley of the Vercors mountains with Jeanne and their two children, Paul is nevertheless mired in depression, haunted by the specter of violence: "Every night, when the calm and charm of the valley dissolve into a dark silence, I distinctly hear Horror growling and snoring. Horror under the ground, sleeping, but not so deeply. Night, that faceless cruelty that Giono tried to write, blood on the snow, white silence, crime, the banality of evil; I perceive them, too"[23] (Péju 2005, 232).

Clara travels the world as a photojournalist, following war and suffering wherever it leads her. Her most celebrated essay portrays the ravaged faces of American veterans of the Vietnam War. Memories of torment and death are still inscribed on their faces, seven years after the end of the war (2005, 241).

Le Rire de l'ogre opens with a short prologue: a timeless fairy tale that serves as a connecting thread to the main story lines. It underscores the devastating effect that war has on children. "An ogre lived in a country ravaged by war," the tale begins; "war was everywhere" and "killing had become a way of life" (2005, 11). The ogre meets a boy and his little sister, lost in the forest. They are exhausted, so he sits down with them against a tree so they can sleep. But his hold on them is so tight that he strangles them—just as Moritz will do to his own little boy and girl. The children are resuscitated by a beautiful fairy, who suddenly metamorphoses into an ugly witch, "horrible to see. Tears flowed in her deep wrinkles. An expression of horror twisted her mouth" (2005, 14). Upon seeing the witch, the ogre no longer desires the fresh flesh of the children. Instead, he bursts out laughing: "It was an insane laugh, an immense laugh, echoing through the clearing. A laugh that shook the tree he had been leaning against" (2005, 15). The children take advantage of the ogre's distraction, and escape his grip. He suddenly begins to gorge himself on flowers and plants, and it would seem that the ogre's conversion to vegetarianism would bring a happy ending to the tale. But no. As the children continue on their way, they encounter a knight on a horse; walking beside him are Death and the Devil. And so the tale ends: "The knight rode by, very straight in the saddle. As for Death, she sniffed an odor of children. The Devil gave a hint of a smile. Soon, all was plunged into darkness" (2005, 15).

The tale is a bleak assessment of our constant appetite for war. One battle may end, as one laughing ogre may lose his taste for human flesh. But soldiers will fight on, accompanied by Death and the Devil. An ogre's laugh is cruel and cynical, a false respite from the horror; more wars will break out and feed on any children who happen to get in the way. This is what happens in the pages that follow the prologue: virtually every character is sullied—directly or indirectly—by the violence of World War II.

Time and memory play key roles in Péju's novel. We have seen how Paul and Clara have vague—perhaps inherited—memories of a war they never saw. But the two German soldiers are haunted by a different kind of memory. Lafontaine committed the savage act of taking Klara from her hiding place and pushing her into a line of women walking to their death at the hands of the SS. He is relentlessly tortured by the image of his hands that did the unspeakable; his hands that will never forget: "Hands have a memory! A tenacious, opaque, and brutal memory that vibrates at the surface of the epidermis, and in the flesh of the palms, in each nerve, each fiber, each life line full of sweat, and under each nail, like mnemonic filth. . . . [S]hameful memories are not contained in our skull, but rather in the obscene flesh of these hands. Each fingerprint like a stamp attesting that evil was done" (2005, 102).

Hands are the ogre's tool. This is seen over and over again in the works we are reading: oversized hands and oversized teeth betray the predator. Moritz's hands too, like Lafontaine's, will remember his atrocity, for he is

> an ogre who, at twilight, crushes the hands of children before smashing their beautiful faces between his jaws. . . .
> Disproportionate hands hang by Moritz's side. Wherever he goes, he will have to drag along these hands. (2005, 107–8)

The careers of Clara and Paul also depend on a memory of hands. Clara, her hands dipped in developing fluid, will conjure up recollections of suffering and war. Paul, chisel in hand, will form out of marble the cruel shapes of a vaguely remembered horror that inexorably pursues him. Both are striving to answer the question that Marianne Payot poses in her review of the novel: "Can the horror only be told through art?" (Payot 2005).

Le Rire de l'ogre closes with an epilogue that is the continuation and conclusion of the prologue tale. The brother and sister, free from the ogre, wander through a countryside devastated by war. Like Moritz and Lafontaine in the Ukraine, however, they are radically perverted by their experience, and become as cruel as the men fighting around them: "[A]ll this butchery gave birth to unspeakable temptations. The little boy took a saber abandoned on the ground, swaggered about as he waved it in the air, and awkwardly swung it at the dying men he found along his way. He had let go of his little sister's hand, and she was robbing the corpses of their possessions. Soon they were loaded down with jewelry and daggers" (Péju 2005, 306).

Suddenly they arrive at a village that has been miraculously spared from the war. "[A]t the foot of a mountain covered with fir trees" (2005, 306), and not far from Black Lake, the village resembles Clara's Kehlstein. It is in fact the children's village, and they are reunited with their parents. Like Kehlstein, all is peaceful, at least in appearance. Yet after the father proposes an outing the next day to Black Lake—as Moritz probably did to his children the day before he strangled them—the tale ends on an ominous note. In the middle of the night, the father's scythe, hanging from a nail on the stone wall, crashes to the floor, "the blade facing slightly upward, threateningly" (2005, 308). The father hangs it back up, but in vain. The scene is repeated several times, and the scythe always falls, its blade vibrating "for a long time after it hit the floor, with a sinister meowing" (2005, 308). The family is terrified, and passes a sleepless night:

> The darkness was complete. The dawn far away. Their bodies were petrified.
> Only the great scythe seemed alive, and everyone could hear its malevolent blade murmuring in the darkness. (2005, 308)

The epilogue ends with the same three words as the prologue: *"dans le noir"* ("into darkness" or "in the darkness"). A gloom pervades humanity, forever mired in war. We have seen that the scythe, symbol of time and death, is attributed to Cronus/Saturn, himself identified with Father Time, devouring his children the Hours. Moreover, the "malevolent blade" of the father's scythe recalls the astrological appellation of Saturn: the malevolent planet.[24] So ends the novel: in darkness. The reader knows that dawn will bring, not brightness, but the murders of two more children.[25]

Paul Lacombe, *Isis*. Musée d'Orsay, Paris, France. Réunion des Musées Nationaux/Art Resource, NY.

4
The Dark Side of Aphrodite: The Ogress

> Eros lends a certain smile to the faces of Cronus.
> —Durand 1984

> Eternal Venus . . . is one of the Devil's seductive forms.
> —Baudelaire 1968

IF CRONUS IS THE MYTHOLOGICAL PROTOTYPE OF THE OGRE, THE OGRESS has different roots. She descends not from the Titanic symbol of time, but rather from his half-sister Aphrodite. Aphrodite is but one aspect of the many-faceted great goddess archetype, whose dark, anthropophagous side is perhaps best illustrated by the Hindu goddess Kali: "dark, all-devouring time, the bone-wreathed lady of the place of skulls" (Heinrich Zimmer, "Die indische Weltmutter;" quoted in Neumann 1955, 150). After studying the nature of the relationship between ogress and goddess in Chessex's *A Father's Love,* I will consider Tournier's "Veronica's Shrouds," Cerf's *Ogres et autres contes* and *Le Verrou.*

JACQUES CHESSEX: *A FATHER'S LOVE*

In chapter 3, we saw how Jean Calmet's suicide is induced by his inability to deal with the various ogres that dominate him. He imagines, for example, that he is being "devoured alive" (Chessex 1975, 187) by his deceased father. But it is Thérèse, the art student he meets in a café, who will push him to his final, fatal act. Jean endows her with ambivalent mythical qualities that make of this very beautiful but otherwise normal nineteen-year-old a seductive and terrifying goddess, a devouring Aphrodite. When they first meet, she is knitting, a task akin to weaving, an invention of women (Freud 1953–74, 22:132), a symbol of control over time and destiny, and thus associated with many of the great ancient goddesses (Chevalier 1982, 951). Her enigmatic demeanor leads him to call her the Cat Girl: "[H]e had given her that name right away, it was law and magic, right away she had plunged him into the mad, mysterious joy of Dionysus" (Chessex 1975, 78).

With Thérèse, Jean is thus initiated into the ecstatic but perilous realm of the effervescent god of wine and mystical joy, whose orgiastic cult merges with that of the goddess of love. Like Aphrodite, Thérèse is a "mixture of freshness and very old wisdom" (1975, 176), and incarnates the love that Jean sorely needs. This Swiss Aphrodite is a goddess of the water: she roams the shores of Lake Geneva, sharing time between her mother's house in Montreux and her apartment in Lausanne.

Chessex's descriptions of Thérèse recall the goddess of Botticelli's *Birth of Venus* (1482). When Jean meets her at the café Apollo in Montreux, Thérèse, like Venus, is outlined against the lake and the sky, and he admires her long blond hair floating on her shoulders (1975, 137, 139). Later, at her apartment in Lausanne, Jean observes her as she bathes, struck again by the sight of her golden hair falling around her shoulders, and the soap on her wet body, which brings to mind the birth of Aphrodite, "risen from the foam" (Grimal 1986, 39). In this erotic scene, Jean cannot overcome the feeling that he is and always will be the ogre's victim. Caressing her toes one by one like rosary beads, he likens himself to little Tom Thumb, lost in the forest with his brothers, hunted by the ogre: "Length of her legs, toes that Jean Calmet counts and re-counts like jacks, like the beads of a smooth, warm rosary, my daughter, my little girl, I love you oh my tenderness, oh my child, I'll finger your pink nails, Tom Thumb, I'll strew your toes in the forest, thanks to you I'll find my way. . . ." (Chessex 1975, 180).

Jean does not specifically invoke the goddess of love in reference to Thérèse, but she does inspire in him thoughts of other magical women bound to water. He calls her Melusine, the fairy of the fountain, half woman, half serpent; Circe, the fair-haired sorceress who transformed Odysseus's men into swine; Morgan, bane of Merlin and of the Knights of the Round Table; and finally, Hamlet's Ophelia, driven to a watery death (1975, 145, 181): enchantresses all whose legends remind us that water can destroy just as it can sustain life. Here he dreams that Thérèse turns him into an animal, as the witch Pamphile does to the hero of *The Golden Ass,* the Roman tale by Apuleius (c. AD 150), that Jean was teaching to his Latin class: "Was he going to be changed into an animal by this the golden tressed sorceress? And why not? With pleasure, he imagined himself in the fairy's power. The Pamphile of the tale. And Circe. And Morgan. All the mediatresses of gloom"[1] (1975, 88).

The Apuleius tale haunts Jean and fascinates Thérèse. When he discovers the book in her apartment, it is the evidence that she is having an affair with one of his students. One can suppose that he identifies Thérèse not only with the witch Pamphile, but also with Isis, who reveals herself in a dream to the hero of *The Golden Ass:* "I am Nature, the universal Mother, mistress of all the elements, primordial child of time, sovereign of all things spiritual, queen of the dead, queen also of the immortals, the single manifestation of all gods and goddesses that are" (Quoted in Pratt 1994, 20). Isis is one of the incarnations of the Aphrodite archetype, inspiring contradictory emotions of love and terror (Campbell 1964, 42–43; Pratt 1994, 117–19).

From the beginning, the narrator associates Thérèse with Dionysus as much as Aphrodite. Jean's imagination leaps to this joyous scene—the only one in the novel—the moment he lays eyes on the "Cat Girl": "[H]e felt cascades gushing deep within him; precipices opened up in his bones, sonorous, where millennial stones fell. The mountain wind whistled in the pines, the sea wind assailed the fig trees. He found himself born by those forces, lifted, hurled; sap bounded into his blood, new humors shook him, starry skies, volcanoes in flames, springs, storms, stampedes of horned herds, leaps of goats on slopes made wild with the smells of flowers" (Chessex 1975, 79). Jean feels far from Lausanne; the sight of the Cat Girl has plunged him into a wild, exotic tableau. Sea, fig trees, and herds of goats recall ancient Greece, and a kind of mystical excitement evokes the madness and ferocity of Dionysian rituals.

Thérèse's room is sparsely furnished. One of her few possessions is, above the bed, a poster of a panther. Jean initially approves of this metonymical connection, in which the "feminine animal" and the "tigress girl" (1975, 86)—descriptions that, as we will soon see, could also fit Tournier's Veronica—form a mesmerizing couple. Later he will remember that what he loved about Thérèse was her "spirit of fairies", part "cradle," part "cat" (1975, 176). As the relationship deteriorates, however, Jean begins to imagine the cat as a mocking and hateful animal. While walking along Lake Geneva one day, Jean encounters a cat, and a curious conversation ensues. The cat admonishes Jean for his timidity with Thérèse, and his failure to fully embrace Dionysus, to which the only alternative is death: "You're half-alive. You're eating yourself up. You're more ash than your father. And your blood? Your flesh that's still young? Your head full of foolishness? You're kidding, Jean Calmet. It's the spirit of Dionysus or nothing. Pan or death. Salvation through one's works or the last ravine at the bottom of the last hole in the last mountain in Greece or elsewhere. Go to the end of the oldest mythologies or into each hour's brazier" (1975, 101–2).

But Jean does not heed the cat's warning, and as jealousy consumes him, he can no longer bear the feline gaze. When Thérèse draws a picture of a cat, its eyes seem to "transpierce Jean Calmet with their white fire" (1975, 137). The pain is blinding: "the green ink has striped, pricked, scratched the picture with slight wounds that spread in a star toward the edges of the paper like explosions or rays, which the eye follows almost painfully. Wicked cat" (1975, 137).

In a long chapter entitled "The Perfumed Panther," Marcel Detienne reflects on this great feline, which the Greeks consecrated to Dionysus. A cunning hunter, the panther uses its pleasant odor—an oddity among wild animals—to attract its prey (Detienne 1998, 38). The seductive nature of the panther's hunt led the Greeks to eroticize the wild beast: "For Aristophanes and his contemporaries a courtesan is in reality a 'panther.' . . . Like the panther, the beautiful courtesan practices a kind of hunt that the Greeks call 'the hunt of Aphrodite'" (1998, 39–40). For Jean Calmet, Aphrodite's charm is fatal; unable to cope with Thérèse's seduction, he chooses—as the cat predicted—death.[2]

After Jean turns away from the "detestable" (Chessex 1975, 138) cat that Thérèse has drawn for him, he turns his attention to the little round knitting basket she carries. His demeanor softens, as the excruciating cat image fades. The basket brings to mind a more innocent Thérèse: "[H]e thinks about Little Red Riding Hood in the woods, about the basket hung over the little girl's arm; it is a tender, heart-rending picture, the gift, a dream sprung from the bottom of childhood. . . . How many fresh little baskets are crossing how many forests at just this moment. How many wolves lying in wait" (1975, 138).

The wolf—like the seducer of Little Red Riding Hood—is a double of the ogre, and for an instant Jean fears that Thérèse might be its prey. But this loving moment ends abruptly when Jean opens the basket and discovers a stiff handkerchief bearing the initials M. B.—Marc Barraud, his student who has become his rival: "He takes hold of it: the handkerchief is compact, as if starched. He lifts it to his nose: the handkerchief smells of dry sperm. That odor of rancid milk, dried fish, feverish night. . . . A handkerchief full of sperm. Marc's sperm. His student in Classics 2G" (1975, 139). Jean knows now that he has lost Thérèse. No longer is she the innocent little girl venturing into the woods. In his mind, she has metamorphosed into the wolf, "the witch, the succuba, the terrible silky fairy" (1975, 141) who will consume him.

Jean is slowly devoured by jealousy. He imagines the "exquisite vampire" (1975, 96) Thérèse devouring both him and his rival. Finally, all men become her prey: "Thérèse crawls over him, adorable succuba, ghoul on the move, vampire coifed with light gold. . . . Witch, executioner, wicked fairy, the Cat Girl has the neighborhood boys delivered, she grinds up their flesh, she feeds on it, she thrives on it, that blood-covered creature!" (1975, 124). The woman of his dreams becomes a creature of nightmares and his ecstasy turns to despair, like the victim in Robert Graves's poem "The Succubus":

Thus will despair
In ecstasy of nightmare
Fetch you a devil-woman through the air,
To slide below the sweated sheet
And kiss your lips in answer to your prayer. (Graves 1977, 42)

In *L'Eau et les rêves* (*Water and Dreams*), Gaston Bachelard analyzes the "Ophelia complex," the fatal, romantic, and melancholic attraction to water symbolized by the watery suicide of a young, beautiful, long-haired woman. "For certain souls," writes Bachelard, "water is the material of despair" (1942, 125). Jean Calmet finally dies in his bath after slashing his wrists. These final pages echo the first bathtub scene, in which the water and soap lather symbolized the birth of Aphrodite, and thus desire, Eros. At that time, Jean called Thérèse his "Melusine," his "Ophelia" (Chessex 1975, 181). As Jean dies, the water from the faucet flows with deafening violence, "drill[ing] through his skull," and he recalls aquatic scenes: stormy nights on Lake Geneva that "[strike] him like echoes of the horrible din" (1975, 197). Stained red, water has become the element of death, and Jean ends his life in the murky water of his bath, a bloody Ophelia.

Michel Tournier: "Veronica's Shrouds"

"Veronica's Shrouds" is a short story about a photographer in search of the perfect photograph. Veronica is dissatisfied with traditional methods of photography, which cannot seem to capture the essence of her handsome lover and model, Hector. The narrator observes the couple over several years, during which Hector, healthy and muscular when they first meet, begins to waste away, and suffer from various dermatological problems. It becomes clear that Hector has become the victim of Veronica's ingenious invention, "direct photography" or "dermography," in which the photographer bathes the model in the caustic developing fluid, and then wraps him, dripping wet, in linen cloth treated with silver bromide. These cloths, Veronica's "shrouds," constitute a perfect image of the model, with the unfortunate side effect that he eventually becomes an *écorché*, a skinless cadaver.[3]

The two protagonists' names resonate with mythological connotations. The greatest Trojan warrior was named Hector. He was slain by Achilles, who refused to let the body be buried. Hector's father Priam, aided by Hermes, persuaded Achilles to give him proper burial rites, the description of which brings the *Iliad* to a close. Veronica's namesake is a Jewish woman who wiped the face of Jesus with a veil as he carried the cross to Calvary. The cloth miraculously retained a perfect image of the suffering Christ, and gave the woman her name, from the Latin *vera* and the Greek *eikon,* meaning "true image." So one can understand why Tournier chose to name his photographer Veronica, after the saint who executed that legendary pure, absolute photograph.[4]

But a taker of pictures is not always a saint, as Tournier has shown elsewhere. We have seen how the hero of *The Ogre* revels in the aggressiveness of the camera, which he likens to a one-eyed Cyclops, or a hawk that swoops down on its prey, steals its image, and later consumes it in the darkroom (Tournier 1997b, 103). Photography is a potent tool of conquest and possession that Veronica skillfully wields against her unfortunate lover, who slowly disappears, one layer of skin at a time, as Veronica triumphantly conquers the art scene of the Provençal city of Arles.

Veronica is a photographic fanatic and fetishist (Redfern 1996, 70). Devoid of the tenderness and vulnerability that characterize Abel Tiffauges, dedicated only to her sadistic art, she is, for Walter Redfern, "the one true monster, in any sense, in Tournier's work" (1996, 71). From the beginning, Tournier's narrator characterizes Veronica as an ogress, and Hector as a victim who must be ready to make "sacrifices" (Tournier 1984, 131). Hector's room in the house he shares with Veronica, filled with chemicals and exercise equipment, is a cross between an "operating room" and a "torture chamber" (1984, 133). Apparently he fears Veronica and her "devouring love" (1984, 139), because around his neck he wears a tiger's tooth, a Bengali fetish said to protect the wearer from being "eaten by a tiger" (1984, 132). Indeed, as long as he wears it, Veronica, whom the narrator characterizes as a "tigress" (1984, 139), does not harm him.

The couple lives near Arles in the Camargue, a marshy region bordering the Mediterranean, known for its rich plant and wildlife, among which are a breed of black bulls, relatively small and quite fast, used in the bullfights popular in Arles, Nîmes, and other towns of Southern France. Hector resembles his land: he is a "Mediterranean type" (1984, 131) whose element is water. The narrator describes him in curiously feminine terms, posing in the surf, and one might imagine the birth of a male Aphrodite:

> The model, superbly curvaceous in his nudity, either ran up and down in the surf, or lay flat on his stomach on the sand, or curled up in a fetal position, or walked in the stagnant waters of the pond, warding off seaweed and salty ripples with his sturdy thighs.
> ... He took full advantage of his natural animality, which was in perfect harmony with the simple, primitive things of the region: fresh water or stag-

nant ponds, russet grasses, bluish gray sands, tree stumps whitened with age. (1984, 130–31)

Hector's "natural animality" is accentuated by "a young bull's forehead" (1984, 131). As we see him prancing in the surf, we are reminded of the bull's intimate bond to water. It is the beast of Poseidon, "the animal of the moon: the waning and waxing god, by the magic of whose night dew the vegetation is restored; the lord of tides and the productive powers of the earth, the lord of women, lord of the rhythm of the womb" (Campbell 1964, 60). As the matador leads the bull to its inevitable destiny through a series of maneuvers called *verónicas*,[5] so Tournier's Veronica, with her superior intelligence, will seduce, torture, and destroy her magnificent Hector.

Veronica has an aesthetic attraction to death. She is dissatisfied with her early pictures of Hector on the beach, which she denounces as "[p]ostcard stuff" (Tournier 1984, 131). She seeks an art that emanates from death, in which she finds not only cold truth, but perfect beauty as well. She takes her inspiration from Renaissance art, which she defines as "the discovery of the corpse" (1984, 136). That may seem to be a contradiction, since "Renaissance" implies life rather than death. Indeed, one of the most celebrated Renaissance paintings is Botticelli's *Birth of Venus,* whose bright and graceful figures floating above the sea fuse the two meanings of Eros: sexual love and Freud's life instinct. But although Veronica cites the anatomical illustrations of da Vinci, she is drawn more to the morbid characteristics of sixteenth-century Flemish art rather than to the Italian Renaissance. For it seems that the jump north from Italy to Flanders was a leap from life to death. Botticelli's Venus gave way to lifeless and decomposing bodies, and Veronica remarks that "the nudes of the time began to stink of the corpse" (1984, 136). She is undoubtedly thinking of works like Hieronymous Bosch's nightmarish *Garden of Earthly Delights* (c. 1510) and Pieter Bruegel the Elder's *Seven Deadly Vices* (1557). But she is inspired above all by Renaissance science, in particular the Flemish anatomist Andreas Vesalius, whose magnificently illustrated treatise *De Humani Corporis fabrica* (On the structure of the human body, 1543) earned him the title of father of modern anatomy.[6] Vesalius based his studies on his dissections of human cadavers, an extremely controversial and for the most part illegal practice, and he was rumored to have extended his research to living men. For this he was condemned to death, although his sentence was commuted since he was a personal physician to the Spanish King Philip II.

The correlation between Tournier's Veronica and Aphrodite hinges on the life-death dichotomy that the narrator finds in the two schools of photographic art. The first are pictures "taken from life" (*pris-sur-le-vif*) (Tournier 1984, 135), unposed shots of a fleeting instant of life that will never be reproduced. The narrator calls the second the "school of the immobile," and includes portraits and still lifes (*natures mortes*), "the deliberate, calculated, immobile image that aims at capturing not the instant but eternity" (1984, 135). Veronica prefers the second school: "Death interests me—it more than interests me. One of these days I shall inevitably go and take photographs in the morgue. In a corpse—a real, raw corpse, . . . there is a truth . . . how shall I put it? . . . a marmoreal truth" (1984, 135).

Veronica's "devouring love" (1984, 139) for Hector leads us to contemplate the dark side of Aphrodite. Botticelli's painting does not show how the goddess was born of an act of violence, when Cronus the Titan, encouraged by his mother Gaea, castrated his cruel father Uranus (Hesiod 1993, *Theogony* 1.171–87). As we noted in chapter 3, this act engendered Aphrodite, along with a host of monsters. *The Larousse Encyclopedia of Mythology* describes the nocturnal crime as follows:

> While he unsuspectingly slept, Cronus, who with his mother's aid lay in hiding, armed himself with the sickle, mutilated his father atrociously and cast the bleeding genitals into the sea. From the terrible wound black blood dropped and the drops, seeping into the earth, gave birth to the redoubtable Furies, to monstrous giants and to the ash-tree nymphs, the Meliae. As for the debris which floated on the surface of the waves, it broke into a white foam from which was born a young goddess, Aphrodite. (*Larousse* 1996, 88)

The contrast is startling. This "awesome, beautiful divinity" with "slender feet," as Hesiod describes her (1993, *Theogony* 1.194–95), comes to life amid black blood and monstrous, fearful creatures, the offspring of a vicious father mutilated by her half-brother, the ogre Cronus. From the beginning, then, Aphrodite belongs to the community of monsters, and, if we search for her roots in Assyro-Babylonian mythology as the great goddess Ishtar, personification of the planet Venus, we find cruelty to be one of her important traits. Goddess of love, honored by a cult of sacred prostitution, Ishtar is above all "irritable, violent," and her love often proves fatal to animals, men, and gods alike (*Larousse* 1996, 58). She will become, in Greek mythology, Aphrodite Porne, "goddess of lust and venal love, the patroness of prostitutes" (1996, 130).

Ambivalence was always a characteristic of the great goddess archetype, celebrated variously as Inanna, Ishtar, Cybele, Astarte, Gaea, Aphrodite, Isis, Venus, etc. The height of her worship in the Near East was during the sedentary Bronze Age civilization (around 3000 BC), when she was "the arch personification of the power of Space, Time, and Matter, within whose bound all beings arise and die: the substance of their bodies, configurator of their lives and thoughts, and receiver of their dead. And everything having form or name, including God personified as good or evil, merciful or wrathful, was her child, within her womb" (Campbell 1964, 7).

As the Bronze Age yielded to the Iron Age, the veneration of the goddess was radically transformed by "those suddenly intrusive patriarchal warrior tribesmen whose traditions have come down to us chiefly in the Old and New Testaments and in the myths of Greece" (1964, 7). By a process of "mythological defamation" (1964, 80), the goddess was demonized and her cult reduced to the role of a "counterplayer" in religions dominated by male gods, heroes, and warriors (1964, 70). This triumph of the patriarchal order over the now loathsome feminine principle is illustrated by Yahweh's defeat of the sea serpent Leviathan in the Old Testament (Job 41:1–8), and in Greek mythology by Zeus's victories over Cronus and the Titans, the Giants, and finally over the monstrous serpent Typhon—all children of Gaea, the goddess Earth (Campbell 1964, 22).

Annis Pratt's analysis of the Aphrodite archetype in modern poetry by male authors reveals that, although some poets celebrate the goddess with "reverence" (Pratt 1994, 197), most regard her with "fear and loathing" (1994, 167). She concludes that this "diminishment" (1994, 107) of the goddess of love is due to the male desire to usurp the powers of "sexuality and generativity" (1994, 108). Reverence and awe before the dualistic goddess degenerates into "deep loathing" and "profound gynophobia" (1994, 112).

At the end of Tournier's story, Hector has disappeared, and his skin has become the "Veronica's Shrouds" photography exhibition in Arles. The narrator notices that the tiger's tooth necklace now adorns the neck of Veronica. The tigress-photographer has literally consumed Hector: his skin, peeled off like the layers of an onion, has become the ogress's deadly art.

MURIEL CERF: *OGRES ET AUTRES CONTES*

In chapter 2 we examined the various ogres of Cerf's short stories, all of whom were in some way sexual predators. In the two tales we will consider here, ogress-mothers prey on their own families. "Dieu des pauvres" [God of poor people] takes place somewhere in the French Antilles. The narrator is the metis daughter of a rich white Creole and a poor indigenous black woman. The daughter despises her mother: the woman apparently murdered her husband and her mother, and aborted several fetuses, "[w]ith a needle, like in the old days" (Cerf 1997a, 53). Like a female Zeus, youngest child and sole survivor of an ogre-parent, the narrator promises to avenge these killings. Her mother protests her innocence, claiming that, "blacker than black" (1997a, 54), she has been a sacrificial victim of an unjust society. As she plots her vengeance, the daughter scoffs at the idea of a merciful God, be it a voodoo or Christian deity. All she knows is that "the God of poor people does not forgive" (1997a, 56).

In "Laura qui est ma femme" [Laura who is my wife], the male narrator, ostensibly deranged, fantasizes about his wife's bloodthirsty nature: he imagines her the potential killer of both her daughter and her mother. But although the title indicates that Laura will be the subject of his tirade, he quickly proceeds from the particular to the general. All women are in fact killers—"infanticides" and "Moerae"[7] (1997a, 38)—he declares. The figure of destructive time should not be the male Cronus, but some female divinity, because "it is women who swallow up everything in this world, and often the children they have put there; they can, like nothing, swiftly like the tooth that used to slice the umbilical cord, destroy your life, too, this life that they give" (1997a, 37).

Laura barely escaped the clutches of her own evil mother, according to the narrator. Just yesterday, over a cup of tea, Laura confided that "she ran away from her mother's house just in time; her mother was going to boil her in a caldron and eat her, because this mother, this bad mother, is a woman too, and thus a cannibal" (1997a, 37).

Laura's husband regards every mother, jealous of the youth of her child, a potential infanticide. This is especially true when a young girl reaches puberty. The beauty and reproductive power of the "usurper" enrage the mother: "under the influence of some Paleolithic terror, the mother shakes from head to foot; she'd prayed that would never happen, that this absolute power over the universe would stay with her only" (1997a, 38).

Obviously paranoid, the narrator longs for the time when he could dominate his wife, like that first night they spent together when he beat her to a pulp in a sexual frenzy. Since then, it is she who is the stronger, and he fears for the day when the ogress, on one of "those four days she lives in blood," will "decapitate" and "pickle" him, "like a big piece of fruit that is too soft, too sweet" (1997a, 43).

Both stories open with epigraphs referring to celebrated mythological ogresses. "Dieu des pauvres" (1997a, 51) quotes *The Medea* of Euripides, in which the terrible sorceress—learning that her husband Jason is forsaking her to marry the princess of Corinth—declares: "I would very much rather stand three times in the front of battle than bear one child"

(Euripides 1967, 72). She will later fashion a poisoned dress that kills both the bride-to-be and her father, before she stabs to death the three sons she had born by Jason.

"Laura qui est ma femme" opens with a quote from Flavius Josephus's *The Wars of the Jews* (mentioned briefly above in chapter 1). This section of Josephus's chronicle recounts the Roman siege of Jerusalem in the first century A.D, and the ensuing famine. It focuses on Mary, a wealthy and honorable woman who, like all the inhabitants of the city, is "pierced through her very bowels and marrow" (Josephus 1987, 737) by hunger. Declaring that her infant son's life would not be worth living as a slave to the Romans, she snatches him up and proclaims: "O, thou miserable infant! For whom shall I preserve thee in this war, this famine, and this sedition? . . . Come on; be thou my food, and be thou a fury to these seditious varlets and a byword to the world, which is all that is now wanting to complete the calamities of us Jews" (1987, 737). She kills her infant, roasts him, and eats half, saving the other half for the Roman soldiers. Cerf (1997a, 35) quotes Mary, taunting the horrified soldiers: "[S]he said to them, 'This is mine own son; and what hath been done was mine own doing! Come, eat of this food; for I have eaten of it myself! Do not you pretend to be either more tender than a woman, or more compassionate than a mother.'" (Josephus 1987, 737–38).

Both epigraphs describe spectacular infanticides, committed by mothers in desperate situations. As we have seen, this crime haunts the narrators of the two tales, who are convinced that their mother, wife—or even women in general—are ogresses: killers and eaters—actually or metaphorically—of their children. These crimes are biological in origin: women are ogresses, reason the narrators, because they are associated with the blood of menstruation and of childbearing. Cerf thus brings to light long-held beliefs that associate the menses with sickness and death. Gilbert Durand has shown that since menstruation is linked to the moon,[8] it is also associated with destructive time, since the moon—waxing, waning, then disappearing—is "the great dramatic epiphany of time" (Durand 1984, 111). Simone de Beauvoir also refers to common beliefs that associate the changing moon with the serpent that sloughs its skin. Thus menstruating women consort with the moon and its "dangerous caprices": "Woman is part of that fearsome machinery which turns the planets and the sun in their courses, she is the prey of cosmic energies that rule the destiny of the stars and the tides, and of which men must undergo the disturbing radiations" (Beauvoir 1953, 149).[9]

Blood, Gaston Bachelard reminds us, "is never happy" (1942, 84), and contact with menstrual blood in particular is a universal taboo.[10]

Durand concludes his analysis by stating that menstrual blood "is terrifying first because it is the master of life and death, but also because its feminine essence makes it the first human clock, the first sign associating humans with the lunar drama" (1984, 122).

From this viewpoint, all women are condemned to play the role of femmes fatales. And lest one think that this attitude is merely one of less "enlightened" cultures, it was certainly existent in post-Enlightenment France, and even in recent years. Let us consider the case of Jeanne Weber, the notorious "ogress of the Goutte-d'Or"—named after the Paris working-class neighborhood where she lived—who strangled at least five children (including her son and three nieces), between 1902 and 1908. Geneviève Morel wrote a study, published by the University of Nancy school of medicine in 1927, on Weber and women who kill children. She found that, while fathers who kill their children are often driven by "alcohol and the sex instinct" (Morel 1927, 8), a mother is more likely to kill because of melancholy or depression: the murder is often a kind of suicide, since she has a "constant and necessary relationship" with this child who "comes from her flesh" (1927, 6). This is certainly true of Mary in Josephus's account; however Jeanne Weber's murders do not fit that mold. Rather, she is the kind of woman who has a "complete absence of the maternal instinct, . . . a deep lesion" that makes possible an "exquisite cruelty of which only a woman is capable, as she is given to extreme passions" (1927, 7–8). A woman is especially prone to criminal acts, Morel believes, when she is having her period, and is thus "in a state of morbid vulnerability and receptivity" (1927, 12). Jeanne Weber, up to her death in 1918 during a fit, "remains particularly dangerous each time she has her period" (1927, 75).

Some seventy years after Morel's research, Barbara Cowen, in "Women and Crime," remarks that while men commit the vast majority of crimes, it is rare that these crimes are given a biological origin: typically, economical or social causes are named. Women, however, even today, are "victims of their biology" (Cowen 1995, 157): "Biological processes were, and still are, believed to cause women to behave either irrationally or irresponsibly or both; consequently, biological events such as menstruation, childbirth, or menopause were thought to be the most likely reasons to explain female criminality" (1995, 157–58). Cowen goes on to cite recent studies that still claim that female criminality increases during the menstrual cycle. She concludes, however, that this "myth" (1995, 159) has lost credibility, and that current research proves that female crime, like male crime, most often has economic or social roots (1995, 166).[11] The blood-soaked ogress is, it seems, fortunately once more a character of myth and folklore.

Muriel Cerf: *Le Verrou*

In chapter 2 we studied Massimo Cuori's ogreish obsession with sixteen-year-old Nora Neumann. Although the poor Austrian girl suffers under the cruel domination of the wealthy Milanese, she is never entirely subjugated by him; indeed, we noted how early on Massimo compares her to an evil "Gretel with teeth of a marten" (Cerf 1997b, 46), and years after she robbed him and disappeared from his life forever, he remembers how her eyes were brilliant with "tears that never flowed, which lay beneath her eyelids like hard bits of gravel, the gravel of her hate" (1997b, 551). As we have so often seen in ogre stories, the victim turns on the oppressor and becomes an ogre, or, in this case, an ogress.

It is not surprising that the beautiful Nora is an ogress, given that it runs in the family. Her mother, a cook, is one of the most vicious characters of the novel: desperate to rise above her social class, she has prostituted Nora since the girl reached puberty. Massimo's mother repeatedly calls her the "sow" (1997b, 20–21) and, writing to her confessor, provides this colorful description of the hypocritical and scheming Magda Neumann:

> Like Tartuffe she prays with us before dinner, then she dives into her food. It's not like she has a respectably feminine sweet tooth; no, this woman has the look and voracity of an ogress, she's a Michelin Man that Fellini would hire on the spot, and can't control her appetites at all: she satisfies the most basic one after grace, but the second is even more frightening, because its objective no doubt is our patrimony and, more specifically, my son's money. (1997b, 17)

Nora is the physical antithesis of her bloated mother. She has, however, inherited her ogreish personality, which manifests itself in two ways. First, like her mother, Nora knows how to manipulate men to obtain the wealth she desires. Magda does this by attracting men with her skillful cooking, and of course by ruthlessly marketing her daughter's body. Nora uses her beauty, "her only weapon" (1997b, 191), and her dexterous lovemaking, learned at a tender age. Massimo is both attracted and repulsed by Nora's talent, which inspires dreams of infamous women of antiquity. Nora's stripteases remind him of Salomé (1997b, 181), and her effortless orgasms liken her to Messalina, the notoriously debauched empress of Rome (1997b, 182). Massimo's pious mother, Carla, considers Nora as yet another example of "feminine perversity," and fears that her son will fall prey to the femme fatale, just like "Adam and so many . . . heroes enslaved by descendants of the serpent: Samson, Solomon, and Merlin the Enchanter" (1997b, 27). Carla hates and fears this demon living in her house, masquerading as her son's fiancée. She despises her "long teeth and eyes of a she-wolf" (1997b, 35, 255), "her Luciferian attributes, those of a downy archangel with cruel eyes that just swooped down on a garden with the suddenness of celestial fire and the vehement radiance of the scythe of death" (1997b, 255).

The second characteristic of this petite ogress is the prodigious appetite she shares with her mother. We previously saw how Massimo wants to devour her—in every way possible. He, in turn, is fascinated by Nora's oral fixations; he often employs metaphors derived from myths or fairy tales to describe the greedy young girl: "[N]othing in the world will keep Nora from eating and drinking, and this charms me more than ever, again and again, because she is the same gluttonous chimera, the same Lilliputian Gargantua as the prepubescent child who wolfed down the leftovers from another party"[12] (1997b, 289). Once again, Massimo evokes the Hansel and Gretel tale to describe their relationship. Nora eating a chocolate cake is transformed into a voracious Gretel devouring both the witch's marzipan house and the witch inside,[13] washed down with the entire Danube. Nora seems made of sugar. "I concluded," writes Massimo, "that this girl's stomach was an abyss more infinite than her dark blue eyes; she would have eaten human flesh without hesitation, as long as someone put some sugar on it, because she so loved sweets; in fact it was as if she had rolled in an ocean of sugar that still sparkled on her skin so white" (1997b, 116).

At first a victim—of her mother who prostitutes her, of her father and her clients who beat her, and finally of Massimo who, far from giving her love, jealously locks her away "in order to keep her close to my claws and my fangs" (1997b, 555)—Nora becomes a figure of the devouring feminine. Carla suspects her wickedness—she is "the demon," "the Adversary," and numbers among the "Powers of the Shadows" (1997b, 585)—and Massimo confirms that the ondinism they practice is "one of the rarest and most revolting sexual perversions" (1997b, 585), a ceremony of the "occult" (1997b, 545). Nora epitomizes the rebellious adolescent that Beauvoir describes in her chapter on "the formative years." Crude, insolent, insincere, and sadistic, "[f]louting nature and society, the young girl challenges and braves them in a number of peculiar ways" (Beauvoir 1953, 353). She might eat and drink disgusting things (urine, in Nora's case); she "feels disgust for her too carnal body, for her menstrual blood, for adult sexual practices, for the male to whom she is destined; she denies the feeling by enjoying with familiarity precisely what is repugnant to her" (1953, 353–54). She does not seek to transcend the social order, but is content to remain within the accepted order but break its rules. Beauvoir calls this behavior "demoniac": "the good is recognized in order to be flouted, the rule is laid down in order to be broken, the sacred is respected to make possible further sacrilege" (1953, 357). This is precisely what Nora does by outraging Massimo's proper, conservative family, living with him and committing the secret "sexual crime" (Cerf 1997b, 314) behind the locked attic door, becoming his "fiancée," then robbing him,[14] and fleeing before the marriage.

Beauvoir evokes the "demoniac" period of a girl's adolescence as it is portrayed in literature, from Anouilh to Woolf (Beauvoir 1953, 358–68), and clearly, Muriel Cerf's Nora fits into this tradition. The young girl, objectified, becomes "disarmed, disposable, . . . now only an offered flower, a fruit to be picked" (Beauvoir 1953, 358). Yet this "disarmed" victim becomes a predator, and men, "demanding to be lured" (1953, 358), are her quarry: "He finds seductive only the girl who spreads these snares; though herself on offer, she is lying in wait for prey; her passivity serves an enterprise, and she makes her weakness the instrumentality of her power; since she is not allowed to attack openly, she has to depend on stratagem and calculation; and it is to her advantage to seem to be freely given" (1953, 358). Tiny Nora, possessing the "heart-rending beauty of undernourished children" (Cerf 1997b, 359), suggesting comparisons to Victor Hugo's Cosette in *Les Misérables*, Gretel and Beauty from fairy tales, proves herself the vanquisher, and with the help of her manipulative mother, conquers the powerful family from Milan, finally driving her fiancé to despair and thoughts of suicide.

We see then how Aphrodite/Venus, the goddess of love, has metamorphosed into a goddess of death. Roman mythology provides a source for a psychoanalytic commentary on this union of opposites. Libitina was an ancient Roman deity associated with Venus. Her name comes from *libitum*, desire, or libido. For reasons that are not clear, funereal objects were sold in her temple, and she became the goddess of funerals (*Larousse* 1996, 213; Durand 1984, 221–22). Love, death, and time—Eros, Thanatos, and Cronus—merge in Venus Libitina, who represents, according to Gilbert Durand, the euphemisation of our dread of time into less overwhelming erotic fears. He quotes the psychoanalyst Marie Bonaparte, who writes that "one of the most constant traits of Eros is to drag after him his brother Thanatos" (1984, 221).[15] The closeness of the two "brothers"—life and death—is made evident by the widespread male fear of menstrual blood, which feminizes death and leads to the symbolic ambivalence we see in divinities like Venus Libitina. She is a reminder of the ambivalence of the libido, which plays between poles of attraction and repulsion, expressing itself sometimes as erotic desire, and sometimes as manifestations of the death instinct, externalized as sadism, masochism, or a striving for peace, quietude, and nothingness.

Gustave Doré, p. 9, "Le Petit Poucet," by Charles Perrault. Bibliothèque Nationale de France, Paris, France.

5
Conclusion: *JE est un ogre*

Car JE est un autre.
—Rimbaud 2005, Letter to Paul Demeny, May 15, 1871

All the soppy talk about the inner child has not laid to rest deep fantasies about the inner ogre.
—Warner 1999, 146–47

"Every fiction inscribes itself in our space as a journey," writes Michel Butor, "and one can say that this is the fundamental theme of any novel" (Butor 1964, 50). All narratives—even if they do not explicitly recount a voyage—entail movement between the space of the writer (or reader) and the space of the narration. In the introduction we briefly mentioned Bunyan's allegorical novel *The Pilgrim's Progress* as a typical example of what Northrop Frye calls "apocalyptic" (heavenly) imagery (Frye 1957, 141). We follow the protagonist, Christian, on his epic voyage from earth (the City of Destruction) to heaven (the Celestial City of Mount Zion). The ogre's progress is in the opposite direction. The "demonic imagery" (1957, 147) of the stories we have studied tells of characters bound for hell, journeying through hopeless lives in a world marked by the sign of devouring.

Though fictions, most of our ogre stories recount barbarous cruelty that is not relegated to literature. Violence is pervasive, and our first tendency is to attribute it to other people, those who do not "dream of equality and fraternity" (Olivier 1998, 7) as we do. Yet the authors we have studied confirm Christiane Olivier's notion that we all have our "inner ogre"—akin to Freud's death instinct—that contains the seed of violence. All it needs in order to thrive is the proper environment, which our dysfunctional world all too readily supplies. The sociologist Michel Juffé observes, "Everyone sees it: 'social cohesion' is threatened, the 'social fabric' is torn. Countries and ethnic groups kill one another, professional and social exclusion is rampant, racism and xenophobia flourish" (Juffé 1995, 11).

In the following sonnet, Michel Butor describes this brutal world of horrors as a grotesque "Danse des ogres." Butor's dancing ogres—like Péju's laughing ogre—prefer to eat tender children, but occasionally will enjoy the spice of terrorist attacks on airports and hospitals, or perhaps the refined taste of a slow death from radioactivity or from some other virulent man-made poison:

> Pour la plupart nous préférons la chair bien fraîche
> En particulier celle des petits enfants
> La vie qui croque sous la dent
> Et qui gémit encore longtemps dans l'estomac
>
> Mais il y en a qui préfèrent le cadavre
> En particulier quand il a bien saigné
> Et il faut avouer qu'il y a d'excellentes recettes
> Avec des épices d'aéroport et des paniques d'hôpitaux bombardés
>
> Et certains raffinés recherchent les charognes
> En particulier celles qui avaient été travaillées pendant leur vie
> Par certaines races de microbes particulièrement ingénieuses
> Des émissions radioactives ou des poisons rares
> Qui laissent un arrière-goût d'horreur exquise
> Dont ils se pourlèchent les babines[.][1]

The stories we have examined in the preceding chapters include a certain number of monsters whose inner ogre probably ruled them from the beginning: Hitler, Goering (*The Ogre*), the SS officers at Auschwitz and Treblinka (*Le Dixième Cercle*), the murderous Nazi cannibals of the department store (*The Scapegoat*). Perhaps more disturbing, however, are the innocents whose inner ogre leaps out in response to abuse or injustice. Abel Tiffauges's (*The Ogre*) love for children is subject to the "malignant inversion" that he discerns everywhere; his innocence is perverted first by society's rejection of him and then by the Nazi war machine that employs him. Nora Neumann (*Le Verrou*) is beaten and prostituted by her parents and then abused by Massimo Cuori before she grows to be a femme fatale and exacts her revenge. Similarly, Lucie Daubigné (*The Medusa Child*) is transformed into a sullen, friendless creature bent on vengeance, after her brother rapes her and brings her idyllic world to a jarring end. Finally, timid Jean Calmet (*A Father's Love*), loving son and devoted teacher, demonstrates ogreish tendencies of his own—lusting after his students, shouting anti-Semitic insults—as a response to the various ogres who victimize him.

JE est un ogre, our authors seem to be saying, echoing the sixteen-year-old Rimbaud's famous declaration *"JE est un autre"* ("I is someone else") (Rimbaud 2005, 375). Rimbaud prefigured by a generation the Freudian topography of the human mind split into various parts, some of which seem to be the "I" we know (the conscious, the ego), and others that are more like "someone else" (the preconscious, the unconscious; the id, the superego). The poet also anticipated Jung's writings on the unconscious, which make clear how little we know about ourselves. A man's "anima" and a woman's "animus" (Jung 1978 et al., 186–207)—individual personifications of the opposite sex—are largely hidden from consciousness.

Rimbaud saw the poet not only as a seer but also as a monster among men. The poet's "soul must be made monstrous," and suffer "[u]nspeakable torture where he needs all his faith, all his superhuman strength, where he becomes among all men the great patient, the great criminal, the one accursed—and the supreme Scholar!—Because he reaches the *unknown!*" (Rimbaud 2005, 377). He is made of the same stuff as other humans, but through a "derangement of all the senses" (2005, 377) he assumes a sublime form, as some lucky piece of wood might become a violin (2005, 371), or a billet of brass a trumpet (2005, 375).

Tortured, sick, criminal, and cursed, the poet as seen by Rimbaud is not unlike our vision of the ogre. Psychoanalysts have shown the devouring instincts of the baby, "monster of greed and gratification and excess," "murderously voracious," insatiably ingesting the milk of its mother (Warner 1999, 146). From the beginning we are all prospective ogres, but only a few of us reach our dubious potential, as only a handful will develop into poets like Rimbaud. The authors examined here are the heirs of Rimbaud. They too have participated in the monstrous, showing us the monsters among us,[2] exposing them so that they might be comprehended, if not apprehended.

Yet as evil as he is, the ogre, like all great mythological figures, is ambivalent—even duplicitous, as he can represent evil or good, the other or the self. Primarily a personification of evil, the ogre can nonetheless be—like his double the dragon[3]—a positive force. Let us consider for a moment the gentle side of the two Greek divinities most readily associated with the ogre: Cronus and Dionysus.

We have more often than not depicted Cronus as a true monster, a sadistic despot who castrated his father and devoured his children. Yet in Hesiod's tale of the five ages of men (gold, silver, bronze, heroic, and iron), Cronus ruled the idyllic Golden Age, when the world approached perfection:

> Golden was the first race of articulate folk
> Created by the immortals who live on Olympos.

> They actually lived when Kronos was king of the sky,
> And they lived like gods, not a care in their hearts,
> Nothing to do with hard work or grief,
> And miserable old age didn't exist for them.
> From fingers to toes they never grew old,
> And the good times rolled. And when they died
> It was like sleep just ravelled them up.
> They had everything good. The land bore them fruit
> All on its own, and plenty of it too. Cheerful folk,
> They did their work peaceably and in prosperity,
> With plenty of flocks, and they were dear to the gods.
> (Hesiod 1993, *Works and Days* l.129–41)

By contrast, the other ages—all governed by Cronus's son Zeus—are characterized by war, suffering, crime, and other miseries. Unlike the men of the Golden Age, who "were dear to the gods," these men constantly incur the anger of Zeus.

Like Hesiod, Plato, in his *Statesman*, heaps praise on Cronus. The Titan reigned as a "shepherd" might, "in every way sufficient for his flock, so that savagery was nowhere to be found nor preying of creature on creature, nor did war rage nor any strife whatsoever" (Plato 1992, 28). The texts of Hesiod and Plato remind us of the bond between the Titans and humans. The Olympian Zeus was constantly at odds with humans, and attempted to destroy them all, first by sending them Pandora with her fateful vase, then by burying them beneath the waters of an enormous flood. Prometheus, however, a Titan like Cronus, always took the side of the human race, and eventually succeeded in saving it from the wrath of Zeus.

For Marcel Detienne and Claire Caillaud, the ambivalent nature of the ogre links him above all to Dionysus. Coming from Lydia or Thrace—thus foreign to the Greeks—Dionysus is "the Other, the Savage," the "eater of raw flesh" (Caillaud 2000, 8–9) who drives women to murder and cannibalism; yet he is admired as "the god of inspiration, of enthusiasm, who ignores the limits imposed by the social order," symbolizing the "vital spark" (2000, 9) of the divine in humankind. His story is that of a god with an insatiable appetite, but it also recounts his sacrifice at the hands of the Titans, who cooked and ate him, inciting Zeus's fury. Like the ogre, Dionysus represents the anguish of humanity, traumatized by its own cruelty: he is both "executioner and victim of the savage appetite inscribed in human nature" (2000, 9).

At times evil, at times good, the ogre can also symbolize either the self or the other. We have seen myriad forms of the ogre as other: for Zola he is the "belly of Paris" and the tyrant Napoleon III, who alike swallow up the poor; for other authors he is the Nazi oppressor, the sexual aggressor, or war personified. Yet the ogre is not always the hostile other. The fear of the ogre is also "the fear of the Self: the primordial taboo, violated by the barbarian, exposes the buried desire of each of us" (Caillaud 2000, 7). Tournier's Abel, Cerf's Nora, Germain's Lucie, Chessex's Jean: all innocents whose ogre within—surfacing like Jung's "shadow," the dark part of the unconscious—takes over their lives and transforms them from victims to aggressors.

It is clear that the ogre is much more than a monstrous fiction. For a sociologist like Michel Juffé, the ogre is one of three archetypes describing the social bond among human beings. In *Les Fondements du lien social: le justicier, le sage et l'ogre* [Foundations of the social bond: the prosecutor, the sage and the ogre], he writes that our "recognition" (1995, 19) of the other depends in part on our ability to deal with the known and the unknown. The "Ogre" cannot bear the unknown. He is the type of person who attempts to destroy, possess, or absorb others: "only people like him exist; it is the world of the *sacrifice*—of Ogres—where the unknown is terrifying, where for reassurance one aspires to Unity, and where all difference must disappear" (1995, 19). The "Prosecutor" tolerates others but inevitably evaluates them: "he hierarchizes people who are like and unlike him; it is the world of the *exchange*—of Prosecutors—where knowledge never ceases to spread, pushing back the limits of the known, in a permanent Duality" (1995, 19–20). Finally, only the "Sage" really succeeds in recognizing individuals, in knowing others: "the place of the other is always open, without exclusion; it is the world of the *gift*—of Sages—where the known and the unknown cohabit in peace, in the midst of infinite Multiplicity" (1995, 20).

For Juffé, nothing can explain the real world like tales and myths, which express "the most profound, the most complete, the most concentrated truths . . . of life in society" (1995, 17). At the center of myths is the plot (*mythos*), which reflects the struggle between the known and the unknown: "[Plots] show us the unending combat between the Same and the Other, between the fear of being nothing and the desire to be one among others. Hence the tendency to want to possess the other, which one can call cannibalism" (1995, 23).

Thus defined, the archetypal plot might be that of Perrault's "Little Tom Thumb" ("Le Petit Poucet"). Juffé writes that at the crux of most plots is "confusion and distinction," the classic example of which is Oedipus's slow progress from ignorance to truth (1995, 36–37). In Perrault's tale, the ogre is absolute confusion: for him, all life is but meat fit for consumption, whether it be animal or human. He fails to distinguish between his daughters and Tom Thumb and his brothers, and ends up slaughtering his little girls instead of the boys. He cannot tolerate difference: anyone unlike him—save his wife—must be eliminated and absorbed as dinner. Tom Thumb, on the other hand, is the sage in a world of ogres, the rare person whose actions are "in another dimension," who "sees what the others do not see" (Juffé 1995, 38), and succeeds in "reestablishing a human order where it is crumbling or being destroyed by force" (1995, 40). He "exposes a cannibal order and escapes it" (1995, 46).

The tale of Tom Thumb accomplishes the goal of the traditional ogre stories of myth and folklore. Just as Zeus finally vanquishes his ogre father Cronus, Tom Thumb overcomes the ogre of the forest. The lesson here, as Marina Warner observes (Warner 1999, 77), is that in a healthy society the older generation gives way to the younger. The future belongs to the young hero who slays the old giant, ogre, or dragon, thus ridding society of corruption and paving the way for a new beginning. And indeed, this occurs in some of the stories we have studied. Benjamin Malaussène (*The Scapegoat*) prevails over the department store ogres, and the future seems rosy for him and his younger siblings. Lucie Daubigné (*The Medusa Child*), after a long descent into hell, appears to be free of her ogres and ready to begin life at forty. The novel ends amid reassuring images of light and joy.

Yet most of our authors are not so optimistic, and the lesson of the modern ogre myth is an overwhelmingly bleak one. At the end of his "exergue" to *Of Grammatology*, Derrida, like Rimbaud, ties the monstrous to the unknown. Rimbaud admires the poet-seer, who is monstrous because he dares make contact with the unknown; for Derrida, what is monstrous is the future, simply because it is unknowable. His analysis of writing implies "a way of thinking that is faithful and attentive to the ineluctable world of the future," which "can only be anticipated in the form of an absolute danger. It is that which breaks absolutely with constituted normality and can only be proclaimed, *presented,* as a sort of monstrosity" (Derrida 1976, 4–5). In a later interview, he adds that "the future is necessarily monstrous: the figure of the future, that is, that which can only be surprising, that for which we are not prepared, you see, is heralded by species of monsters. A future that would not be monstrous would not be a future" (1995, 386–87).

The works we have studied show that the ogre usually wins—and will continue to win—in our decidedly unhealthy world. As in *The Belly of Paris,* the fat will persist in oppressing the thin; as in *Ogres et autres contes* and *Le Verrou,* lovers will keep on abusing their loved ones. With a sly wink Bruckner's ogre offers his own flesh to infect the children with his cruelty; with a cynical laugh Péju's ogre abandons one war, only to begin another. The monstrous lesson that—like a monstrance—our authors are holding up for us to see is that the future belongs to the ogres.

One important question remains: why did the literary ogre begin to reappear with such regularity precisely in late twentieth-century France? To answer that question, let us consider more closely two of the most disturbing ogres we have studied. First, there is the ogre of political tyranny, like the one who terrorizes the poor and "thin" people of *The Belly of Paris*. In novels published after 1970, like *The Ogre*, *The Scapegoat*, *Le Dixième Cercle*, and *Le Rire de l'ogre*, the "political" ogre—who does violence to all the weak, but above all to children—is most often incarnated by Nazi Germany and its Vichy collaborators. Second, there is the abuser of women and children, the "sexual" ogre. We have seen him as the perverted Nazis in Pennac's and Zimmermann's novels, and he especially haunts the works of the two major women authors we have studied: Muriel Cerf and Sylvie Germain. At roughly the same time, the crimes of these two ogres finally broke through the surface of the French consciousness and began to occupy a significant share of the national social and historical discourse.

Tzvetan Todorov, in *Les Abus de la mémoire* [The abuses of memory], claims that as one millennium wanes and another begins, contemporary Europe—and especially France—is obsessed by "the cult of memory" (Todorov 1995, 51). We are living in an age of "commemorative mania" (1995, 51), which is helping to bring memories of the Holocaust into clearer focus, with the potentially constructive result that the French nation is at long last coming to terms with its responsibility for the deaths of 76,000 French Jews deported to the Nazi death camps.

I say "potentially" constructive, because the point of Todorov's essay is that memory can be abused; remembrance of atrocities can lead as often to hate as to healing. He distinguishes two ways in which a people can recall crimes inflicted against it. The first he calls "literal memory" (1995, 30–33). This occurs when remembrance is "intransitive"; that is, an act is remembered in such a way that the memory leads nowhere—at least nowhere productive. The memory cannot escape the past with which it is contiguous, inspiring more often than not thoughts of hate and revenge. Todorov implores those touched by the Holocaust to go beyond literal memory to the second way of remembering: "exemplary memory" (1995, 30–33). Exemplary memory learns from past crimes and encourages solutions to prevent their recurrence: in this way it is "transitive," and helps a wronged society free itself from its past, thus leading it, finally, from suffering to justice. Following Todorov's linguistic terminology, one could say that exemplary memory is metaphorical: "I open this memory to analogy and generalization, I make it an *exemplum* and I learn a lesson from it; the past thus becomes a basis of action for the present. In this case, the associations that I evoke in my mind are triggered no longer by contiguity, but by similarity" (1995, 31).

The novels of Tournier, Pennac, Zimmermann, and Péju all express the crimes of National Socialism by means of an ogre metaphor resurrected from myths and fairy tales. Their fictions contribute to a kind of national psychoanalysis—coinciding with the long and agonizing investigations and "trials of memory" (Golsan 1998, "Introduction" 14) of French collaborators like Paul Touvier and Maurice Papon[4]—in which repressed horrors and guilt are brought to light. Zimmermann's *Le Dixième Cercle* explicitly condemns the involvement of the French police in the arrest and deportation of French Jews, graphically describing their brutality in Paris and Drancy, the transit camp just north of Paris. Published in 1997, Zimmermann's unsettling novel appeared just two years after the French government finally acknowledged its own guilt in the deportations. Then president Jacques Chirac admitted that France had committed a "collective fault" (Depaulis 2007, 182). He apologized exactly fifty-three years after the infamous roundup of nearly 13,000 Parisian Jews, who were temporarily imprisoned in the fifteenth arrondissement's Vélodrome d'Hiver, before being deported to Auschwitz:

> France, country of the Enlightenment and of the Rights of Man, land of welcome and asylum; on that day France committed the irreparable. Breaking its word, it delivered those it protected to their executioners. . . . Other round-ups, other arrests would follow. In Paris and in the provinces. Seventy-four trains would leave for Auschwitz. Seventy-six thousand Jews deported from France would not come back.
> We owe them an imprescriptible debt. (2007, 180)

Toward the end of his speech, Chirac urged that recalling France's role in the Holocaust be a cautionary act, like Todorov's exemplary remembering, and that it help overcome the still-powerful force of racism, both in France and in Europe: "These values [liberty, justice, tolerance], upon which our democracies are founded, are today being mocked right here in Europe, before our eyes, by the proponents of ethnic cleansing. Let us learn lessons from history. Let us not accept being passive witnesses, or accomplices, to the unacceptable" (2007, 183).

The essays in Richard Golsan's *Fascism's Return* demonstrate what a remarkable admission Chirac's words were, when compared to the attitude of former presidents like Georges Pompidou and François Mitterrand. Chirac's call for transparency regarding the Vichy years contrasts sharply with Pompidou's and Mitterrand's desire to bury the past. Like many postwar historians and politicians, they wanted to avoid scandal and to "normalize" or "rehabilitate" Vichy (Golsan 1998, "History and the Responsibility of Memory" 185). Pompidou, shortly after he pardoned Paul Touvier, declared in 1972 that "the time for national reconciliation had come where the Occupation was concerned, and that it was necessary to 'draw a veil over the past'" (1998, 188). Mitterrand also showed sympathy for Touvier, whom he described as "just an old man," adding that "[o]ne cannot sustain oneself forever on memories and rancor" (1998, 193). More troublingly, Mitterrand shocked the public by praising as "a man of 'exceptional stature'" (1998, 194) his old friend René Bousquet, former head of the Vichy police, and thus ultimately responsible for the deaths of thousands of deported French Jews.[5] For Golsan, the *Affaire Mitterrand* was one of the more glaring symptoms of what has been called the "Vichy Syndrome," (1998, 182–83, 193–95; also Gordon, in Golsan 1998, 154), a long, excruciating national psychological malady born from France's struggle to recognize and admit its role in implementing the Nazis' "Final Solution" to the Jewish question.

Around the same time that France was coming to terms with the Vichy Syndrome, another long-buried ogre was being confronted. For a long time, the subject of violence against women and children had been a dark secret, not often discussed openly. The research of Anne-Marie Sohn and Alain Corbin shows that, historically, in cases of sexual aggression against women and girls, there was a reluctance to believe in the innocence of the victim. Indeed, the roles of aggressor and victim were often reversed, and the man—seen as an innocent prey of woman's "threatening" (Corbin 1989, 11) or "devouring" (Sohn, in Corbin 1989, 101) sexuality[6]—would be acquitted. All women were thus considered to be descendants of the ogress, wicked daughters of Eve: "The investigation of evidence of the attack is transformed into an inquest to find the proof of impurity, and the judgment is overturned against the false victim; when all is said and done, the greatest fault could be said to lie with Eve the temptress" (Corbin 1989, 11). There was indeed, as some contemporary writers still argue, a "war against women."[7]

Finally, in the 1970s the veil of silence covering violence against women was lifted. The history of sexuality became a subject of intense study, "mainly from the angle of illegitimate births and prostitution, while volume 1 of Michel Foucault's *The History of Sexuality* attracted attention to the 'biopolitical' techniques of power that bring into play the control of the body and of reproduction" (Sohn, in Corbin 1989, 71). Western society's *scientia sexualis*—procedures developed "for telling the truth of sex" (Foucault 1990, 58)—finally began to reveal rather than hide the truth, thanks to post–World War II research such as that carried out in the United States by Kinsey in the 1950s, and Masters and Johnson in the 1960s and 1970s. The secret of sex[8] gained new transparency, and the secret of sexual violence was also exposed.

The rise of feminism in France during the 1970s encouraged a new openness concerning both violence against women and violence against children. The physician and psychiatrist Marie-France Hirigoyen, citing staggering statistics proving the high frequency of domestic violence in France, writes of a "social plague." She declares that "it is only since the 1970s, with the actions of the feminists, that the impact of domestic violence on women has begun to be studied. Until then, people hesitated to intervene, under the pretext that it was a private matter" (Hirigoyen 2005, 8). As for violence against children, also a "plague," according to Gérard Lopez, a psychotherapist at the University of Paris (Lopez 1999, 4), it too has come under scrutiny thanks to organizations—many of which were created under the impetus of the feminist movement (1999, 10)—devoted to the protection of victims.

With the exception of Zola, all the authors we have been studying published their books in post-1970 France. They have both contributed to, and been influenced by, the "cult of memory" that Todorov discerns in contemporary Europe. They have not forgotten the fairy tale ogres that were their standard childhood reading fare; they have displaced these monsters into their own metaphorical fictions, which are seasoned by the dark lessons of modern history. "It is the Devil who writes History in letters of blood," writes Michel Tournier in *The Mirror of Ideas* (1998, 55). Tournier and our other authors are not necessarily *engagés* in the Sartrean sense of political activism, but the bloody letters of their writings effectively employ the vehicle of the ogre to decry the violence that, like the ogres of their youth, devours countless young victims of war, genocide, and sexual aggression.

Appendix:
The Resurgence of the Ogre:
Interviews with Michel Tournier and Pascal Bruckner

Interview with Michel Tournier in Choisel, France
May 19, 2002

JK: Why is the myth of the ogre important to you?

MT: For my work, the ogre is an especially rich theme. First of all, the ogre is a mythological character. Polyphemus, the Cyclops in Homer's *Odyssey*, is an ogre. Colin-Maillard was a famous blind warrior of the Middle Ages.[1] Saint Christopher was a giant with a giant appetite who transported children on his back. Next comes literature, with characters that descend from this mythology. For example, Shakespeare's Falstaff, Rabelais's Pantagruel and Gargantua, the countess of Ségur's General Dourakine. Also, Porthos, one of Alexandre Dumas's three musketeers, was enormous and strong, ate a lot, and was naïve. So these are the first two areas where the ogre appears: mythology and literature.

And then there is a third place we find ogres: in life. Because in life we meet ogres, don't we? Fellini was an ogre. He ate a lot, he had a broad face, and his films are ogre films, in the sense that one of their main subjects is eating. For example, at the beginning of *Satyricon* there is the great *festa*. In Fellini's films, every time people sit down to eat, it's extraordinary! In *Roma* there is a character who sits down at a kitchen table and eats noodles; this simple act immediately becomes grandiose.

So what are the traits of the ogre? It's first of all a character who eats a lot, who has a big belly, and who suffers from digestive and defecation problems: an anal individual. Look at Rabelais: urination and defecation play a very important role, don't they? On the other hand, the ogre's sexuality is quite weak. Look at Fellini: everything concerning sex is ridiculous. His Casanova is grotesque; Casanova should be sexy, but for Fellini he can only be grotesque, because for him there is no sex.

The ogre's sense of smell is extraordinary: he lives by his nose. On the other hand, his vision is very poor. The most famous ogre in French literature is in Charles Perrault's tale, "Little Tom Thumb." He is a giant who lives in the forest. Remember that in Perrault's time "country" meant civilization, and "forest" meant untamed, uncivilized. Etymologically, "savage" means "forest." The ogre was a savage, a man of the forest, and he ate little children. Tom Thumb's parents abandon him and his brothers in the forest; they hide in the ogre's house. The ogre arrives and declares to his wife: "I smell fresh flesh." During the night he tries to slit the throats of Tom and his brothers, but instead he kills his daughters, because of his poor eyesight. That's typical of the ogre, and you see the same thing with Homer's ogre, Polyphemus. He only has one eye, which Ulysses pokes out, so then he only has his sense of smell to guide him.

JK: Because of this powerful sense of smell, is there a relationship between the ogre and the dog or wolf?

MT: Yes, the dog, in effect, is an animal with an extraordinary sense of smell, and bad eyes; but this inverse relationship between smell and sight is highest in the rabbit and hare. Rabbits and hares see almost nothing. They are completely myopic, but what a sense of smell! They have a second brain, called the olfactive bulb. In the human brain, the olfactive bulb is tiny; in the hare and rabbit it is a second brain. That is to say, one cannot imagine what the world of a hare or rabbit is like, because they see—first and foremost—odors. Their world is above all a landscape of smells.

JK: We find the ogre-dog in Egyptian mythology with Anubis.

MT: Yes, the god with the head of a jackal. Like the ogre, the dog is very scatological. Many dogs eat excrement, and when two dogs meet, the first thing they do is sniff one another's anus. It's their way of communicating. And Anubis . . . it's really Anus-bis, anus twice over! There is truth in words!

So, the ogre is myopic, his sense of smell is highly developed, his sexual drive is weak, and he is an anal person who lives for defecation . . . Anubis. The ogre is also obsessed with freshness. He wants fresh things, like the ogre in "Little Tom Thumb" who adores "fresh flesh." It's a characteristic I give to Abel Tiffauges in *The Ogre*. He wants milk, he wants salad, he wants raw vegetables, fresh eggs, and raw oysters. The ogre likes raw food. And personally, that's my only affinity with the ogre: I'm fixated on freshness.

JK: In *The Ogre*, it is especially Nazism that is symbolized by the ogre.

MT: Yes. And also "The Erl-King," Goethe's ballad.

JK: There is the same Nazi symbolism in Pennac's *The Scapegoat,* where the ogres are Nazis, and Chessex's *A Father's Love,* in which one of the characters is a neo-Nazi. How do the ogre and Nazism go together?

MT: Let's talk about Nazism, which I experienced as a child. I often went to Germany while it was under Nazi rule, and I saw clearly how Nazi propaganda was directed at me, a child. The main reference to Goethe's "Erl-King" is these two phrases spoken by the Erl-King: "Mich reizt deine schöne Gestalt," and "komm, . . . Gar schöne Spiele spiel' ich mit dir."

The first phrase is very difficult to translate, because you can go from one extreme to the other. Most translators write something like "I'm charmed by your beautiful face," but one could also correctly write "Your beautiful body excites me." It's not incorrect, but in my opinion it would be excessive; something between the two is needed. I wrote "Your beautiful body tempts me," which isn't as strong as "excite."

The second phrase means "Come, . . . such lovely games I'll play with you." And that was the Nazi propaganda: "Come with us, and you'll see horses, weapons, airplanes, Panzers, drums." They made the military seductive in order to attract the adolescent. And it's always been the same. Remember the words of Napoleon, who said to the young French peasants: "Come with me; we'll conquer Europe together, and there is perhaps a marshal's baton in your pack." So "komm, . . . Gar schöne Spiele spiel' ich mit dir."

But Napoleon was trying to attract twenty-year-old boys, while the Nazis wanted children practically from birth. Nazism is a philosophy of biology, blood, and race. Children had to be educated, and they had to correspond to the blond, blue-eyed Nordic ideal. The Nazis were obsessed with biology. They would have liked to start indoctrination while the mother was still pregnant, before the child was born. There was really a kind of pedophilia or pedomania with the Nazis that one didn't find with Napoleon, or in modern propaganda from developing countries trying to attract young people to the army. They are taken at the age they are useable, around eighteen. They won't be taken at six years of age; what can you do with a child of six in the army? But with the Nazis, yes . . . and that's their affinity with "The Erl-King," because the child of Goethe's poem is not eighteen; he's six, or seven, or eight, a little boy in the arms of his father. That's why "The Erl-King" symbolizes so well the pedomania of the Nazis; one mustn't forget that while the Nazis were in power, the German child was forced into service at ten years of age. Boys had to join the *Jungvolk,* and girls went into the

Jungmädelbund. At fourteen, boys became members of the *Hitlerjugend* ("Hitler Youth"), and girls entered the *BDM*, or *Bund der deutschen Mädel* ("Union of German Girls"), where they remained until they were eighteen. Then the girls were left alone, but the boys went into the *Reichsarbeitsdienst* ("Work Service") at eighteen, and the *Militärdienst*—the army—at nineteen. In other words, the government owned them from ten to twenty-two.

JK: That is well documented in Leni Riefenstahl's 1934 film, *The Triumph of the Will.* You see the young German men with their shovels and other tools.

MT: Yes, that's the *Reichsarbeitsdienst.* They built highways, which Germany was one of the first countries in the world to have. I believe that Mussolini built the first highway, but there was just one in Italy; I think it was Milan-Rome. And then Hitler, from 1933 on, built a whole network of highways, which obviously were of great strategic military importance for transporting weapons.

JK: In *The Ogre* and in Chessex's *A Father's Love,* it seems that ogres are often victims as well as persecutors. In Chessex's novel, for example, the young teacher is very shy and fragile, and his ogreish character hides a fundamental weakness. I wonder if the ogre is always a victim, persecutor and persecuted at the same time. The ogre Abel Tiffauges is a victim of the Nazis, who in turn are victims of the Russians. And Gilles de Rais was victimized by the Catholic Church in a sense.

MT: The ogre can have a character trait that one could call either stupidity (rather negative) or naïveté (relatively positive). General Dourakine is a likeable idiot. And Falstaff, too. The ogre is at the same time pleasant and frightening.

JK: In *The Scapegoat,* René Girard recounts the myth of Cronus and Zeus. Cronus, devourer of his own children, is one of the first ogres, symbol of destructive time. But he too ends up a victim, defeated by Zeus, who casts him into hell. This story hints that there is something very human about the ogre, who descends from the race of the Titans, enemies of the gods. And certain Titans—like Prometheus—were also friends of the human race. Perhaps one could interpret the popularity of the ogre myth as a revalorization of humans at the expense of the gods, a sort of humanist revolt, like Nietzsche's declaration of the death of God.

MT: It's an interesting thesis, but I see Cronus more like a monster. Cronus eats his children. The most terrible ogre is the one who practices "infantiphagia": eating his own children.

JK: You are currently working on a vampire story. Can one put these two monsters—the ogre and the vampire—in the same category, or are there more differences than similarities between the two?

MT: There is no similarity, because the ogre is interested in solids, the vampire in liquids: blood. And blood resembles wine, which the vampire—more than the ogre—has a taste for. One mustn't forget that in the Christian religion, wine is transformed into Jesus's blood: thus there is an affinity between wine and blood.

JK: Yes, wine wouldn't interest the ogre, because it is not fresh.

MT: Wine is not and cannot be fresh, while flesh must be.

JK: Another difference between the two monsters is that the ogre is a brute, whereas the vampire is very subtle.

MT: Yes, that's true. The vampire is no brute.

Interview with Pascal Bruckner in Paris, France
May 21, 2002

JK: What inspired your short story, "Les Ogres anonymes"?

PB: I had just won the Prix Renaudot for *Les Voleurs de beauté,* and I wrote the short story for fun. I don't know how I got the idea, but I have a little girl who was one at the time, and I began telling her a story about a wolf who had problems digesting children. It was annoyed because it didn't want to become a vegetarian. The idea began to germinate like that, and so I imagined this story of a modern ogre, a business attorney from a good family, torn between his appetites and accepted morals, which forbid cannibalism. So he tries to cure himself with modern therapy: psychoanalysis, acupuncture, behaviorism, etc. At first the story was just a way of entertaining myself, but then it grew into a little tale. I retell myths, rereading them in an ironic way.

JK: The second tale in your book, "L'Effaceur" (The eraser) is also an ogre story, isn't it? It's about a man who kidnaps and literally erases children.

PB: Yes, he's a misanthropic ogre who hates children, while Balthus in "Les Ogres anonymes" loves them too much. In tales, a child learns about life's risks, which can hurt him, but also about his own aggressive drives, which horrify him. But I don't have a particular lesson to give, it's more the pleasure to play on a myth, to play with the taboo on pedophilia by inventing ogres who are monsters, of course, but also normal people tortured by digestive problems, by moral problems, due in part to contemporary life. They are trying to free themselves of these troubles. I used the model of Alcoholics Anonymous, where addiction is treated through group work. My anthropophagous attorney signs up for Ogres Anonymous, where old repentant ogres try to wean him of his taste for children's flesh. They meet each week, proclaiming in funereal voices: "Hello, I haven't eaten any little children for over a week, and I'm doing fine." The others applaud this good resolution.

JK: In contemporary novels about ogres, there is a recurrent theme: the ogre who in turn becomes a victim. Thus the same person unites victim and torturer, like in Baudelaire's "L'Héautontimorouménos" ("The Self-Tormenter") in which the poet calls himself "the wound and the dagger! . . . victim and executioner!" You speak about that in *The Temptation of Innocence*, in reference to Serbia, "the torturer [who] displayed himself as the martyr, and . . . rendered those under attack (Croatians, Bosnians, Kosovar Albanians) responsible for the tragedies that befell them" (Bruckner 2000, 216). In "Les Ogres anonymes," the members of Ogres Anonymous are afraid of being eliminated by normal people and, of course, at the end the hero Balthus gives himself up to the collective revenge of the children. And then in "L'Effaceur," the aggressor becomes in a way the prey of the child he had kidnapped. Did you consciously think about the "tormenter-victim" in writing these tales?

PB: Yes; that is, in today's society, we no longer want to portray evil. Everything cruel, evil, violent—quite visible in medieval society and in the world of the *ancien régime*, where figures of cruelty were personalized—has been eliminated. Modernity is Rousseauan: we think that man is good, thus that evil comes from society, from institutions, and that it is not in us. All Europe wanted to erase and hide the barbarity of fairy tales, which allows the child to exorcise his own violence by portraying it. The stories of Perrault, Grimm, Andersen—which politically correct good souls wanted to clean up—are obviously a very cruel depiction of life, but children adore these tales of cannibalism, murders, cutting up of body parts. That was Bettelheim's thesis, and I think it's pretty accurate. The tale teaches the child to master his fear of the other, but also to master the fear of his own aggressiveness, particularly his desire to kill his parents and his family. Thus the ogres in my story become victims of this modern optimism that consists in erasing completely the negative sides of life. They are a sort of archaism, a barbarian relic; it's the return of the repressed, but very alive repressions because every day we see on the news horrible crimes of which children are victims. I adore horror films. They are not always of the finest quality—with the exception of a few masterpieces—but they are the survival—in our de-Christianized and secular French society—of old religious terrors recycled in the form of popular culture: the revenge of the dead, ghosts, succubi, vampires. All the medieval fears survive in our apparently hyperrational societies. In all horror films there is a very classic schema of the victim who becomes the tormenter and makes his descendants pay for the pain he suffered; and then there is the zombie who contaminates the living by a simple bite or touch. "Les Ogres anonymes" is a kind of rewriting of the vampire myth—the monster is eaten by the children, and since his flesh is contaminated, they in turn become ogres: thus evil is ensured a kind of eternity. Death of the persecutor, who is resurrected in other bodies.

JK: In *The Temptation of Innocence,* you speak of a "cannibal logic" in the consumer society, which behaves like an ogre with a "taste for immediate and easy pleasures" (Bruckner 2000, 83). Mircea Eliade speaks of the millenarian and eschatological character of National Socialism, an idea on which Daniel Pennac elaborates with his anthropophagic Nazis in *The Scapegoat*. The Nazis, galvanized by the glorious past of the Germanic people, believed that the Apocalypse was imminent, and that they must enjoy and live for the present moment. Is there a connection between consumerism and this aspect of the extreme right, in that they both believe in the primacy of the present?

PB: No, there have always been Christian heresies that preferred to take advantage of the moment rather than think about the future in Paradise. There is a greediness in consumerism that covets objects, merchandise, and not living creatures; we are not as much ogres as greedy babies. That said, cannibalism still remains the great taboo of modern society; it is a very rare event. Do you remember that Japanese man living in France who ate Dutch, Swedish, and French women? Today he is a hero in Japan. He was judged insane, so he did some time here, and then was deported to Japan. He wrote a book in which he brags about his culinary exploits, and compares the flesh of French women, Dutch women, etc., as one would in a gastronomical guidebook. It's an extreme case that, far from blurring the taboo, underscores it.

JK: He said he ate them because he loved them, right?

PB: Yes, they were cruel, ritual killings: he cut the women up, and then ate them. The essence of cannibalism is to appropriate the substance of the other. Cannibalism is a ritual in certain primitive societies; they do not eat people because they are hungry, they eat them to steal their soul, their strength.

JK: As in the Holy Eucharist.

PB: Exactly. The Eucharist is a Christian sublimation of anthropophagy. Also in the sex act we eat the other; we devour him, but he escapes whole from this passionate outpouring. There are cases of catastrophes, such as shipwrecks, in which humans draw straws to see who will be eaten, but that remains an exception.

JK: The sociologist Michel Maffesoli, in *The Shadow of Dionysus*, describes two conceptions of time: horizontal, linear, historical time; and the vertical time of the present. Industrial society lives by horizontal time, working to save for the future. On the other hand, vertical time is "a poetic and erotic time, a time of the amorous body" (Maffesoli 1993, 31) enjoying the moment. The symbol of this time is Dionysus, the ogre-god, with his exuberance, his effervescence, his chaos. Living for the present, enjoying the moment can be something positive, revolutionary, because society's traditional values are thus put into question. In *The Temptation of Innocence*, you criticize the modern consumer's desire to have everything immediately. But do you agree with Maffesoli that this impatience, this refusal to save can sometimes be beneficial?

PB: Today we live in a society that is totally hedonistic. Dionysus is at the supermarket everyday, you just have to look at the advertising posters. In the past forty years—more or less since May 1968—our society has completely reversed its fundamental principles. Whereas in the past we were supposed to save, hold back, and learn how to wait, today we should enjoy, buy immediately, and never know the least frustration. Thus our relationship to time has been upended. It is perhaps true that at the beginning of the twentieth century our society was based on saving. But now it is no longer true: pleasure has become the golden rule of the system, while Puritanism now seems an aberration. Capitalism itself has put our happiness at the heart of its operation: it aims at our unlimited satisfaction, it caresses our drives, our desires, and its great fear is that we don't desire enough, that is, that we don't buy enough. There is a very contemporary collusion between libertarians and advertisers. Sex itself has become a commercial argument that sells a lot, but at the same time makes us feel guilty, because we are constantly bombarded with models of pleasure and sexual fulfillment that penalize those who don't correspond to them.

Getting back to "Les Ogres anonymes," what amused me in this book was to highlight the contrasts between man's barbarous roots, that is, the desire to kill and eat the other, and the civilized, smiling, and pleasant side of modern society, where we live in perpetual euphemism, attenuating—or completely refusing to see—evil. There is this contrast between two languages, the one of greed, of the gourmandise of a creature that wants to eat all the little boys and little girls, and our social morals that say no, that's not acceptable. But we don't condemn anymore in the religious sense, like in the past when witches, or people suspected of cannibalism were burned at the stake in the name of religion. Today it's therapeutic. Today evil is treated like an illness. If you are a criminal, it's because you had childhood problems, your parents didn't take care of you, society neglected you, etc. Your problem will be treated by doctors, by psychiatrists, by acupuncturists, by aromatherapy, in short, by all the therapies we have at our disposal today. That was what amused me: how to submit evil to all sorts of therapies derived from Buddhism, Hinduism, personal development, the primal scream, etc. It was more or less an encounter between Bluebeard and the Dalai Lama.

JK: And in *Le Palais des claques* (The palace of slaps), the ogre takes the form of the tyrant, doesn't it?

PB: Yes, he's the president of a small republic. This book was very successful in Eastern Europe, particularly in Romania: it was considered a metaphor for tyranny. The president is broke. He decides to forbid parents to beat their children at home, but he lets them do it on Saturdays and Sundays at the palace of slaps, for a fee. And all the children from two to twelve must spend time at the palace of slaps, as a kind of civic service. The palace consists of several floors: slaps on the first floor, spankings on the second, whipping on the third, and on the fourth there is the total machine, which delivers all the punishments at the same time, and leaves the children groggy and half-dead. It was staged at Avignon, Lyon, and Paris.

Yes, the tyrant is a kind of ogre, perhaps because he believes that his people belong to him, that he has the power of life and death over them. Look at Castro, Saddam Hussein, etc. The ogre, like the vampire, incarnates the phantasm of the creature who steals life. Devouring marks the fine line between love and hate, between the will to adore the other and the desire to suffocate him. When we love—even when we love a child—we say things like "I'm going to eat you," and then cover him with kisses. And this eagerness to love may also suffocate the child who longs to escape from our embrace.

JK: Michel Tournier once said that, according to doctors, death from a vampire's bite, in which one slowly loses all his blood, would resemble an orgasm: Thanatos disguised as Eros.

PB: It is interesting how close passionate love is to hate, and how one can want to possess the other so much as to destroy him or her. Nothing is more difficult than establishing boundaries between normal passion and insane passion. This is particularly true of perverted maternal or paternal attachments to children. This is where the theme of the ogre is interesting, because the ogre is not simply one who wants to do you harm; those who love you can hurt you, too. If those who love you are ogres, they prevent you from living, from growing, from going out. So we must set limits to love. Perhaps that is what ogres teach us: love is not necessarily good, it is dangerous when not balanced by other virtues; left to itself, it overwhelms a person to the point of annihilation.

Notes

INTRODUCTION

1. Citations of French authors are based on published translations, where available. Otherwise, translations from French sources are my own.

2. The notion of "devouring" is more satisfactorily expressed by the now obsolete "devoration" (from the French *dévoration*).

3. Danneels and Dezutter remark that the ogres in contemporary children's literature are rarely anthropophagous, and are generally much less violent than the monster in Perrault's "Little Tom Thumb." They conclude that most modern children only read about sterilized, "denatured" (Watthée-Delmotte 2002, 249) ogres, very different from the frightening, "uncanny" figure of traditional tales.

Bettelheim holds similar views on most children's literature, which he finds "so shallow in substance that little of significance can be gained from them" (1989, 4). These stories only present the sunny side of life, whereas the "fairy tale, by contrast, takes . . . existential anxieties and dilemmas very seriously and addresses itself directly to them: the need to be loved and the fear that one is thought worthless; the love of life, and the fear of death" (1989, 10).

4. Frye prefers "ironic mode" to the more common categories of realism and naturalism. The hero of ironic fiction is "inferior in power or intelligence to ourselves, so that we have the sense of looking down on a scene of bondage, frustration, or absurdity" (Frye 1957, 34). The ironic mode is the last of Frye's five more or less chronologically ordered fictional modes, the first four being myth (in which the hero is divine), romance (including legends and folktales), high mimetic (epics, tragedy), and low mimetic (some works of realism).

5. Gargantua has become the archetype for the "good" ogre, a giant with a giant appetite, a penchant for scatological jokes, and a good heart. Perrault's "Puss in Boots" and "Little Tom Thumb" tell of terrifying ogres who love to eat children. These monsters are paradoxically superhuman because they can change form, but dim-witted enough to be defeated by the children they covet. "Little Red Riding Hood" introduces the ravenous and dangerously seductive wolf, a double of the ogre, while "Bluebeard" warns young wives of the perils of undue curiosity. Jarry's Ubu, while primarily a buffoon, is also a bloodthirsty tyrant whose avatars will be the ogres of Nazism and Fascism. The ogre as tyrant also figures in Sartre's version of the Electra myth, where Jupiter is the defender of order and the enemy of freedom.

6. See Gilbert Durand's analysis of Zola's *The Kill* (*La Curée*) in *Figures mythiques* 258–65.

7. In *La Maison de Claudine,* Colette recounts how her father strictly forbade her to read Zola. She was grateful to her indulgent mother, who would secretly lend her only "certain" (1990, 35) Zola novels.

8. I analyze the links between Zola's naturalism and myth in "Nana: Still Life, *nature morte.*"

Chapter 1. Appetites

1. These characteristics obviously inscribe Zola in the Dionysian spirit. Raymond Geuss, in his introduction to Nietzsche's *The Birth of Tragedy*, describes the contrasting principles of Apollo and Dionysus:

> "Apollo" embodies the drive toward distinction, discreteness and individuality, toward the drawing and respecting of boundaries and limits; he teaches an ethic of moderation and self-control. ... The Dionysiac is the drive towards the transgression of limits, the dissolution of boundaries, the destruction of individuality, and excess. The purest artistic expression of the Dionysiac was quasi-orgiastic forms of music, especially of choral singing and dancing. (Geuss 1999, xi)

2. When Etienne first sees the mine, he describes it as a "pit" [*une fosse*]. The double meaning of *fosse* (pit or grave), along with the name of the mine—Le Voreux—reinforce its deadly, voracious nature.

3. As evidenced by the bracketed original French verbs, the English translation does not render Zola's metaphor of the devouring nature of social upheaval.

4. In "Tom Thumb Runs Away," Michel Tournier also invents a character named Logre. Tall and slim, this vegetarian hippy with a soprano voice is even more an "anti-ogre" than Zola's Logre.

5. The subjugation of the Thin by the Fat is also an important theme in Michel Tournier's writings, but for him the Thin are nomads (wanderers such as shepherds; also Gypsies and Jews), while the Fat are sedentary peoples (those who are tied to the land like farmers; and by extension landed aristocracy and even the German Nazis, who rallied around the cry of *Blut und Boden* [Blood and Soil]). For Tournier as for Zola, the murder of the shepherd Abel by the farmer Cain symbolizes the eternal conflict between these two races. Tournier's protagonist in *The Ogre*, appropriately named Abel, comes to realize that the persecution of the Jews and Gypsies by the Nazis is a reenactment of the primordial murder: "Here he encountered once more the immemorial hatred of the sedentary races for the nomads, now carried to its paroxysm. Jews and gypsies, wanderers, sons of Abel, the brothers he felt so close to in heart and soul, were falling in thousands at Auschwitz beneath the blows of a Cain who was booted, helmeted, and scientifically organized" (Tournier 1997b, 357).

6. The word ogress is appropriate because *Halle* (market), like *bête* (beast), is a feminine noun, which grammatically permits Zola's feminization of this monstrous space, an effect that is lost in the polite English translation of this passage. For example, the "swelling forms" that seem to surround Florent are, in Zola's words, "enormous breasts, monstrous hips" [*des gorges énormes, des reins monstrueux*].

7. Abel's last name is Tiffauges. Tournier borrowed the name from the property of Gilles de Rais (1404–40) in Vendée. This wealthy nobleman fought alongside Joan of Arc, and after her death he fell into the practice of alchemy, black magic, and satanism. Convicted of torturing and murdering hundreds of children, he is the historical basis for the Bluebeard legend, and the subject of Tournier's short novel *Gilles & Jeanne*.

8. The French text uses the German word *Unhold* to describe the blind elk. *Der Unhold* is the German equivalent of "ogre," and it is also the German title of Volker Schlöndorff's 1996 film version of *The Ogre*. Interestingly, *Unhold* negates—and is therefore bound up with—the adjective *hold*, meaning noble, gracious, lovely, and all the other good things a girl or young woman can be for a Romantic.

9. Even though the sex of the smaller figure cannot be determined, the archeologist insists that the two cadavers were probably man and wife. One might consider the ironic possibility, however, that what the scientist considered symbols of the "German soul" (Tournier 1997b, 188) were actually a homosexual couple, given the German tribal prac-

tice of drowning homosexuals in peat bogs. In the "biocracy" of the Third Reich, male homosexuality was criminalized, ostensibly because this "disease" would hinder the propagation of the Aryan race. In *Les Bienveillantes*, Jonathan Littell reports that the Reichsführer-SS Heinrich Himmler regretted the cessation of this lost custom, which he considered an efficient way of dealing with the homosexual "menace" (Littell 2006, 74). Himmler made this remark during a long speech on homosexuality in 1937 (Giles 2002, 263).

10. Zimmermann's novel clearly depicts the explicit role of the Vichy police in rounding up and deporting French Jews. René Bousquet, general secretary of the French police—and later a friend of former French president François Mitterrand—makes a brief appearance in the novel (Zimmermann 1997, 84). However, it is the fictional Drancy guard Van Neste, stinking of alcohol and cigarettes, who most vividly incarnates the brutality of the police. Whip in hand, "assaulting the weak who no longer have the strength to obey quickly enough" (1997, 59–60), the corrupt Frenchman is no less an ogre than his SS counterparts at Auschwitz. Exposing, as Zimmermann does, the guilt of French police and bureaucrats in the mass murder of tens of thousands of its citizens, is a key step to overcoming what historians call the "Vichy Syndrome" (Golsan 1998, 182–83, 193–95; Gordon, in Golsan 1998, 154). We will discuss this dilemma in chapter 5.

11. In his *Theogony*, Hesiod recounts the story of Cronus, leader of the first divine race, the Titans. Cronus (Saturn for the Romans) is told that one of his children will usurp his power; wishing to thwart the oracle, he eats each of his children as they are born. Only Zeus (the Roman Jupiter) is spared: his mother Rhea fools Cronus by giving him a stone in swaddling clothes to eat, telling him that it is Zeus. When Zeus grows up he does indeed overthrow his father and drives him from power. He gives Cronus a drug to make him regurgitate his five older brothers and sisters—Hestia, Demeter, Hera, Hades, and Poseidon—and together, after a long battle, they defeat Cronus and the other Titans. This is the beginning of the reign of the Olympians (*Larousse* 1996, 91; Hesiod 1993, *Theogony* l. 456–885).

12. The eighth circle of Dante's hell was divided into ten *bolgia*, stone ditches connected by arching bridges.

13. A kapo was one of the prisoners placed in charge of his colleagues in exchange for certain privileges. Zimmermann depicts many of the kapos as being as cruel—or crueler—than the SS, an image supported by Holocaust witnesses.

14. The Freud text the prisoner is referring to is *Totem and Taboo*. Freud describes as follows the ancient concept of the "totem meal":

> One day the brothers who had been driven out came together, killed and devoured their father and so made an end of the patriarchal horde. United, they had the courage to do and succeed in doing what would have been impossible for them individually. (Some cultural advance, perhaps, command over some new weapon, had given them a sense of superior strength). Cannibal savages as they were, it goes without saying that they devoured their victim as well as killing him. The violent primal father had doubtless been the feared and envied model of each one of the company of brothers: and in the act of devouring him they accomplished their identification with him, and each one acquired a portion of his strength. The totem meal, which is perhaps mankind's earliest festival, would thus be a repetition and a commemoration of this memorable and criminal deed, which was the beginning of so many things—of social organization, of moral restrictions and of religion. (Freud 1953–74, 13:141–42)

15. This ancient orthodox practice, *mezizah*, was mistakenly thought to sterilize the wound as it stopped the bleeding.

16. In citations of Detienne's book, I will retain spellings used by his translators, which transliterate the Greek rather than Latinize it.

17. Also citing Aristotle, Roberto Calasso remarks that blood sacrifices are required for gods who are anthropomorphic in all ways except that they have no need of human food (they drink nectar and eat ambrosia), and they have no blood in their veins. Blood sacrifices demonstrate the continuum between food, blood, and death: "The gods are immortal because they don't eat our food. They don't have blood because blood gets its nourishment from the food men eat. So food carries death within it, our dependence on death, which forces us to kill for more food, so as to keep death at bay. Though never for long" (Calasso 1993, 294).

18. The ancient Chinese also believed that the liver was the seat of courage, so they would eat the liver of their enemies (Chevalier 1982, 452).

19. See Matt. 8:28–34; Mark 5:1–20; Luke 8:26–39.

Chapter 2. The Ogre as Sexual Predator

1. In *Eléazar,* Michel Tournier describes the houses of poor Irish peasants in the 1840s, at the time of the potato famine: "[A] glance inside revealed the destitution of these people: a table and three wobbly chairs, a cauldron where the ubiquitous potatoes simmered, and, lying on the floor like some monstrous goddess of the house, a grunting sow surrounded by a cluster of children" (Tournier 2002a, 25). Remarkable are both the lofty status of the sow—which has born "children," not "piglets"—and her proximity to the family.

2. Roberto Calasso addresses the ambivalent, antithetical nature of myth in general. The complexities and contradictions of some stories are heightened by their numerous variants: "Myths are made up of actions that include their opposites within themselves. The hero kills the monster, but even as he does so we perceive that the opposite is also true: the monster kills the hero. . . . How can we be sure? The variants tell us. They keep the mythological blood in circulation" (Calasso 1993, 280–81).

3. Because of similarities in spelling and pronunciation, the Titan Cronus (Saturn in Roman mythology), who devoured his children, and Chronos, the personification of time, have long been merged into one. Thus it can be said that time, which devours our lives second by second, is one of the first ogres.

4. Durand comments that there are two phases in the Freudian stage of oral fixation: sucking precedes biting, and the latter is a much more negative action: "We have already suggested *à propos* of the ogre archetype that the traumatism of teething, an inevitable traumatism, painful and more brutal than weaning, reinforced the negativity of biting" (Durand 1984, 131).

5. Michel Tournier's "The Red Dwarf" provides another example of this type of inversion. Lucien, a dwarf, becomes the lover of Edith, dissatisfied with the sexual performance of her husband, whom the narrator describes as "a colossus" (Tournier 1984, 113). A tall, athletic woman, she "was enchanted to discover that such a small, misshapen body should be so fantastically equipped, and so delightfully efficacious. . . . His embrace sent her into ecstasies" (1984, 116).

6. The oral act of licking Catherine's blood recalls the Freudian concept of "incorporation," a feature of the oral stage of childhood, in which the child, because he or she has not yet learned that there are boundaries between the self and others, seeks to interiorize a loved object (Laplanche 1990, 200). Mauperthuis is mad because he carries a dead woman inside himself. He suffers from a pathological form of melancholy, a prolonged state of mind that Freud, in his 1917 essay "Mourning and Melancholia," describes as an unhealthy substitute for mourning, the latter a normal expression of grief that eventually comes to an end.

7. In the French version, "serpent eyes" are "yeux de Vouivre." The villagers believe in the reality of the Vouivre, a green-eyed snake-woman peculiar to Celtic legends surviving in eastern France (Franche-Comté, Burgundy, etc.). She haunts the lakes, ponds, and rivers of the forests. When foolhardy men attempt to steal the ruby from the crown of this Celtic Medusa, they are attacked and killed by the entourage of vipers that always follows her. See Marcel Aymé, *La Vouivre*.

8. In the cosmogony of the ancient Greeks, especially after the teachings of Empedocles, the universe was composed of four "roots": air, fire, water, and earth. The first two came to be associated with the masculine principle. Air and fire, light elements with a tendency to ascend, symbolized intellectual qualities, long considered the province of men. Water and earth, heavier, base elements, were thought of as feminine, and thus linked to fertility and reproduction. The French language reflects this ancient dichotomy: air and fire are masculine nouns, water and earth feminine.

9. "Saturnine" is one possible translation of *le ténébreux*, "the dark one." (In French, the first line of Nerval's poem reads: "Je suis le ténébreux,—le veuf,—l'inconsolé.") "Saturnine," rather than conjuring up the romantic picture of a mysterious dark stranger, emphasizes the gloomy state of mind of the poet. This rather learned adjective is consistent with the cosmic "black sun" metaphor that follows.

10. The image of the black sun is particularly striking in Georges Bataille's writings. In "The Solar Anus," written in 1927, Bataille names the black sun "the Jesuve," a cynical neologism that connotes both spirituality (Jesus) and violent, cosmic orgasm (Vesuvius):

> Love, then, screams in my own throat: I am the *Jesuve*, the filthy parody of the torrid and blinding sun.
> I want to have my throat slashed while violating the girl to whom I will have been able to say: you are the night.
> The Sun exclusively loves the Night and directs its luminous violence, its ignoble shaft, toward the earth, but finds itself incapable of reaching the gaze or the night, even though the nocturnal terrestrial expanses head continuously toward the indecency of the solar ray.
> The *solar annulus* is the intact anus of her body at eighteen years to which nothing sufficiently blinding can be compared except the sun, even though the *anus* is the *night*. (Bataille 1985, 9)

Ferdinand in *The Medusa Child* is a "Jesuvian" figure: outwardly a handsome solar hero, but inwardly a depraved, dark, and uncontrollable ogre. When Bataille conjures up images of Jesuve "violating the girl" or the sun raping the earth, he could be describing Ferdinand's crime against Lucie, who is, as we shall see shortly, a daughter of the earth.

11. The *Oxford English Dictionary* (see "Saturn" and "melancholy") informs us that a person born under the influence of Saturn is said to be gloomy and melancholy. Furthermore, the predominant Greek sense of melancholy is "anger," due to an excess of black bile. This is the ogreish temperament par excellence.

12. Turning once again to the *Oxford English Dictionary* (see "saturnine"), we learn that the toad was considered a saturnine animal. The song of Melchior, while it brings comfort to Lucie, nonetheless will reinforce her melancholy temperament.

13. In "Medusa's Head" (1922), Freud links the gaze of Medusa—which in this novel appears literally to frighten Ferdinand to death—to the "terror of castration" (Freud 1953–74, 18:273). The snakes of the Gorgon's head symbolize for a man the troubling "female genitals . . . surrounded by hair" (18:273). Freud reminds us that "[t]his symbol of horror is worn upon her dress by the virgin goddess Athene. And rightly so, for thus she becomes a woman who is unapproachable and repels all sexual desires" (18:273). Lucie is a violated *Athena parthenos* (Athena the virgin); her anorexia and her petrifying stare constitute a double shield to fend off her rapist.

14. The influence of Miller's *Tropic of Cancer*, which Cerf affirmed when I interviewed her on May 24, 2002, is apparent in the fluidity of her interior monologues, which correspond to a plethora of descriptions of bodily fluids. Some would brand her language and subject matter obscene. Like Miller's novel, Cerf's work is quite personal: "I only recount what I have lived" (Douin 2001).

15. A pareu is a Tahitian wraparound skirt.

16. Assurbanipal, sometimes identified with Sardanapalus, was the last king of ancient Assyria, and ruled during the seventh century BC. He is as famous for his love of books as for his brutality. Kali is the terrible Hindu mother and death goddess, often depicted encircled by skulls, smeared with blood, wielding a sword, and devouring human body parts. She is similar to the Sumerian and Babylonian goddess Ereshkigal, who narrates the hallucinatory tale "Between the Rivers" that concludes Cerf's collection.

17. Olivier's use of the "shadow" metaphor underscores her brutal assertion that the anorexic is on a course to death, and that she "has almost nothing human left" (Olivier 1998, 121).

18. Sexologists have unfortunately usurped the name of the gentle and innocent Ondine (played magnificently by a young Isabelle Adjani in a production of Giraudoux's *Ondine* by the Comédie Française in 1974) to refer to Cuori's favorite sexual practice with Nora. Ondinism, or urophilia, denotes finding sexual pleasure in urine, and guilt haunts Cuori for the rest of his life: "One day, the forbidden liquid will burn my tongue and my stomach, or perhaps suddenly poison me" (Cerf 1997b, 306).

19. Verena Kast opens her essay on "How Fairy Tales Deal with Evil" by stating: "The first thing that strikes us in investigating the question of evil is that fairy tales always show us that evil is not simply evil. Most characters can be both good and evil at the same time. For instance, wolves devour baby goats and grandmothers, but they can also be helpful" (Jacoby, Kast, Riedel 1992, 16). The ambivalence of mythic and fairy-tale figures concurs with Jung's descriptions of the anima and animus, which can be either benevolent or malefic (Jung et al. 1978, 186–207). For Massimo Cuori, Nora is both the eternal feminine and the femme fatale, even the devil himself: "This Lucifer who lived in her velvety body was, unmistakably, the most beautiful of angels" (Cerf 1997b, 385). In chapter 4 we will consider this aspect of Nora: the diminutive ogress who subjugates her lover.

20. In "Infantile Sexuality," Freud discusses the two stages of pregenital sexuality: "The first of these is the oral or, as it might be called, cannibalistic pregenital sexual organization. Here sexual activity has not yet been separated from the ingestion of food; nor are opposite currents within the activity differentiated. The *object* of both activities is the same; the sexual *aim* consists in the incorporation of the object. (Freud 1953–74, 7:198)

Earlier in the same essay, Freud refers to Lou Andreas-Salomé's research on anal eroticism: "The clear-cut distinction between anal and genital processes . . . is contradicted by the close anatomical and functional analogies and relations which hold between them. The genital apparatus remains the neighbour of the cloaca, and actually (to quote Lou Andreas-Salomé) in the case of women is only taken from it on lease" (7:187).

Chapter 3. Avatars of Cronus

1. In Greek, only the first letter differentiates the two figures. Cronus (also written "Kronos") begins with kappa (κ), and Chronos with chi (χ).

2. Zagreus is a Cretan god with whom Dionysus is identified in Orphic mysticism. He is the son of Zeus and Persephone, and sometimes called the "first Dionysus." He was a particular favorite of Zeus, and thus aroused Hera's jealousy. It is said that she was responsible for his murder by the Titans. (See *Larousse* 1996, 160; Grimal 1986, 477.

3. As we mentioned in chapter 1, Michel Tournier explores the fascinating relationship between the ogre and the saint in a short novel entitled *Gilles & Jeanne* (1983).

4. Frye cites Frazer's research on ritual murder of the kings. In *The Golden Bough*, Fraser gives numerous examples of this practice from both myth and history.

5. In "Plato's Pharmacy," Jacques Derrida remarks on the ambivalence of the Greek root *pharmako-* in Plato's dialogue on writing and rhetoric, the *Phaedrus*. Derrida notes the difficulty of translating *pharmakon*, commonly rendered as "remedy," but which could also designate "poison"(Derrida 2004, 99–101). Similarly, *pharmakos*, before it came to signify "scapegoat," could be translated as "wizard," "magician," or "poisoner" (2004, 133). The scapegoat retains this ambivalence: "The origin of difference and division, the *pharmakos* represents evil both introjected and projected. Beneficial insofar as he cures—and for that, venerated and cared for—harmful insofar as he incarnates the powers of evil—and for that, feared and treated with caution. Alarming and calming, sacred and accursed" (2004, 134).

6. Nestor affectionately refers to Abel as "M'Abel," short for "mon Abel" ("my Abel"). Homonym of "ma belle," Nestor's diminutive both establishes and destabilizes gender identity.

7. The strangeness of Abel's "sinister writings" recalls Freud's note in "The Uncanny" (1919) that "sinister" is one of the most common translations of "uncanny."

8. Alcibiades (450–404 BC) was an Athenian general, a favorite of Socrates, but haunted by accusations of scandal and sacrilege. Pontius Pilate (first century AD) was the Roman military governor of Judea who let Jesus be crucified; some say he later committed suicide. Caligula (12–41 AD) was a demented, murderous Roman emperor. Hadrian (76–138 AD), an extremely cultivated emperor of Rome, deified his favorite, the youth Antinoüs, after his death. Frederick William I of Prussia (1688–1740) was known for kidnapping tall men for his elite Potsdam Guard. Paul Barras (1755–1829), a French revolutionary credited with arresting Robespierre, was later exiled by Napoleon. Talleyrand (1754–1838) was the powerful, unscrupulous rival of Napoleon. Grigory Yefimovich Novykh (1872–1916) came to be known as Rasputin (the debauched one) because of his scandalous sexual exploits. He was counselor to Nicholas II, and seemed to have a mysterious healing power over the hemophiliac Alexis, heir to the Russian throne. *The Ogre* is dedicated to the "slandered memory" of Rasputin, "murdered for his opposition to the 1914 war" (Tournier 1997b).

9. In 1969, St. Christopher was dropped from the Catholic church's universal calendar of saints, since his saintly deeds, largely legendary, could not be authenticated.

10. In *The Wind Spirit,* Tournier explains that Goethe's Alder King "is trying to win the child's favor, and finally takes the boy from his father's arms and kills him" (1988, 97), much in the way Abel Tiffauges plucks little boys from their parents' arms and forces them to join the Nazi military school at Kaltenborn. The French title of *The Ogre, Le Roi des Aulnes,* is a literal translation of Goethe's "Erlkönig," meaning the king of the alders. The black alder thrives in European marshlands, like those of East Prussia where most of *The Ogre* takes place.

11. Marina Warner notes that the correlation between bearing children and bearing children away is a key element of the Cronus-Zeus myth. Like Tiffauges, Cronus is "a surrogate mother" (Warner 1999, 54), because the children he has swallowed are reborn from his belly when Zeus gives him an emetic. Zeus himself will twice become a bearer

of children. When told that he will be dethroned by any child of his first wife Metis, he swallows the goddess when she is pregnant; shortly thereafter, Athena, fully armed, is born from his head (*Larousse* 1996, 98, 108). When the mortal Semele is made pregnant by Zeus, a jealous Hera convinces Zeus to show himself to Semele in all his majesty. Semele is consumed by fire, so Zeus sews her premature son—little Dionysus—into his thigh, and brings him to term (1996, 157). These stories corroborate the close link between "ingestion and gestation" (Warner 1999, 65) or, as we noted in chapter 2 à propos of Freud, the symbolic proximity of the "digestive belly" and the "sexual belly."

12. This is one of the most unforgettable scenes in Volker Schlöndorff's 1996 film, *The Ogre*, starring John Malkovich as Abel Tiffauges. The movie ends as an exhausted Tiffauges bears the child—"so heavy"—through the marsh, away from the battle and into the setting sun. Schlöndorff brings to life the rich iconography of Christopher the Christ-Bearer, as Tiffauges, staff in hand, struggles through the water to save the child.

13. Tournier reflects on erotic photography in "L'Image érotique," a short text on Lewis Carroll and his passion for the little girls he photographed—or had photographed—in suggestive poses (and perhaps nude, although this is disputed). Photography, for the Victorian author and mathematician as well as for Tournier's fictional character, sublimates the sex act: "To possess the photo of one's object of desire gives great satisfaction, but it is much better to take this photo oneself, 'take' in photo (like one 'burns in effigy') the desired body" (Tournier 1979, 107). Like Tiffauges, Lewis Carroll keeps his predatory nature somewhat in check: "Eroticism? Certainly, but of the highest kind: eroticism-love, eroticism-passion, eroticism-tenderness that invests the entire life of a genius and crystallizes in a sublime work" (1979, 108).

14. This passage recalls the "ogre" of Patrick Süskind's remarkable 1985 novel *Perfume (Das Parfum)*. Gifted with an incomparable sense of smell, Jean-Baptiste Grenouille becomes morbidly obsessed with the scent of young virgins.

15. Rastenburg was Hitler's headquarters in East Prussia.

16. Morbier is a small town in the French Jura mountains, famous for its clocks.

17. Although Chessex does not mention it, Bern's "Ogre Fountain" personifies the anti-Semitic past of Western Europe. According to Bernese legend, the pointed hat of the ogre, and its earlier yellow color, identified it as a Jewish figure. In the Middle Ages, two Jews were blamed for the ritual murder of a Bernese boy; this death was a pretext to ban Jews from the city. Jean Calmet, a few days after his trip to Bern, and shortly before his suicide, visits the apartment of a neo-Nazi acquaintance, Mollendruz. Mesmerized by his rantings, and angry at Thérèse, Jean shouts "Dirty Jew!" (Chessex 1975, 183) at an old friend he later meets on the street. Jean is disgusted with himself, and realizes that he too is an ogre, hurting his friend and perpetuating an eternal hatred revived by the Nazis: "Oven-ogre, thought Jean Calmet. . . . Spineless vampire. Jean Calmet-ogre. And me out of revenge. What baseness" (1975, 191).

18. In 1900, in a chapter of *The Interpretation of Dreams* analyzing dreams of death wishes against siblings and parents, Freud wrote that "Zeus emasculated his father" (Freud 1953–74, 4:256). In 1909, he added a corrective footnote stating "[o]r so he is reported to have done according to some myths."

19. Susanna Lee compares the "spectacle" of the department store as recounted by Zola in 1883 and Pennac in 1985. The former enthusiastically displays a "reverence for consumerism and conspicuous consumption" (Lee 2003, 46). For the latter, situating the ritual murders of Jewish children in the store recalls "the atrocities of the Holocaust" (2003, 47); what was once the epitome of capitalistic vitality has degenerated into a derisive symbol of the chaos, disorder, and brutality of the twentieth century.

20. See *Totem and Taboo* (Freud 1953–74, 13:141–42; cited above in chapter 1,

n14), and Girard, *The Scapegoat*. After analyzing the myths of the murders of Remus and later Romulus, Girard writes that it was not just Rome that was built on a crime: "The foundation and structure of every community is based on violence that is and should have remained destructive at its very essence, but by some miracle the community has been able to *ward off* this violence which, for the time being, has become constructive and has achieved a means of reconciliation through some divinely bestowed reprieve" (Girard 1986, 94).

21. "Orgy" and "orgiasm," in Maffesoli's texts, are not always charged with sexual meaning. The *Oxford English Dictionary*'s first definition of "orgy" refers to secret rites practiced in the worship of Dionysus, "celebrated with extravagant dancing, singing, drinking, etc." In modern usage, it may of course refer to group sex, but it may also be "excessive indulgence in any activity." Maffesoli's translator is careful to explain his double use of "orgiasm,"

> referring to both the celebration of orgies and a state of excited or exalted feeling which should not be confused with orgasm. One sees here the slide of meaning, rooted in the word orgy, that encompasses both the corporal elements of sexuality and the psycho-sexual drive apparent in emotional outburst. Just as one may speak of orgies in reference to events other than group sex, one may speak of orgiasm in reference to elation not directly caused by physical sexuality. (Maffesoli 1993, xvii)

That said, it is impossible not to think of the Marquis de Sade when orgies are the subject. In the violent group sex scenes of works like *The 120 Days of Sodom* (written in 1785; not published until 1904) and *Philosophy in the Bedroom* (1795), Sade's libertines, like Pennac's ogres, live entirely in the present; that is, in the constant repetition of rigorously organized sexual pleasures. Timo Airaksinen explains the cyclical nature of time in Sade: "Sadean time entails circularity. The circles are small but numerous, and time is a set of small circles of real life. Every pleasure is independent of any other pleasure, and after a discharge the person returns to the point from which he started. He achieves nothing, simply because he cannot add more pleasures to the pool of them which he already possesses" (Airaksinen 1995, 84–85).

22. It is difficult to comprehend the enormity of the massacre committed against Ukrainian Jews by the Nazis. An exhibition at the Memorial of the Shoah in Paris estimated that 1.5 million perished between 1941 and 1944, including over 33,000 in just two days at Babi Yar in Kiev ("Les Fusillades" 2007–8). *The Holocaust Encyclopedia* confirms the number of deaths at Babi Yar, but estimates the total death toll of Ukrainian Jews at about 700,000, stating that "[t]he scope of the mass executions and the speed with which they were carried out . . . make it nearly impossible to determine with accuracy the number of victims" (Tzur 2001, 652).

The ferocity of the Ukrainian genocide is also recounted in Jonathan Littell's massive novel, *Les Bienveillantes* (Prix Goncourt 2006). After observing the executions of thousands of Jews, their corpses piling up higher and higher in the Babi Yar ravine, the narrator (an SS officer) comes to realize that the Nazis have invented an evil greater than war itself, heretofore considered the greatest evil possible: "Even the insane butchery of the Great War, which our fathers or some of our older officers had experienced, seemed almost clean and just compared to what we had introduced to the world. I found that extraordinary. It seemed to me that there was something crucial in that thought, and if I could understand it I could understand everything and finally be at peace" (Littell 2006, 127).

23. The Vercors plateau was an Alpine base of the French Resistance during World War II, perhaps one reason that Paul is drawn to the region. It is just west of the Trièves, the setting of Giono's *Un Roi sans divertissement* [A king without distractions], and

north of the author's native Manosque. In Giono's novel, two men—a murderer and the policeman who pursues him—are driven to violence by the fatal boredom imposed by a long, snowy winter, and also, like modern avatars of Chrétien de Troyes's Perceval, by their fascination with the sight of blood on the snow. *Un Roi sans divertissement* explores the natural cruelty of human beings, which Giono symbolizes by the voracious appetites of his characters, and also by the ravenous wolves that roam the mountains.

24. The *Oxford English Dictionary*'s article "malevolent" (astrological meaning) quotes the seventeenth-century Welsh author James Howell: "Saturne that dull and malevolent planet."

25. Michel Tournier and Jonathan Littell also strikingly convey the victimization of children by the ogre war. *The Ogre* ends with the massacre by the Russian army of the young students of Kaltenborn military school. These children, for the narrator, are proof of "the fundamental affinity that exists between war and boys" (Tournier 1997b, 291). War is adults acting like children; men who have forgotten how to play playing with deadly toys. Boys who not long ago carried around their toys are now carried by adult toys like tanks and planes. A perverse version of phoria, Tiffauges describes warring children as "the overturning of phoria by malign inversion" (1997b, 292).

Like Péju, the narrator of *Les Bienveillantes* describes war as a twisted and lethal fairy tale: "So was that war, a perverted fairy world, the playground of an insane child who breaks his toys while he screams with laughter, who gleefully throws the dishes out the window?" (Littell 2006, 127).

CHAPTER 4. DARK SIDE OF APHRODITE

Portions of this chapter are based on a previously published article: "The Dark Side of Aphrodite: the Ogress in the Fiction of Michel Tournier and Jacques Chessex." *Hermes and Aphrodite Encounters.* Edited by Metka Zupancic. Birmingham: Summa Publications, 2004. 99–108. Reprinted by permission of the publisher.

1. For Simone de Beauvoir, the alleged magical power of woman "reflects the most ancient and universal of myths," and helps entrench her as the Other, forever the adversary of man: "[S]he is not subject, transcendence, creative power, but an object charged with fluids. In the societies where man worships these mysteries, woman, on account of these powers, is associated with religion and venerated as priestess; but when man struggles to make society triumph over nature, reason over life, and the will over the inert, given nature of things, then woman is regarded as a sorceress" (Beauvoir 1953, 164).

2. In Balzac's short story "A Passion in the Desert," a French soldier wandering in the Egyptian desert—a magical place he calls "God without man" (Balzac 1985, 15)—apparently falls under the charm of Dionysus and Aphrodite. He falls in love with a panther, and this "beauty of the desert" (1985, 14) returns his love. The narrator explains, however, that this exotic and wonderful affair "ended as all great passions end," poisoned by "falsity," "obstinacy," and pride (1985, 15): through a "misunderstanding" (1985, 15), the soldier kills the animal with his dagger. In Balzac's story, as in Chessex's, the male lover proves to be unworthy of his "Cat Girl," and unable to rise to the heights of the "spirit of Dionysus."

3. As preposterous as this idea might seem to the modern reader, Tournier, in an essay on photography, *Le Crépuscule des masques,* reports that Balzac, who posed for the great photographer Nadar in 1842, espoused a strange and terrifying theory of photography. He believed that all bodies in nature are made up of infinite layers of specters,

and that each photograph literally attacks the body, peeling off and transferring to the photographic plate the outermost layer (Tournier 1992, 28).

4. In a chapter of *Le Crépuscule des masques* dedicated to women photographers, Tournier blithely declares that Saint Veronica is the true inventor of the photographic image (1992, 172).

5. This maneuver is named after the saint, because the matador's cape, likened to Veronica's veil, almost grazes the bull's head. The *Oxford English Dictionary* explains that the matador, holding his cape in two hands, is said to resemble Veronica, as she is depicted holding her veil out to Jesus.

6. "Vésale." *Le Petit Robert: Dictionnaire universel des noms propres.* 1994 ed.

7. Hesiod describes the three Moerae, or Fates, who control the destiny of the individual. Death occurs when the Moerae cut the thread of life (*Larousse* 1996, 163; Hesiod 1993, *Theogony* l. 217–22).

8. It is called, for example, "the moment of the moon" in French folklore, and "the lunar sickness" in the Maori culture (Durand 1984, 112).

9. Beauvoir writes that menstrual blood is said to harm organic substances especially. Not surprisingly, French folklore warns to keep it out of the kitchen, where it will turn sugar black, make bacon spoil, prevent cider from fermenting, and, most insidiously, doom a mayonnaise to failure (Beauvoir 1953, 149).

10. Among the examples that Durand cites are the Polynesians, where the word *tabu* is related to *tapa*, or menses. Closer to our own tradition, *Leviticus* "teaches us that menstrual blood is impure, and prescribes in great detail the conduct that must be followed during the menstrual period" (Durand 1984, 119).

In "Menstrual Taboos," Elisa J. Sobo gives an account of the power of "menstrual magic" (Sobo 1997, 145) in rural Jamaica. It is believed that women may "tie" men to them, "and thus secure men's love and money" (1997, 154), by putting menstrual blood in their food. A reddish brown dish of rice and red beans is the food most commonly used for tying. This shared blood creates a lifelong bond between the man and the woman of the kind that an unborn child has with its mother. Jamaican men are thus strong supporters of a complex set of menstrual taboos, one of which requires menstruants to keep away from men's food (1997, 156).

11. See Cowen for references to several studies that refute the biological connection between women and crime. Other researchers arriving at the same conclusion include Horney (1978) and Harry and Balcer (1987). Neither article finds evidence to link menstrual cycles and crime; moreover, Horney argues that menstrual cycles—which some lawyers have tried to use to expand the insanity defense—do not diminish criminal responsibility.

12. They first met at a New Year's party in Munich, when Nora was twelve, and Massimo twenty-three. Massimo was struck by the girl's smile, her insolence, and her gourmandise (Cerf 1997b, 106).

13. Bettelheim maintains that the witch who longs to devour Hansel and Gretel represents the "threatening mother," "personification of the destructive aspects of orality" (Bettelheim 1989, 162). The children eating the gingerbread house prove the danger of "unrestrained giving in to gluttony" (1989, 161). Nora's oral obsessions are predictable, given the ogreish nature of her mother.

14. Kleptomania is a form of "sexual sublimation," according to Beauvoir (1953, 355), and a common habit of the demoniac teen.

15. In *Life Against Death*, Norman O. Brown states that our incapacity to accept "the unity of life and death" is at the source of human neurosis (Brown 1985, 175). That Freud's two instincts are more brothers than enemies is illustrated by the confusion regarding the Nirvana principle. Freud postulates that the Nirvana principle, which

aims at rest, inactivity, or sleep, belongs to the death instinct, since it is a condition of stasis, in which desire is extinguished. Brown points out, however, that Nirvana is more properly considered a part of the life instinct and the pleasure principle, since it describes a profound contentment, "a balanced equilibrium between tension and tension release" (1985, 90).

Chapter 5. Conclusion

1. "The Dance of the Ogres"
   For the most part we prefer nice fresh flesh
   Especially that of little children
   The life that crunches under the tooth
   And moans lingeringly in the stomach

   But there are some who prefer the cadaver
   Especially after it has nicely bled
   And one must admit that there are excellent recipes
   Seasoned with the panic of bombed airports and hospitals

   And some with refined tastes search for carrion
   Especially if while alive it had been worked on
   By some especially ingenious kinds of germs
   From radioactive emissions or rare poisons
   That leave an exquisite after-taste of horror
   That they lick from their lips[.] (Butor 1986)

2. The French noun *monstre* (monster) and verb *montrer* (to show) both derive from the Latin *monstrarer* (to show) and *monstrum* (prodigy). Jacques Derrida remarks that the monster frightens in part because it shows itself as something new, unnatural, unrecognizable. "But as soon as one perceives a monster in a monster, one begins to domesticate it, one begins . . . to compare it to the norms, to analyze it, consequently to master whatever could be terrifying in this figure of the monster" (Derrida 1995, 386).

3. Jean Burgos devotes several pages to the symbol of the dragon, and reminds us that, although it is often an evil obstacle that the hero must overcome, the dragon also performs a service by guarding the treasures of the gods (Burgos 1975, 22).

4. Paul Touvier, after a difficult investigation that lasted decades and at times seemed almost farcical—it featured a pardon by President Georges Pompidou in 1971, and staunch defense by important members of the Catholic Church hierarchy—was finally found guilty of crimes against humanity in April 1994. In Chambéry, he had been a commander of the Vichy paramilitary militia. He was specifically charged with ordering the murders of seven Jewish hostages at the cemetery of Rillieux-la-Pape, near Lyon. Richard Golsan recounts Touvier's story in "History and the Responsibility of Memory" (1998).

Maurice Papon held important government posts from the late 1950s to the early 1980s, including prefect of the Paris police and minister of finance. During the war he had been a Vichy functionary in Bordeaux (Golsan 1998, introduction 9–10). First accused in 1983 of crimes against humanity for his part in rounding up and deporting hundreds of Bordeaux Jews, he was finally brought to trial and convicted in 1998.

5. Bousquet was awaiting trial for crimes against humanity when he was assassinated in his Paris apartment in 1993 (Golsan 1998, "History and the Responsibility of Memory" 194; Gordon, in Golsan 1998, 158).

6. Muriel Cerf's Cuori and Jacques Chessex's Calmet certainly reflect this attitude. Both fancy themselves victims of young, ruthless ogresses.

7. See, for example, the following two essays: (1) Mariana, Jessica. *Une Guerre contre les femmes?: Femmes et enfants, même souffrance.* Le Kremlin-Bicêtre: Les points sur les i, 2006; (2) Blaise, Suzanne. "Une guerre contre les femmes ou Assez d'hypocrisie." *Femmes et violences dans le monde.* Edited by Michèle Dayras. Paris: L'Harmattan, 1995.

8. Literature on the history of sex and sexual violence abounds with references to secrets. For example, Bruno Bettelheim maintains that fairy tales help children "transcend infancy" (Bettelheim 1989, 123) by suggesting ways of overcoming the Oedipal conflict. The riddle of the Sphinx involved "sexual knowledge" (1989, 128) for Oedipus, as it does for all children: "To a child the greatest riddle is what sex consists of; that is the secret of adults which he wishes to discover" (1989, 128).

Foucault comments on the great paradox of sex, the repressed secret that we are never able to talk about enough: "What is peculiar to modern societies, in fact, is not that they consigned sex to a shadowy existence, but that they dedicated themselves to speaking of it *ad infinitum,* while exploiting it as *the* secret" (Foucault 1990, 35).

Finally, Thierry Petitot, in his book on pedophiles in the classroom, states that students may be attracted to their teacher because "knowledge is charged with an erotic power. The teacher in front of his class is the one who knows the Secret, and he could share this Secret" (Petitot 2007, 71).

Appendix

This is a translation of two interviews previously published in French: "Les Résurgences de l'ogre dans la littérature contemporaine: entretiens avec Michel Tournier et Pascal Bruckner." Héroïsation et questionnement identitaire en Occident: Héroïsation/antihéroïsation—civilisation/barbarie. *Cahiers électroniques de l'imaginaire* 2 (2005), 155–66. http://www.e-montaigne.com/. Reprinted by permission of the publisher.

1. In France, the children's game Blind Man's Bluff is called Colin-Maillard.

Bibliography

Aeschylus. *Prometheus Bound.* 5th century BC. *Aeschylus II.* Edited by David Grene and Richmond Lattimore. New York: Washington Square, 1967.

Airaksinen, Timo. The Philosophy of the Marquis De Sade. London: Routledge, 1995.

Arendt, Hannah. *The Origins of Totalitarianism.* 1951. New York: Harcourt, Brace & World, 1966.

Audeguy, Stéphane. *Fils unique.* Paris: Gallimard-Folio, 2006.

Aymé, Marcel. *La Vouivre.* Paris: Gallimard, 1943.

Bachelard, Gaston. *L'Eau et les rêves: Essai sur l'imagination de la matière.* Paris: José Corti, 1942.

———. *La Terre et les rêveries du repos: Essai sur les images de l'intimité.* Paris: José Corti, 1948.

Balzac, Honoré de. "A Passion in the Desert." Gloucester: Alan Sutton, 1985. Translation of "Une Passion dans le désert." (1830. Colomars: Mélis, 2001).

Bataille, Georges. *Visions of Excess: Selected Writings, 1927–1939.* Edited by Allan Stoekl. Translated by Allan Stoekl, et al. Minneapolis: University of Minnesota Press, 1985.

Baudelaire, Charles. *Mon coeur mis à nu. Oeuvres complètes.* Edited by Marcel Ruff. Paris: Seuil, 1968, 622–42.

Beauvoir, Simone de. *The Second Sex.* Edited and translated by H. M. Parshley. New York: Alfred A. Knopf, 1953. Translation of *Le Deuxième Sexe.* Paris: Gallimard, 1949.

Bettelheim, Bruno. *The Uses of Enchantment: The Meaning and Importance of Fairy Tales.* 1976. New York: Vintage, 1989.

Bond, David J. "Jacques Chessex: The Ogre Within." *The International Fiction Review* 16, no. 2 (1989): 109–12.

Bouloumié, Arlette. *Michel Tournier: Le Roman mythologique.* Paris: José Corti, 1988a.

———. "Le mythe de l'ogre dans la littérature." *L'Ecole des lettres II* 13 (1985–86): 27–40.

———. "L'ogre dans la littérature." *Dictionnaire des mythes littéraires.* Edited by Pierre Brunel. Paris: Rocher, 1988b. 1071–86.

———, ed. *Recherches sur l'imaginaire, Cahier 26: Les Mythes de l'ogre et de l'androgyne.* Angers: Presses Universitaires d'Angers, 1996.

Bourbonnais, Nicole, et al. *Incidences 2–3: Analyse plurielle, "Les suaires de Véronique" de Michel Tournier.* Ottawa: Editions de l'Université d'Ottawa, 1979.

Brown, Norman O. *Life Against Death: The Psychoanalytical Meaning of History.* 1959. 2nd ed. Hanover: University Press of New England, 1985.

Bruckner, Pascal. *Les Ogres anonymes, suivi de L'Effaceur: Deux Contes.* Paris: Grasset & Fasquelle, 1998.

――. *The Temptation of Innocence: Living in the Age of Entitlement*. New York: Algora, 2000. Translation of *La Tentation de l'innocence*. Paris: Grasset & Fasquelle, 1995.

――. *Les Voleurs de beauté*. Paris: Grasset & Fasquelle, 1997.

Burgos, Jean. "Le Monstre, même et autre." *Le Monstre (1): Présence du monstre—mythe et réalité*. Edited by Jean Burgos. Paris: Lettres Modernes, 1975. 11–24.

Butor, Michel. *Danse des ogres*. Bois gravé de Gérard Blanchet. Lyon: Galérie Alma, 1986.

――. "L'espace du roman." *Essais sur le roman*. Paris: Gallimard, 1964.

Caillaud, Claire. "L'Ogre en littérature: Figure de l'Autre, peur du Moi." *Textes et documents pour la classe* 791 (March 2000): 6–17.

Calasso, Roberto. *The Marriage of Cadmus and Harmony*. 1988. Translated by Tim Parks. New York: Knopf, 1993.

Campbell, Joseph. *The Masks of God, Vol 3: Occidental Mythology*. New York: Arkana, 1964.

Cazenave, Michel, ed. *Encyclopédie des symboles*. Paris: Librairie Générale Française, 1996.

Cerf, Muriel. *Ogres et autres contes*. Arles: Actes Sud, 1997a.

――. *Le Verrou*. Arles: Actes Sud, 1997b.

Chessex, Jacques. *A Father's Love*. Translated by Martin Sokolinsky. New York: Bobbs-Merril, 1975. Translation of *L'Ogre*. Paris: Grasset, 1973.

Chevalier, Jean, and Alain Gheerbrant, eds. *Dictionnaire des symboles*. 1969. Paris: Laffont et Jupiter, 1982.

Clot, René-Jean. *Le Miroir de l'ogre: Nouvelles*. Lausanne: L'Age d'Homme, 1987.

Colette. *La Maison de Claudine*. 1930. Paris: Librairie Générale Française, 1990.

Corbin, Alain, ed. *Violences sexuelles*. Paris: Imago, 1989.

Cowen, Barbara. "Women and Crime." *Violence and the Prevention of Violence*. Edited by Leonore Loeb Adler and Florence L. Denmark. Westport, CT: Praeger, 1995. 157–168.

Danneels, Pascaline, and Olivier Dezutter. "Des ogres (mal)traités dans la littérature de jeunesse contemporaine." Watthée-Delmotte 239–49.

Depaulis, Jean-Jacques and Pascal Marchaud. *Le Dernier Secret de Jacques Chirac*. Paris: Editions du Moment, 2007.

Derrida, Jacques. *Of Grammatology*. Translated by Gayatri Spivak. Baltimore: Johns Hopkins University Press, 1976. Translation of *De la Grammatologie*. Paris: Minuit, 1967.

――. "Plato's Pharmacy." *Dissemination*. Translated by Barbara Johnson. London: Continuum, 2004. 67–186. Translation of *La Dissémination*. Paris: Seuil, 1972.

――. *Points . . . : Interviews 1974–1994*. Edited by Elisabeth Weber. Translated by Peggy Kamuf et al. Stanford: Stanford University Press, 1995.

Detienne, Marcel. *Dionysos mis à mort*. 1977. Paris: Gallimard, 1998.

Douin, Jean-Luc. "Muriel Cerf, passion et réclusion." *Le Monde* [Paris] November 2, 2001: III.

Durand, Gilbert. *Figures mythiques et visages de l'oeuvre: De la mythocritique à la mythanalyse*. 1979. Paris: Dunod, 1992.

――. *L'Imaginaire: Essai sur les sciences et la philosophie de l'image*. Paris: Hatier, 1994.

———. *Les Structures anthropologiques de l'imaginaire*. 1960. 10th ed. Paris: Bordas, 1984.

Eliade, Mircea. *Aspects du mythe*. Paris: Gallimard-Folio, 1963.

———. *Mythes, rêves et mystères*. Paris: Gallimard-Idées, 1957.

Empedocles. *The Extant Fragments*. 5th century BC. Edited by M. R. Wright. London: Gerald Duckworth, 1995.

Euripides. *The Bacchae*. 405 BC. Translated by William Arrowsmith. *Euripides V.* Edited by David Grene and Richmond Lattimore. New York: Washington Square Press, 1968. 145–228.

———. *The Medea*. 431 BC Translated by Rex Warner. *Euripides I.* Edited by David Grene and Richmond Lattimore. New York: Washington Square Press, 1967. 59–117.

Fleutiaux, Pierrette. "La femme de l'Ogre." *Métamorphoses de la reine*. Paris: Gallimard-Folio, 1984. 15–49.

———. "Préface." *Métamorphoses de la reine*. Paris: Gallimard-Folio, 1984. 9–12.

Foucault, Michel. *The History of Sexuality*. Translated by Robert Hurley. Vol. 1. New York: Vintage, 1990. Translation of *Histoire de la sexualité*. Vol. 1. Paris: Gallimard, 1976.

Freud, Sigmund. *The Standard Edition of the Complete Psychological Works of Sigmund Freud*. Edited and translated by James Strachey et al. 24 vols. London: Hogarth, 1953–74.

Frye, Northrop. *Anatomy of Criticism: Four Essays*. Princeton: Princeton University Press, 1957.

"Les Fusillades massives des Juifs en Ukraine, 1941–1944: La Shoah par balles." Exhibition Brochure. Musée de la Shoah, Paris. June 20, 2007–January 6, 2008.

Germain, Sylvie. *Days of Anger*. Translated by Christine Donougher. Sawtry, Cambs: Dedalus, 1993. Translation of *Jours de colère*. Paris: Gallimard, 1989.

———. *The Medusa Child*. Translated by Liz Nash. Sawtry, Cambs: Dedalus, 1994. Translation of *L'Enfant Méduse*. Paris: Gallimard, 1991.

Geuss, Raymond. Introduction. Nietzsche, *The Birth of Tragedy* vii–xxx.

Giles, Geoffrey J. "The Denial of Homosexuality: Same-Sex Incidents in Himmler's SS and Police." *Sexuality and German Fascism*. Edited by Barbara Loomis and William N. Bonds. Spec. issue of *Journal of the History of Sexuality* 11, nos. 1–2 (2002): 256–90.

Girard, René. *The Scapegoat*. Translated by Yvonne Freccero. Baltimore: Johns Hopkins University Press, 1986. Translation of *Le Bouc émisssaire*. Paris: Grasset & Fasquelle, 1982.

———. *Violence and the Sacred*. Translated by Patrick Gregory. Baltimore: Johns Hopkins University Press, 1979. Translation of *La Violence et le sacré*. Paris: Grasset, 1972.

Godo, Emmanuel. "Une violente utopie, *Le Roi des Aulnes* de Michel Tournier." Watthée-Delmotte 287–303.

Golsan, Richard J., ed. *Fascism's Return: Scandal, Revision, and Ideology Since 1980*. Lincoln: University of Nebraska Press, 1998.

———. "History and the Responsibility of Memory: *Vichy: Un Passé qui ne passe pas* and the Trial of Paul Touvier." Golsan, *Fascism's Return* 182–99.

———. "Introduction." Golsan, *Fascism's Return* 1–18.

Gopnik, Adam. *Paris to the Moon*. New York: Random House, 2000.

———. "Two Cooks." *The New Yorker.* September 5, 2005: 91–98.
Gordon, Bertram M. "World War II France Half a Century Later." Golsan, *Fascism's Return* 152–81.
Graves, Robert. *New Collected Poems.* Garden City: Doubleday, 1977.
Grimal, Pierre. *Dictionnaire de la mythologie grecque et romaine.* 1951. Paris: Presses Universitaires de France, 1986.
Guillemin, Henri. Préface. Zola, *Le Ventre de Paris* 9–27.
Guiol, Elsa. *Tous Pédophiles?*. Paris: La Martinière, 2005.
Harry, Bruce, and Charlotte M. Balcer. "Menstruation and crime: A critical review of the literature from the clinical criminology perspective." *Behavioral Sciences & the Law* 5, no. 3 (1987): 307–21.
Hecker, Jurgen. "Prison Cannibal Attack Chills France to the Bone." *Agence France Presse* January 7, 2007.
Heers, Jacques. *Gilles de Rais.* Paris: Perrin, 1994.
Hesiod. *Works and Days and Theogony.* 8th century BC. Translated by Stanley Lombardo. Indianapolis: Hackett, 1993.
Hirigoyen, Marie-France. *Femmes sous emprise: Les ressorts de la violence dans le couple.* Paris: Noyelles, 2005.
Horney, Julie. "Menstrual Cycles and Criminal Responsibility." *Law and Human Behavior* 2, no. 1 (1978): 25–36.
Huet, Marie-Hélène. *Monstrous Imagination.* Cambridge: Harvard University Press, 1993.
Jacoby, Mario. "C. G. Jung's View of Fairy Tale Interpretation: General Reflections on Hermeneutics in Depth Psychology." Jacoby, Kast, Riedel 3–15.
Jacoby, Mario, Verena Kast, Ingrid Riedel. *Witches, Ogres, and the Devil's Daughter: Encounters with Evil in Fairy Tales.* 1978. Translated by Michael H. Kohn. Boston: Shambhala, 1992.
Jaton, Anne Marie. *Jacques Chessex: la lumière de l'obscur.* Geneva: Editions Zoé, 2001.
Josephus, Flavius. *The Wars of the Jews.* C. 75 AD. *The Works of Josephus.* Translated by William Whiston. Peabody, MA: Hendrickson Publishers, 1987. 543–772.
Juffé, Michel. *Les Fondements du lien social: le justicier, le sage et l'ogre.* Paris: Presses Universitaires de France, 1995.
Jung, C. G., et al. *Man and His Symbols.* 1964. London: Pan, 1978.
Kast, Verena. "*Bluebeard:* On the Problem of the Destructive Animus." Jacoby, Kast, Riedel 86–104.
———. "How Fairy Tales Deal with Evil: Thematic Approaches to the Fairy Tale as a Dynamic Process." Jacoby, Kast, Riedel 16–39.
Knapp, Bettina L. *Pierrette Fleutiaux.* Atlanta: Rodopi, 1997.
Krell, Jonathan F. "The Dark Side of Aphrodite: the Ogress in the Fiction of Michel Tournier and Jacques Chessex." *Hermes and Aphrodite Encounters.* Edited by Metka Zupancic. Birmingham: Summa Publications, 2004. 99–108.
———. "Nana: Still Life, *Nature Morte.*" *French Forum* 19, no. 1 (1994a): 65–79. Reprinted in *Bloom's Modern Critical Views: Emile Zola.* Edited and with an introduction by Harold Bloom. Philadelphia: Chelsea House, 2004. 83–97.
———. "L'ogre réécrit, l'ogre réhabilité." *Cahiers de l'Imaginaire 16: Esthétique, littérature et modernité.* Paris: L'Harmattan, 1998. 15–20.
———. "Les ogres de la littérature française contemporaine: Tournier, Chessex, Pen-

nac." *Mythes dans la littérature contemporaine d'expression française.* Edited by Metka Zupančič. Ottawa: Editions du Nordir, 1994b. 247–55.

———. "Les Résurgences de l'ogre dans la littérature contemporaine: entretiens avec Michel Tournier et Pascal Bruckner." *Héroïsation et questionnement identitaire en Occident: Héroïsation/antihéroïsation–civilisation/barbarie. Cahiers électroniques de l'imaginaire* 2 (2005). 155–66. http://www.e-montaigne.com

———. *Tournier élémentaire.* West Lafayette, IN: Purdue University Press, 1994c.

Kristeva, Julia. *Black Sun: Depression and Melancholia.* Translated by Leon S. Roudiez. New York: Columbia University Press, 1989. Translation of *Soleil noir: Dépression et mélancolie.* Paris: Gallimard, 1987.

Laplanche, Jean, and J.-B. Pontalis. *Vocabulaire de la psychanalyse.* 1967. 10th ed. Paris: Presses Universitaires de France, 1990.

The Larousse Encyclopedia of Mythology. Translated by Richard Aldrington and Delano Ames. London: Chancellor Press, 1996.

Lee, Susanna. "*Au Bonheur des ogres* and *Au Bonheur des dames:* The Dismantling of Foundations in the *Série noire.*" *Dalhousie French Studies* 63 (2003): 45–52.

Lévy, Bernard-Henri. *La Barbarie à visage humain.* Paris: Grasset & Fasquelle, 1977.

Littell, Jonathan. *Les Bienveillantes.* Paris: Gallimard, 2006.

Lopez, Gérard. *Les Violences sexuelles sur les enfants.* Paris: Presses Universitaires de France, 1999.

Macé, Gérard. *Le Goût de l'homme.* Paris: Gallimard, 2002.

Maffesoli, Michel. *Essais sur la violence banale et fondatrice.* Paris: Méridiens-Klincksieck, 1984.

———. *Du Nomadisme.* Paris: Librairie Générale Française, 1997.

———. *The Shadow of Dionysus: A Contribution to the Sociology of the Orgy.* Translated by Cindy Linse and Mary Kristina Palmquist. Albany: State University of New York Press, 1993. Translation of *L'Ombre de Dionysos: Contribution à une sociologie de l'orgie.* Paris: Méridiens-Klincksieck, 1985.

———. *Le Temps des tribus: le déclin de l'individualisme dans les sociétés de masse.* Paris: Méridiens-Klincksieck, 1988.

———. *La Violence totalitaire: Essai d'anthropologie politique.* Paris: Presses Universitaires de France, 1979.

Mitterand, Henri. "Notice." Zola, *Le Ventre de Paris* 443–58.

Monès, Philippe de. "Abel Tiffauges et la vocation maternelle de l'homme." Postface. Tournier, *Le Roi des Aulnes* 585–600.

Morel, Geneviève. *Les Tueuses d'enfants ("L'ogresse" Jeanne Weber): Etude psychopathologique et médico-légale.* Nancy: Faculté de Médecine de l'Université de Nancy, 1927.

Narjoux, Cécile. "L'écriture des commencements de Sylvie Germain ou le lyrisme 'au bord extrême du rêve'." *Roman 20–50* 39 (2005): 73–84.

Neumann, Erich. *The Great Mother: An Analysis of the Archetype.* Translated by Ralph Mannheim. New York: Pantheon, 1955.

Nietzsche, Friedrich. *The Birth of Tragedy.* 1872. Edited by Raymond Geuss and Ronald Speirs. Translated by Ronald Speirs. Cambridge: Cambridge University Press, 1999.

———. *Twilight of the Idols.* 1888. *The Portable Nietzsche.* Edited and translated by Walter Kaufmann. New York: Viking, 1968. 463–563.

Olivier, Christiane. *L'Ogre intérieur: De la violence personnelle et familiale.* Paris: Fayard, 1998.
Oxford English Dictionary Online. Oxford University Press, 2006. http://dictionary.oed.com
Payot, Marianne. "L'ogre de barbarie." Review of *Le Rire de l'ogre*, by Pierre Péju. *L'Express.* September 5, 2005. http://livres.lexpress.fr/critique.asp?idC=10590&idR=9&idTC=3&idg=3
Péju, Pierre. *Le Rire de l'ogre.* Paris: Gallimard, 2005.
Pennac, Daniel. *The Scapegoat.* Translated by Ian Monk. London: Harvill, 1999. Translation of *Au Bonheur des ogres.* Paris: Gallimard-Folio, 1985.
Perrault, Charles. *Contes.* 1697. Paris: Gallimard-Folio, 1999.
Petitot, Thierry. *Le Pédéraste et le pédophile à l'école.* Paris: L'Harmattan, 2007.
Plato. *Statesman.* 4th century BC. Edited by Martin Ostwald. Translated by J. B. Skemp. Indianapolis: Hackett, 1992.
Platten, David P. "The *Geist* in the Machine: Nazism in Tournier's *Le Roi des Aulnes*." *Romanic Review* 84, no. 2 (1983): 181–94.
Pratt, Annis. *Dancing with Goddesses: Archetypes, Poetry, and Empowerment.* Bloomington: Indiana University Press, 1994.
Quignard, Pascal. *Terrasse à Rome.* Paris: Gallimard, 2000.
Redfern, Walter. *Michel Tournier:* Le Coq de Bruyère. Madison, NJ: Fairleigh Dickinson University Press, 1996.
Rimbaud, Arthur. *Rimbaud: Complete Works, Selected Letters (A Bilingual Edition).* Translated by Wallace Fowlie. Chicago: University of Chicago Press, 2005.
Roberto, Eugène. "Du symbole taurin au complexe de Nessos." Bourbonnais 41–50.
Sobo, Elisa J. "Menstrual Taboos, Witchcraft Babies, and Social Relations: Women's Health Traditions in Rural Jamaica." *Daughters of Caliban: Caribbean Women in the Twentieth Century.* Edited by Consuelo López Springfield. Bloomington: Indiana University Press, 1997. 143–70.
Sohn, Anne-Marie. "Les attentats à la pudeur sur les fillettes en France (1870–1939) et la sexualité quotidienne. Corbin 71–111.
Todorov, Tzvetan. *Les Abus de la mémoire.* Paris: Arleá, 1995.
Tournier, Michel. *Le Bonheur en Allemagne?.* Paris: Maren Sell, 2004.
———. *Des Clefs et des serrures: Images et proses.* Paris: Chêne/Hachette, 1979.
———. *Le Crépuscule des masques.* Paris: Hoëbeke, 1992.
———. *Eleazar, Exodus to the West.* Translated by Jonathan F. Krell. Lincoln: University of Nebraska Press, 2002a. Translation of *Eléazar ou La Source et le buisson.* Paris: Gallimard-Folio, 1996.
———. *The Fetishist.* Translated by Barbara Wright. Garden City: Doubleday, 1984. Translation of *Le Coq de bruyère.* Paris: Gallimard-Folio, 1978.
———. *Friday.* Translated by Norman Denny. Baltimore: John Hopkins University Press, 1997a. Translation of *Vendredi ou les limbes du Pacifique.* 1967. Paris: Gallimard-Folio, 1972.
———. *Gemini.* Translated by Anne Carter. Garden City: Doubleday 1981. Translation of *Les Météores.* Paris: Gallimard-Folio, 1975.
———. *Gilles & Jeanne.* Translated by Alan Sheridan. New York: Grove Weidenfeld, 1990. Translation of *Gilles & Jeanne.* Paris: Gallimard-Folio, 1983.
———. *Journal extime.* 2002b. Paris: Gallimard, 2004.

———. *The Mirror of Ideas*. Translated by Jonathan F. Krell. Lincoln: University of Nebraska Press, 1998. Translation of *Le Miroir des idées*. Paris: Mercure de France, 1996.

———. *The Ogre*. Translated by Barbara Bray. Baltimore: Johns Hopkins University Press, 1997b. Translation of *Le Roi des Aulnes*. Paris: Gallimard, 1970.

———. "The Red Dwarf." Translation of "Le Nain rouge." *The Fetishist* 113–25.

———. "Tom Thumb Runs Away." Translation of "La Fugue du Petit Poucet." *The Fetishist* 38–49.

———. "Veronica's Shrouds." Translation of "Les Suaires de Véronique." *The Fetishist* 130–43.

———. *The Wind Spirit*. Translated by Arthur Goldhammer. Boston: Beacon, 1988. Translation of *Le Vent Paraclet*. Paris: Gallimard-Folio, 1977.

Tzur, Eli. "Ukraine." *The Holocaust Encyclopedia*. Edited by Walter Laqueur and Judith Tydor Baumet. New Haven, CT: Yale University Press, 2001. 645–53.

Warner, Marina. *No Go the Bogeyman: Scaring, Lulling, and Making Mock*. 1998. New York: Farrar, Straus and Giroux, 1999.

Watthée-Delmotte, Myriam, ed. *La Violence: représentations et ritualisations*. Paris: L'Harmattan, 2002.

Woods, David. "The Origin of the Cult of St. Christopher." Oct. 1999. http://www.ucc.ie/milmart/chrsorig.html

Zimmermann, Daniel. *Le Dixième Cercle: L'Anus du monde*. Paris: Cherche Midi, 1997.

Zola, Emile. *The Belly of Paris*. Translated by Ernest Alfred Vizetelly. Los Angeles: Sun & Moon Press, 1996. Translation of *Le Ventre de Paris*. 1873. Paris: Gallimard, 2002.

———. *Correspondance*. Edited by B. H. Bakker. Vol. 5. Montréal: Presses Universitaires de Montréal, 1985.

———. *The Dram Shop (L'Assommoir)*. Translated by Robin Buss. London: Penguin, 2000. Translation of *L'Assommoir*. 1877. Paris: Flammarion, 1969.

———. Préface. *La Fortune des Rougon*. By Zola. 1871. Paris: Flammarion, 1969. 35–36.

———. *Germinal*. Translated by Peter Collier. Oxford: Oxford University Press, 1993. Translation of *Germinal*. 1885. Paris: Fasquelle, 1977.

Index

Page numbers in italics indicate illustration pages

Aeschylus, 18
Airaksinen, Timo, 151 n. 21
anorexia, 63, 69–70, 147 n. 13
anthropophagy, 42, 45, 107, 138–40, 143 n. 3. *See also* cannibalism
Aphrodite, 21, 91, 107–21, 152 n. 2. *See also* Venus
Apollo, 54, 81, 108, 144 n. 1
Apuleius: *The Golden Ass*, 108
Aristotle, 44, 45, 146 n. 17
atmospheric density (in *The Ogre*), 51, 86–87, 96
Audeguy, Stéphane, 25
Auschwitz, 37–43, 100, 124, 130, 140 n. 5, 145 n. 10
Aymé, Marcel, 147 n. 7. *See also* Vouivre

Bachelard, Gaston, 55, 57, 111, 117
Balcer, Charlotte M., 153 n. 11
Balzac, Honoré de, 152 nn. 2 and 3
Bataille, Georges, 147 n. 10
Baudelaire, Charles, 25–26, 107, 138
Beauty and the Beast, 73–74, 121
Beauvoir, Simone de, 117, 120–21, 152 n. 1, 153 nn. 9 and 14
belly: digestive vs. sexual, 75, 150 n. 11
Bettelheim, Bruno: *The Uses of Enchantment*, 16, 74, 138, 143 n. 3, 153 n. 13, 155 n.8
black sun, 20, 60–62, 77, 147 nn. 9 and 10
Blaise, Suzanne, 155 n. 7
Botticelli, Sandro: *Birth of Venus*, 108, 113–14
Bouloumié, Arlette, 16, 49, 50
Bousquet, René, 131, 145 n. 10, 154 n. 5
Brown, Norman O., 153–54 n. 15
Bruckner, Pascal, 16, 22, 137–42; *Les Ogres anonymes*, 21, 97–100, 128, 137–41; *Le Palais des claques*, 141; *The Temptation of Innocence: Living in the*

Age of Entitlement (La Tentation de l'innocence), 97–100, 138–40
Bunyan, John: *The Pilgrim's Progress*, 17–18, 123
Burgos, Jean, 45–46, 154 n. 3
Butor, Michel, 123, 124, 154 n. 1

Caillaud, Claire, 44, 46, 126–27
Calasso, Roberto: *The Marriage of Cadmus and Harmony*, 15, 78–79, 146 n. 17 (chap. 1), 146 n. 2 (chap. 2)
Campbell, Joseph, 109, 113, 115
Canada, 34
cannibalism, 15, 16, 18, 19, 40–45, 50, 62, 69, 70, 72–73, 79, 83, 89–91, 96, 98–99, 116, 124, 126–28, 137–39, 141, 145 n. 14, 148 n. 20. *See also* anthropophagy
Carroll, Lewis, 150 n. 13
castration, 91–92, 147 n. 13
cat, 38, 107, 109–10, 152 n. 2. *See also* panther; tiger
Cerf, Muriel, 98, 107, 129, 148 n. 14; *Ogres et autres contes*, 20, 21, 63, 65–70, 75, 115–18, 148 n. 16; *Le Verrou*, 20–22, 58, 71–75, 119–21, 127, 148 nn. 18 and 19, 153 n. 12, 155 n. 6
Chessex, Jacques: *A Father's Love (L'Ogre)*, 16, 19, 21, 80, 88–92, 96, 100, 107–11, 124, 127, 135, 136, 150 n. 17, 152 n.2, 155 n.6
Chevalier, Jean, 60, 107, 146 n. 18
Chirac, Jacques, 130
Christopher, St. (Christophoros), 32, 37, 51, 82–84, 86, 133, 149 n. 9, 150 n. 12
Clastres, Pierre, 45
Clot, René-Jean, 49
Cocaigne, Nicolas, 15–16
Colette, 143 n. 7
consumerism, 97–99, 139, 140, 150 n. 19
Corbin, Alain, 131

163

Cowen, Barbara, 118, 153 n. 11
Cronus, 17–20, 22, 54–55, 61, 77–79, 89–92, 99, 104, 107, 114–16, 121, 125–26, 128, 136, 145 n. 11, 146 n. 3, 148 n. 1, 149 n. 11. See also Saturn; time; Titan(s)

Danneels, Pascaline, 143 n. 3
Dante: *The Inferno*, 38, 39, 41, 145 n. 12
defecation, 19, 22, 25, 33–36, 38–40, 133, 134
demonic imagery, 17–19, 80, 123
Depaulis, Jean-Jacques, 130
Derrida, Jacques, 128, 149 n. 5, 154 n. 2
Detienne, Marcel: *Dionysos mis à mort*, 19, 43–44, 110, 126, 145 n. 16
Dezutter, Olivier, 143 n. 3
digestion, 19, 22, 25, 27, 28, 30, 36, 75, 98, 133, 137, 138, 150 n. 11
Dionysus (Dionysian), 19, 26–27, 35–36, 43–44, 78–79, 94–96, 108–10, 125, 126, 140, 144 n. 1, 149 n. 2, 150 n. 11, 151 n. 21, 152 n. 2
Douin, Jean-Luc, 148 n. 14
dragon, 54, 65, 70, 125, 128, 154 n.3
Durand, Gilbert, 19, 25–26, 53–56, 60, 61, 75, 77, 80–81, 83, 95, 107, 117–18, 121, 143 n.6, 146 n. 4, 153 nn. 8 and 10

ecphrasis, 59
Eliade, Mircea, 80, 92–93, 139
Empedocles, 18, 147 n. 8
Eros, 22, 55, 107, 111, 113, 121, 141
Eucharist, 18, 50, 72, 140
Euripides, 116–17

Fates. See Moerae
Fellini, Federico, 119, 133
Flaubert, Gustave, 17
Fleutiaux, Pierrette: "La Femme de l'ogre," 16, 20, 51–56, 75
Foucault, Michel, 67, 131, 155 n. 8
Fragonard, Jean-Honoré: *Le Verrou*, 71
Freud, Sigmund (Freudian), 22, 42, 43, 45, 55, 64, 69, 73, 75, 78, 83, 91, 94, 107, 113, 123, 125, 145 n. 14, 146 nn. 4 and 6, 147 n. 13, 148 n. 20, 149 n. 7, 150 nn. 11, 18, and 20, 153 n. 15
Frye, Northrop: *Anatomy of Criticism: Four Essays*, 17–21, 80, 123, 143 n. 4, 149 n. 4

Gaea, 19, 61, 64, 90, 114, 115
Gargantua, 19, 61, 120, 133, 145 n. 5

Germain, Sylvie, 51–52, 75, 98, 129; *Days of Anger (Jours de colère)*, 20, 56–58, 64; *The Medusa Child (L'Enfant Méduse)*, 20, 58–65, 124, 127, 128, 147 n. 10
Geuss, Raymond, 144 n. 1
Gheerbrant, Alain. See Chevalier, Jean
Giles, Geoffrey J., 145 n. 9
Gilles de Rais, 79, 136, 144 n. 7, 149 n. 3
Giono, Jean, 101, 151–51 n. 23
Girard, René, 94; *The Scapegoat (Le Bouc émissaire)*, 21, 78–79, 136, 151 n. 20
Goering, Hermann, 33–35, 81, 87, 124
Goethe, Johann Wolfgang von, 34, 56, 83, 135, 149 n. 10
Golsan, Richard J., 130–31, 145 n. 10, 154 nn. 4 and 5
Gopnik, Adam, 15, 25
Gordon, Bertram M., 131, 145 n. 10, 154 n. 5
Goya, Francisco: *Saturn Devouring His Child*, 20, 21, *24*, 40, 43, 45, 77
Graves, Robert, 110–11
Grimal, Pierre, 108, 149 n. 2
Guillemin, Henri, 27, 31

"Hansel and Gretel," 16, 73–74, 119, 120, 121, 153 n. 13
Harry, Bruce, 153 n. 11
Hecker, Jurgen, 15
Heers, Jacques, 79
Hermes, 111
Hesiod, 90–92, 114, 125–26, 145 n. 11, 153 n. 7
Hirigoyen, Marie-France, 132
Hitler, Adolf, 34, 81, 87, 93, 98, 124, 136, 150 n. 15
Holocaust, 22, 129–30, 145 n. 13, 150 n. 19, 151 n. 22
Homer, 91; *Odyssey*, 44, 85, 108, 133, 134; *Iliad*, 81, 111
Horney, Julie, 153 n. 11
Hugo, Victor, 25–26, 121

incest, 20, 26, 45, 62, 63, 68–70, 74
infanticide, 40, 43, 101, 116–17, 136
Isis, *106*, 108–9, 114

Jacoby, Mario, 68, 148 n. 19
Jarry, Alfred, 19, 52, 143 n. 5
Jaton, Anne Marie, 89
Josephus, Flavius, 43, 117, 118
Juffé, Michel, 123, 127–28
Jung, C. G., 125, 127, 148 n. 19

INDEX

Kali, 67, 68, 107, 148n. 16
Kast, Verena, 68, 148n. 19
Kindlifresserbrunnen (Ogre Fountain), 76, 90, 98, 150n. 17
Knapp, Bettina L., 51–52
Kristeva, Julia, 20, 60, 62

Lacombe, Paul, *106*
Laplanche, Jean, 146n. 6
Lee, Susanna, 150n. 19
Lévi-Strauss, Claude, 49–50
Littell, Jonathan, 145n. 9, 151n. 22, 152n. 25
Lopez, Gérard, 132

Macé, Gérard, 42, 45–46, 49
Maffesoli, Michel, 94–96, 140, 151n. 21
Mariana, Jessica, 155n. 7
Medusa, 61, 64, 65, 147nn. 7 and 13
Melusine, 108, 111
memory, 21, 22, 61, 68, 71, 100–103, 129–32. *See also* Cronus; Saturn; time; Titan(s)
menstruation (menstrual blood), 67, 117–18, 120, 121, 153nn. 9–11
Miller, Henry: *Tropic of Cancer*, 66, 148n. 14
Mitterand, Henri, 30
Mitterrand, François, 130–31, 145n. 10
Moerae (Fates), 116, 153n. 7
Monès, Philippe de, 84
Morel, Geneviève, 118

Napoleon I, 135, 149n. 8
Napoleon III, 26–28, 30, 126
narcissism, 58, 75
Narjoux, Cécile, 59
naturalism, 19, 20, 52, 143nn. 4 and 8. *See also* Zola, Emile
Nazism (National Socialism, Nazi Party, Nazis), 17, 21, 22, 34–46, 78, 80, 84, 87–88, 92–94, 96, 99–100, 124, 126, 129–31, 134–36, 139, 143n. 5, 144n. 5, 149n. 10, 150n. 17, 151n. 22
Nerval, Gérard de, 60, 62, 77, 147n. 9
Neumann, Erich, 107
Nietzsche, Friedrich, 26, 136, 144n. 1

Oedipus (Oedipal), 21, 84, 90, 127, 155n. 8
Ogre Fountain. *See* Kindlifresserbrunnen
Olivier, Christiane: *L'Ogre intérieur*, 15, 58, 62, 63, 69–70, 123, 148n. 17

Ondine, 72, 148n. 18
Ophelia, 108, 111
orgy, 94–96, 108, 151n. 21

panther, 109, 110, 152n. 2. *See also* cat; tiger
Papon, Maurice, 130, 154n. 4
Paracelsus, 56
Payot, Mariannne, 103
pedophilia, 135, 138, 155n. 8
Péju, Pierre: *Le Rire de l'ogre*, 21, 100–104, 124, 128, 129, 130, 152n. 25
Pennac, Daniel: *The Scapegoat (Au Bonheur des ogres)*, 21, 80, 92–96, 98, 124, 128–30, 135, 139, 150n. 19, 151n. 21
Perrault, Charles, 14, 16, 19, 122, 138; "Bluebeard" ("La Barbe bleue"), 16, 35, 49, 68, 141, 143n. 5, 144n. 7; "Little Red Riding Hood ("Le Petit Chaperon rouge"), 16, 20, 48, 49, 52, 143n. 5, 110; "Little Tom Thumb" ("Le Petit Poucet"), *14*, 16, 20, 51–56, 108, *122*, 127–28, 134, 143nn. 3 and 5, 144n. 4; "Puss in Boots" ("Le Chat botté"), 16, 143n. 5
"Petit Poucet, Le." *See under* Perrault, Charles, "Little Tom Thumb"
Petitot, Thierry, 155n. 8
Pharmakos. *See* scapegoat
phoria (phoric), 21, 35, 37, 51, 82–86, 152n. 25
photography, 21–22, 84–86, 111–12, 114, 115, 150n. 13, 152–53n. 3, 153n. 4
Plato (Platonic, Platonistic), 26, 36, 53, 126, 149n. 5
Polyphemus, 18, 85, 133, 134
Pompidou, Georges, 130, 154n. 4
Pontalis, J.-B. *See* Laplanche, Jean
Poseidon, 44, 64, 113, 145n. 11
Pratt, Annis, 109, 115
Prometheus (Promethean), 18, 25–26, 126, 136. *See also* Titan(s)
Propp, Vladimir, 53
Prussia, 26, 33, 36, 37, 87, 149nn. 8 and 10, 150n. 15

Quignard, Pascal, 77

rape, 63, 64, 69, 70, 71, 147n. 13
Redfern, Walter, 112
Riedel, Ingrid, 68, 148n. 19

Riefenstahl, Leni, 136
Rimbaud, Arthur, 123–25, 128
Rougemont, Denis de: *Love in the Western World*, 67

Sade, D. A. F., Marquis de, 151 n. 21
Sagawa, Issey, 15–16, 49, 139
Saturn (saturnine), 20–21, 24, 40–43, 45, 60–61, 74, 77, 104, 145 n. 11, 146 n. 3, 147 nn. 9, 11, and 12, 152 n. 24. *See also* Cronus; Goya; time; Titan(s)
scapegoat, 17, 21, 78, 79–80, 92, 149 n. 5. *See also under* Pennac, Daniel; Girard, René
Schlöndorff, Volker, 144 n. 8, 150 n. 12
Serbia, 99–100, 138
Sobo, Elisa J., 153 n. 10
Sohn, Anne-Marie, 131
Süskind, Patrick, 150 n. 14

Tarot, 54, 60
Thanatos, 22, 55, 121, 141
tiger (tigress), 109, 112, 115. *See also* cat; panther
time, 17, 20–21, 36, 52, 54–55, 59–61, 75, 77, 80–82, 84–89, 92–95, 102–4, 107, 109, 115–17, 121, 136, 146 n. 3, 151 n. 21; circular vs. linear, 87–88; narrative, 68–69; vertical vs. horizontal, 94–95, 140. *See also* Cronus; memory; Saturn; Titan(s)
Titan(s), 18–19, 22, 26, 43, 61, 77–79, 90–92, 99, 107, 114, 115, 126, 136, 145 n. 11, 146 n. 3, 149 n. 2. *See also* Cronus; Prometheus; Saturn
Todorov, Tzvetan: *Les Abus de la mémoire*, 22, 129, 130, 132
Tournier, Michel, 17, 19, 22, 132–37, 141; *Le Bonheur en Allemagne?*, 77–78; *Des Clefs et des serrures: Images et proses*, 150 n. 13; *Le Crepuscule des masques*, 152–53 n. 3, 153 n. 4; *Eleazar, Exodus to the West (Eléazar ou La Source et le buisson)*, 146 n. 1; *Friday (Vendredi ou les limbes du Pacifique)*, 95; *Gemini (Les Météores)*, 15; *Gilles & Jeanne*, 144 n. 7, 149 n. 3; *Journal extime*, 49; *The Mirror of Ideas (Le Miroir des idées)*, 132; *The Ogre (Le Roi des Aulnes)*, 16, 20–21, 25, 32–38, 50–51, 72, 80–88, 93, 96, 112, 127, 130, 144 nn. 5, 7, and 9, 149 n. 8, 150 n. 13,

152 n. 25; "The Red Dwarf" ("Le Nain rouge"), 146 n. 5; "Tom Thumb Runs Away" ("La Fugue du Petit Poucet"), 144 n. 4; "Veronica's Shrouds" ("Les Suaires de Véronique"), 21–22, 107, 109, 111–15; *The Wind Spirit (Le Vent Paraclet)*, 82, 149 n. 10
Touvier, Paul, 130–31, 154 n. 4
Treblinka, 38, 39, 41, 43, 44, 124
Twilight of the Gods, 88, 93
Tzur, Eli, 151 n.22

Ukraine, 100–103, 151 n. 22

vampire, 67, 68, 110, 137, 139, 141, 150 n. 17
Venus, 107, 108, 113, 114, 121. *See also* Aphrodite
Veronica, St., 111–12, 153 nn. 4 and 5
Vesalius, Andreas, 113
Vichy, 38, 129–31, 145 n. 10, 154 n. 4; Vichy Syndrome, 131, 145 n. 10
Vouivre, 57, 147 n. 7. *See also* Aymé, Marcel

Warner, Maria: *No Go the Bogeyman: Scaring, Lulling, and Making Mock*, 40, 43, 49, 77, 89–92, 123, 125, 128, 149–50 n. 11
Watthée-Delmotte, Myriam, 143 n. 3
Weber, Jeanne, 118
Woods, David, 83
wolf, 16, 20, 21, 50, 54, 59–60, 63, 67, 110, 120, 134, 137, 143 n. 5

Zeus, 78–79, 90–92, 115, 116, 126, 128, 136, 145 n. 11, 149 n. 2, 149–50 n. 11, 150 n. 18
Zimmermann, Daniel: *Le Dixième Cercle: L'Anus du monde*, 19, 38–46, 72, 124, 129, 130, 145 nn. 10 and 13
Zola, Emile, 17, 19–20, 26–27, 52, 132, 143 n. 7, 144 n. 1; *The Belly of Paris (Le Ventre de Paris)*, 19–20, 25, 27–31, 126, 128, 129, 144 nn. 5 and 6; *The Dram Shop (L'Assommoir)*, 27; *Germinal*, 27, 144 n. 3; *The Kill (La Curée)*, 143 n. 6; *The Ladies' Paradise (Au Bonheur des dames)*, 92, 150 n. 19; *The Rougon-Macquart Cycle*, 20, 26–27, 29; *Nana*, 143 n. 8. *See also* naturalism